The Long Distance
~~Grandmother~~
Grandparent

✳ ✳ ✳ ✳

# The Long Distance Grandmother

## How to Stay Close to Distant Grandchildren

FOURTH EDITION

Selma Wassermann

Hartley
&Marks
PUBLISHERS

Published by
HARTLEY & MARKS PUBLISHERS INC.
P. O. Box 147    3661 West Broadway
Point Roberts, WA    Vancouver, BC
98281    V6R 2B8

LIBRARY OF CONGRESS CATALOGING-IN-PUBLICATION DATA
Wasserman, Selma.
The long distance grandmother : how to stay close to distant grandchildren / by Selma
Wasserman.—4th ed.
p.   cm.
Includes bibliographical references and index.
ISBN 0-88179-188-1
1. Grandparent and child—United States.    2. Grandmothers—United States.    I. Title.

HQ759.9 .W37 2001
306.874'5—dc 21                          00-052984

Typeset in Minion by
The Typeworks
Printed in the U.S.A.

This book is dedicated to the memory
of my grandmother, Fanny Goldstein,
who taught me the "little virtues."

# CONTENTS

# Introduction

IT DOESN'T SEEM that long ago—that summer afternoon when my friend Patsy Arrott persuaded me that writing about being a long distance grandparent had some merit for grandparents everywhere. Our own grandchildren were toddlers at the time, and untapped resources of stories and tall tales that would fill many pages of the first edition of this book. Now, more than a dozen years later, the book is finding its way into a fourth edition—a testament to Patsy and her insight into what grandparents wanted to know about establishing and maintaining loving relationships with their beloved and distant grandchildren.

The idea for the first book was born when we were having lunch outdoors, on a rare summer day, warm enough to sit in the sun, but not so hot that you felt you were frying. Patsy and Tony, longtime friends, had just become long distance grandparents. Their son, Matthew, had just become a father and the thought of it was unnerving. Wasn't it only yesterday that Matthew was a boy himself, urging his father not to risk his life and climb the tree to rescue our cat?

Matthew had just finished graduate school in the Los Angeles area and he and his wife both had job opportunities there that were promising. While Patsy and Tony were delighted with these career prospects for the young couple, they mourned the idea of being at such a distance from the new baby. As with most grandparents, Patsy was already feeling the "itch"—that excruciating longing to hold one's grandchild in one's arms. And the distance between Los Angeles and the grandparents' home made the itch tough to scratch.

Our friends were not unique in their geographical separation from their new granddaughter. While in our own growing-up days, most of us could count on our grandparents living just down the block, or at least in the same town or city, today it is more often the case that grandparents live at different ends of the continent, if not in different countries. With so many miles between us and with the toll that these miles take on our human relationships, how do grandparents maintain a loving connection with their offspring? If frequent visits and the coming together of families on a regular basis was simply not possible, were there other options open to us that would permit us to develop a growing relationship with our grandchildren, even at a distance? Was it possible to find ways to bridge the distance between us, so that grandparents would not be remote strangers—names on birthday parcels with colored wrapping?

What had I done? Patsy asked me. How had I managed to maintain my connection with our boys who lived 400 miles away? She convinced me that the ideas I had developed and that had worked for me would be useful for other long distance grandparents. And as we counted them, we realized that in our own close circle of friends, long distance grandparents outnumbered the "live-nearby" group by more than two to one. Friends who had read the first edition of the book later reproached me. Why on earth have you excluded other significant adults in children's lives? What about long distance aunts and uncles? Godmothers and godfathers? Good friends? The ideas in the book seemed to have meaning now for many adults who lived at a distance from much-loved children.

The first edition of *The Long Distance Grandmother* began to take shape from Patsy Arrott's inspiration, that summer day on the deck of the house on Eagleridge Drive. During the writing, a friend, whose opinion I valued greatly, argued persuasively that I change the working title to *The Long Distance Grandparent*. He made a strong case for inclusion of grandfathers, and I was sympathetic to his concerns. The book is, after all, for grandparents (as well as significant others), and some of these may be put off by what they perceive to be such exclusion by title.

Yet, when push came to shove, I kept the original name and have kept it through the succeeding three editions. Writing from personal experience helped me to make the book more real, more immediate to me, and therefore, I believed, of more practical help to readers. In keeping the original name, I realized I would be taking some risks. Some grandfathers and other significant adults might be offended at this personalization. They might be put off by too many female references. Grandfathers might feel that they had been excluded and therefore that they were not important.

There is no question in my mind that grandfathers and grandmothers are equally important. There is no question that each plays a particularly crucial role in the healthful growth and development of grandchildren. In some families, it may well be grandfather, rather than grandmother, who plays *the* role of consequence. To write this book from a grandmother's perspective is not to slight grandfathers. It was done first as a literary convenience, since it is awkward and tedious to give equal treatment in the text to both "grandmothers and grandfathers" and too impersonal, I believe, to refer always to the collective "grandparents." Finally, I chose to take the risk and stay close to personal experience. That the book has sold through three editions, and is now entering its fourth evolution, has been taken as a sign that such a choice was not altogether wrong.

Having made that choice, I want to reiterate my message to grandfathers, aunts, uncles and other significant adults in the lives of children they love. You are valued! You are terribly important! I sincerely hope you will know this, as you read a text that is tilted strongly toward a grandmother's experiences, and that you will be able to translate *grandmother* into the appropriate label, without wrath or malice toward this writer.

> The wise man looks into space and does not regard the small as too little nor the great as too big for he knows that there is no limit to dimension. (Lao-tse)

A book is never the work of one person alone. Many contribute behind the scenes, to inspire, as well as to give specific and practical help to produce what is finally found in the bookstores. I'd like to express my gratitude to each, making their significant contributions explicit. Paula and John, our daughter and son-in-law, and Simon and Arlo, our remarkably grown up grandsons, have been the source of most of my stories. They were, and continue to be, my teachers in the subject of interpersonal relationships across the generations. Now that the boys are grown to young adulthood, with our connections stronger than ever, it seems clear that maintaining loving relationships across distance is not only possible, but imperative. Jack, my husband of fifty awesome years, is a constant support system for everything I write.

Toronto grandmother Myra Krangle sent many creative ideas that found their way into the second and subsequent editions. Numerous other grandparents, with whom I've talked over the years, have shared ideas and talked openly of their concerns. The editor of the first edition, Sue Tauber, must also be remembered for her tireless encouragement, her enthusiasm, and for her shepherding the original edition from first draft to finished product. Friends and colleagues contributed their stories: Cherie Smith, Jaap Tuinman and Marv Wideen. Fran Yee and her grade one students allowed me to use their "Ideal Grandmother" stories. Computer whiz Mark Cohen was enormously generous in reading every word of the new Chapter 14, pointing me in the right directions of the high-tech wired world. Linda Hof, my good buddy and ally at the Centre for Technology in the Faculty of Education at Simon Fraser University, provided valuable help with the citations of informational websites for children of all ages. And finally, to Patsy Arrott, who told me at the very beginning: "Write this book!"— heartfelt thanks to all of you for making it possible.

# 1

# In Praise of Grandmothers

*"My ideal grandma would be loving and kind."*

MY GRANDMOTHER was the most important person in my early childhood. During those critical early years when my mother was wrestling with her own demons, it was my grandmother who stepped in and filled my world with nurturing. She had a lap bigger than Miami Beach, and when she took me into it, I knew I was safe. It didn't matter what atrocities I committed in my childish enthusiasm for investigating the unknown—from (they tell me) cutting the beads off her precious new living room lamps to "playing doctor" with the boy next door; I knew, without a moment's equivocation, that her love for me would never diminish. And even when she was angry, I knew, from the depths of my being, that her anger was of the moment and that our heart-to-heart connection could never be in jeopardy.

It was from my grandmother that I learned the most important things about myself—that I was loved and therefore lovable; that I was appreciated, even though I had flaws; that I was special. When my mother's patience for my childish mischievousness wore thin, it was my grandmother who tried to help me understand. She, more than any other person, taught me about unselfishness, about care-

In the days when extended families lived in close proximity, grandparents often filled in the gaps left by parents.

Upstairs-downstairs relationships between grandparents and grandchildren are for many families a thing of the past.

giving, about forgiving. Her great heart was as open and as loving as any child's dream could have conjured. If not for her, my life would have had a vacancy as large and as bitter as the Dead Sea.

In the years when I was growing up (in those olden days when dinosaurs roamed the earth), the extended family of three generations commonly lived quite closely together. Suburbs had not yet been invented; and if you lived on a farm, or in a small town, parents and parents of parents, along with all offspring, lived within touching distance of each other. If you lived in a large city, the chances were more than good that parents of parents lived in the same neighborhood. The most removed were a short city bus or train ride away. When I was very young, my grandparents lived on the street floor of our rented two-family house and there was no differentiation between "our" place and "theirs." I was as much with them as I was upstairs; perhaps even more. When we had to give up the house and move to two entirely separate apartments, my mother and I easily traversed the six city blocks between us—at least four or five times a week. My grandparents were my first and only babysitters, and I always considered it a major treat to be left with them—an especially sweet occasion if my grandmother was cooking or baking, which was almost all the time. I remember my mother lightly reprimanding me about my not caring if, let alone when, she ever came to fetch me home.

Friends and colleagues of my generation have remarkably similar connections to their grandparents, who were strong presences in their lives both in a physical and a psycho-social sense. We may, however, have been the last generation to have had such close physical ties. Grandparents today are too often much more remote geographically, and for some, the physical distance understandably plays havoc with opportunities for closer emotional connections. Among my close circle of friends, only one pair of grandparents lives in the same city.

Many of the others live thousands of miles away—in different cities, different states or provinces, different countries. And such a set of physical estrangements of parents from parents of parents is very much an accepted part of our complex, sophisticated, career-led, urbane lives. Perhaps that is why long distance telephone calls have so greatly increased in number and decreased in cost; they are the primary and most frequently used mode of contact-across-the-miles between loved ones.

Our own grandchildren live 400 miles from us. We may wish it were different, but the conditions that dictate our places of residence are not likely to change soon. My daughter, who is very much caught up in her own professional life, runs her own business and financial consulting firm in the small town where she lives. She does not care for big city life and there does not seem to be the slightest possibility that she would consider moving next door. My own work running an educational software company makes it imperative that I remain within commuting distance of my activities. Love alone does not make it possible for me to relocate to her territory.

In short, each of us is involved in our own affairs, in our own communities, and living lives that are physically disconnected from one another. And, along with so many other community-rooted grandparents and their grown offspring who have chosen to take root elsewhere, this is the compact we have made and accepted. The danger of such a physical disconnection lies, of course, in the risk of an emotional disconnection from those delicious, delightful, precious early years. For until the grandchildren may come to visit under their own power, or unless the parents or grandparents are entirely free in such matters as visiting times or airfare expenditures, such conditions of physical distance are all too likely to set grandparents off as remote strangers.

When I was a new grandmother, facing the challenge of a long distance relationship with my own grandsons, I was determined not to let this happen. Perhaps I could not have the same kind of upstairs-

Career choices largely shape today's living arrangements, often leaving extended families scattered over hundreds and sometimes thousands of miles.

downstairs relationship with our boys that my own grandparents had with me. But surely there were ways to bridge the physical distance between us, to keep the connection alive. Beyond the long distance telephone calls. Beyond the once-a-year birthday and Christmas parcels. Beyond the hungry longing for more visits. Even if the results are never an entirely adequate substitute for real-life cuddling (It's true: There is nothing that can quite match the feelings of those little arms around you in a loving embrace.), there are ways of making long distance connections that forge the vital links—so that grandparents and grandchildren are not strangers when they meet, but loving relations who have found ways to transcend the miles that keep them physically apart.

## Grandmothers Come in Many Shapes and Sizes

My grandmother was a large woman, old before her years. By today's standards, she would have been considered unattractive, even ugly. Her face was pitted like the craters of the moon, marked for life in a childhood bout with smallpox. Her hair, mousegray, was as fine as silken thread and could not even hold a hairpin. Overweight, diabetic and infirm at 50, the result of years of bad nutrition, she was very much a traditional, immigrant grandmother, fully involved with her husband, her six children and, when they were grown, their spouses and families. Being a wife and mother was what she did; and going shopping meant going to the market to secure the best plump chicken for the Sabbath dinner. She could neither read nor write and her English was, at best, limited to about twenty odd-lot words, none of which could be combined in a sentence.

Her preoccupation with the cooking and offering of food was typical of the cultural milieu in which she lived. Sometimes, we jokingly refer to this as the "Jewish Mother" syndrome. But it was no joke that the offering of food (largely because of its scarcity in the Old Country and because food is so intimately connected with care-giving) was how all of us in the family felt her presence most. Food was the gift she had to give us, and through food, she expressed her love, individually and collectively. She took special pains to bake the Sabbath bread herself, because my father much preferred home-made to store bought, even when she would have done better to stay off her feet. She would make a special beef entrée for my uncle, her youngest son, when the rest of us were having chicken, because he disliked chicken. Her potato pancakes were a main event for all of us, and we begged for them, not considering the work it took to prepare them in those days before electric grinders and blenders took the pain out of the kitchen. We loved to come to her house for any occasion—and we knew that our visits would be surrounded by the sights and smells and tastes to which we had all grown accustomed.

There was, in and around her gifts of food, a generosity of spirit that was unmistakable. A woman of limited means and meager resources, food was what she could give, and she gave it more generously than her budget would allow. I remember a day in the hard years of the Great Depression—when none of us had enough of anything—that she gave a starving young Russian sailor who had jumped ship, a parcel of food. She did not know him; he had just walked down her street. They talked at length in Russian and when he left, he carried with him half of her own dinner and the next day's lunch.

For me, her gifts of food were an emotional watering trough. I relished them in spite of my increasing waistline, which tended to expand out of proportion to my height.

Whether your own grandmother came from the "Old Country" or not; whether she baked challah, or Irish soda bread or panettone or scones, it is likely that she, like my grandmother, lived in a highly circumscribed world. The boundaries of that world were set by the economic constraints, the role expectations, the concept of family, and the religious traditions of those times. And all of these were further

Today's grandmothers are as likely to wear track shoes or a corporate suit as their own grandmothers were to wear comfy slippers and aprons.

The traditional picture of the grandmother at home in the kitchen, expressing her love through baking and cooking, has largely disappeared.

influenced by the role imposed upon women. Even though it is only fifty years since my grandmother's death, and fifty years doesn't seem such a very long time, the world in which my grandmother lived was radically different from ours today. In my grandmother's day, a grandmother was a GRANDMOTHER. We could recognize one at a glance! We had a vision of grandmothers that was as unambiguous as our vision of Cinderella.

In our present culture that mind-set has been shattered. Grandmothers today come in a wider range of shapes and sizes. Some grandmothers may have gray hair; others are blonde. Some are past sixty; others barely forty. Some are home-makers by preference; others are career bound. Some are active, jogging several miles before breakfast each morning; others prefer more sedentary activities. Grandmothers may enjoy home-making and giving gifts of food, but they may do much more and have talents that extend far beyond the home. Today, grandmothers at sixty are more youthful, healthy and energetic than my grandmother was at forty.

More grandmothers today work outside the home than ever before. Many have businesses of their own. Some run huge corporations that employ hundreds of workers. Some are professionals—interior decorators, architects, lawyers, psychiatrists. Many do volunteer work in libraries, schools, or centers for the aged and infirm. Becoming a grandmother these days does not mean packing up your former life and settling down to your declining years. On the contrary. Today our expectations of grandmothers and what they do are completely different.

There are, of course, many modern grandmothers whose work is still inside the home, but this is often a matter of personal choice. Modern grandmothers have many more life opportunities open to them than did my grandmother.

They may be involved with a variety of home projects that enable them to exploit and expand their innate creative talents—sculpting, cooking, weaving, silversmithing, pottery, gardening, sewing, making

music. They may be entrepreneurs, working out of their homes to provide goods and services that tap their unique abilities. They may have decided to return to school, either to take a degree, or to study for the pure pleasure of learning. The modern grandmother's involvement covers a wide territory of experience. As a consequence, when she gives gifts of herself to her grandchildren, she has much more extensive resources to draw upon.

While you may not have considered yourself a rich resource, think about this: for my grandmother, a trip meant taking a one-hour subway ride to Coney Island. Today's grandmothers are more likely to holiday in Italy or take a one-month camping trip in the RV across the country. Recreation for my grandmother was a chance to sit on a chair outside her house, gossiping with the neighbors. Today's grandmothers watch the latest TV programs, play golf, go to concerts, read best sellers, go cross country skiing. I know one great-grandmother whose passion for her three times a week fitness class has not diminished, even at age seventy-seven.

What all this means, to my way of thinking, is that exercising our individual options and taking advantage of increased life opportunities allows us more freedom to grow and develop in richer and more diverse ways. Therefore, the gifts we have to offer our grandchildren are also much richer and more diverse. We have so much more to draw on, and we draw on such a wide variety of personal experience. In that way, we are very lucky. Not only does this benefit us by adding quality and pleasure to our lives, it enriches our grandchildren in turn, since they are the beneficiaries of who and what we are.

## What's In It for Me?

So far I have written about the gifts of love that grandmothers give, and it would be easy to get the impression that grandmothers are for giving and grandchildren for taking. There is more to the relationship than this one-way street and if you have already been enrolled into the ranks of grandparenthood, you will know immediately that the gifts of love flow in both directions.

There is a special quality to the grandparent-grandchild relationship that transcends, in surprising ways, what we felt as parents. It's hard to explain why this should be so—why our grandchildren are so easily able to wrap their fingers around our hearts and squeeze until it's hard to breathe. Other writers have said that the grandparent-grandchild love connection is special because it is so free—so unencumbered by the day-to-day details of living that steal our attention and get in the way of "total love." After all, we still remember from our own experiences as parents that we did get angry, annoyed, frustrated, disappointed when our child: spilled the milk on the newly waxed floor; pulled the cat's tail; refused to eat the lamb chop that we had taken great pains to prepare; cut holes in the evening paper; forgot to clean up his room. In the twenty-four hour day, seven day a week intimate family, feelings other than love inevitably come into play, diluting the purely loving relationship.

The grandparent-grandchild bond is especially strong—free on both sides from the encumbrances of daily life.

As grandparents we are freed from these encumbrances. Our times together are not so extensive and exhaustive and we are not responsible for the working details of the household. Love can surface unfettered and other, quite normal emotional responses like anger, annoyance, frustration will take a decided back seat. If they do come into play, it is rare. We are free to let the love flow, without restraint. And that powerful emotionality, that unencumbered rush of affection, is not only "received" by our grandchildren. It is reciprocated in kind, growing and maturing as the grandchildren grow and mature, to an indescribably delicious bond between you that can never be extinguished.

There was a new baby on its way in the Anderson household and grandma and mom were having tea, talking with three year-old Jessa about the forthcoming event.

"If you could choose any name that you wanted for your new baby sister—a really *special* name, what name would you choose, Jessa?" asked her mother.

Jessa pondered for a few moments, stroking her grandmother's arm. This was a big question and she was going to bring all of her three year-old intelligence to bear on it. Then she smiled and said, "I think we should call her Grandma."

"Her mother loved her dearly and so did her grandmother who doted on her with even greater tenderness."
CHARLES PERRAULT,
*Little Red Riding Hood*

# 2

# And Now for the Good News: My Daughter, A Mother/ My Son, A Father!

*Soon-to-be grandparents are often torn between feelings of joy and the fear of aging.*

IT STARTS WITH a phone call. When you least expect it. "Hi, mom. I have some news. I'm pregnant."

Few of us greet such news (at least for the first time) with total enthusiasm, for it means that we have to confront our own aging, our own mortality.

"Wait a minute. I'm not ready to be a grandmother," is hardly an appropriate response. Nor is, "Who told you you could become pregnant without my consent!" Nor, "How could you do this to me?" We may be experiencing all of these feelings—(a) I'm not ready; (b) I'm not sure you are ready; (c) you are making me old before my time and I hate it!—but we muster the resources within ourselves and rise to the occasion. It's wonderful news! We are very happy! Are you feeling okay? And we recognize those feelings in ourselves, too—even as we're wrestling with the uneasiness nagging at us. Gradually, gradually, we grow to love the idea. But it takes a bit of work.

Unless you totally accept your own aging and are happy to pay the price of generational seniority by being rewarded with "grand-progeny," you will have mixed feelings about grandparenthood. There is, of course, much joy in the notion that your child has matured, and that there is a new baby coming to bring the pleasures of parenthood just as you have experienced them. There is also joy in anticipating how it will feel to have, once again in your life, little ones who are the bringers of much happiness and inner satisfaction. You will think of so many things you will want to share with them—stories you loved to read to your own children; trips to the zoo; going to the circus; camping trips; holidays—all the activities you used to enjoy doing with your own children and which stopped when they let you know, "We're too old for that stuff, mom." You can have all of that again—and that feels very good.

The good feelings, however, do not completely obliterate the ambivalence. Most of us have difficulty accepting the encroaching seniority that marks our shift from parenthood into grandparenthood. In terms of aging, it means gray hair and/or less hair; it means more wrinkles and sagging flesh under the chin; it means bifocals (oh, dear God! not bifocals!); it means young people getting up to give you a seat on the bus; it means getting into the movies for half price—all those accoutrements of passing time that, up until now, we had associated with "those other folk across the street." How can all of this happen to me . . . when I still feel so young, so virile, so physically infallible? Much resistance to grandparenthood is the result of our desire to defy growing old—for many of us, a common threat.

Contained within those feelings is our unspoken need to see our own offspring as young, immature, even unwise. "How can she possibly handle the responsibilities of motherhood when she's hardly more than a baby herself!" If we continue to think of our children as children, rather than as adults, it somehow helps us to maintain the fiction that we, ourselves, are not getting older. Yet, if we have done our jobs as parents at all well, we have helped our children to become adult, mature and wise—and there is a part of us that knows that, too.

The words grandma and grandpa come armed with stock images of rocking-chairs, grey hair and sensible shoes.

15

At the sound of those magic words: "Hey, mom. It's a boy," any lingering fears and doubts vanish instantly.

We can continue to battle the idea of growing old psychologically as well as physically, through distorted perceptions and face lifts, but I don't know of any human who has actually conquered the process. The best we can do is to accept aging gracefully—and make the most of it.

The most difficult step may be the first one, that of accepting the thought of "my daughter, the mother," "my son, the father." Once you have come to terms with that idea—have rolled it around in your head, turning it this way and that to see its many perspectives; considered its implications for you—you may move to a fuller and more complete acceptance of what is inevitably to come. To be dragged into grandparenthood "kicking and screaming and protesting," serves no one well, least of all yourself.

At the end of your struggle with self, at the end of a long series of "How are you?" telephone calls, there will be, finally, the long-awaited news.

"Hey, mom. It's a boy."

Whew!

And quite remarkably, the doubts evaporate. All the energy is focused on the blessed event. Who cares about wrinkles and bifocals? What you want most of all in your life, in this very moment, is to reach out and have the feeling of that small being warm in your arms. And when you have had that feeling, you know that you have fully become a grandmother.

## Becoming a Grandparent

As grandparenthood is almost always "thrust upon us," preparing ourselves, both physically and emotionally, may take some work.

No one of us sets out consciously to be a grandparent. Without prior experience or preparation for the job, we are parachuted into grandparenthood holus-bolus. Unlike planning for parenthood, where we often decide about having a baby and read lots of books to prepare ourselves for the agonies and ecstasies of parenting (none of which

16

ever tells the real story!), we are not included in the decision-making process about this major milestone in our lives. Instead, we are grateful that we are finally "let in on the news." Unlike preparing for parenthood, there are few serious books that would presume to tell us how to behave as grandparents, what to expect, and how to deal with our own expectations vis-à-vis those of our grown children-turned-parents. The assumption is made that if we have already survived in our roles as parents and lived to tell the tale, we should slip gracefully into grandparenting without effort. While this may be true for some of us, it is certainly not true for most.

Do grandmothers have to dress differently? Should my skirts now be longer? Should I give up high heeled shoes? Should I let my hair go to gray? Is it unseemly for grandfathers to ride motorcycles? To fall in love? To go to school to study art?

Should grandfathers help with the gardening? Be available on call as baby sitters? Pay the orthodontist's bill? Maintain the college fund? Should grandmothers send the children's favorite cookies in the mail once a week? Offer to take the children for two weeks every summer to give the parents a breather?

Should grandmothers set standards of behavior for the grandchildren? For the parents of the grandchildren? Should grandfathers give advice freely—about what the parents and grandchildren *should* do?

Should grandparents take in grandchildren who are angry with the parents and who have (temporarily) left home?

Should the grandchildren and their parents be the grandparents' overriding concern in their lives? Should grandparents' lives be totally devoted to their grandchildren and children? Or are grandparents entitled to interests of their own? To be "selfish," with regard to their time and finances?

Should grandparents expect that grandchildren be grateful and appreciative? Thoughtful about telephoning and writing? Should grandparents expect that grown grandchildren will choose to spend

Like parenthood before it, grandparenthood is a learned experience.

time with them, rather than pursuing only their own friends and their own interests?

Unfortunately, the answer to all of these nagging and troublesome questions is, "It depends." Each question has many answers which will vary, not only from grandparent to grandparent and family to family, but also in different circumstances, within the same family. It is how these questions are answered and what lies behind the answers that make grandparenting "for better" or "for worse."

## Better Grandparenting

Learning to become a "grandparent of quality" is a lot like learning other kinds of interpersonal skills. And yes, Virginia, there are skills to grandparenting, as there are skills to parenting. No matter what the family context—rural, urban, suburban; no matter what the social class; no matter what the size of the family or the ages of family members, there are some important principles that make a difference to the quality of grandparenting. To be aware of these is the first step in learning them. Regrettably, we do not become "perfect grandparents" because we wish it. Nor will perfection occur at the moment of a grandchild's birth when we are endowed with the title. The qualities of good grandparenting can be studied, and learned, over time.

My list contains three qualities that I consider essential. Other lists may be longer, and more comprehensive, but as I reflect upon the qualities that contribute positively to relationships—those that make a big difference in being together and in getting along together—I see that they are really the same for all groups. What works between friends also works between members of a family.

Before any other quality, I would put *respect* at the very top of my list: respect for your grown child, who is now an adult and a parent (although you might think that he or she sometimes doesn't act like one), and respect for your grandchildren, no matter what their age. To communicate respect for others is to give them opportunities to make choices for themselves; to treat them as you would other adults—courteously and with full regard. This means that you are considerate of their feelings and of their ideas; that you allow them the freedom to decide for themselves about matters of consequence in their lives.

This is as important with very young grandchildren as it is for those who are older, even though the choices may be considerably narrower. Small children can make choices about their food preferences, about the stories they enjoy hearing, about whether they'd like to come for a walk with grandpa or stay at home with mum. Wherever they may make choices safely, it is respectful (as well as satisfying to them) to offer as many as we can. If you take your granddaughter for a walk, she can choose the route, or she may choose to stop to watch a bird, or she may choose the library books she'd like. Instead of always telling her what to do and how to do it, invite her opinions. "What do you think?" is a very important question to ask her—showing respect for the child and her ideas. If she chooses not to do something that we'd like her to do—like kiss grandma goodbye, or talk on the telephone, or recite her favorite poem, can we find it in our hearts to respect that choice, even though we may be hurt momentarily? For older grandchildren, freedom of choice is even more imperative, since their growing self-hood is intimately connected with having their options open to decide for themselves. When their options are denied, or seriously circumscribed, when grandparents seek always to tell, rather than to ask, grandchildren are more likely to avoid such restrictions by avoiding the persons that impose them. Respecting older grandchildren's choices, in all conditions where personal safety is not an issue, is a key to maintaining loving connections with them.

Respect is missing when grandparents are frequently critical; when they give unasked for advice; when they believe they know better what is right for the family and often say so; when they show little regard for the feelings and ideas of their children and grandchildren.

How do we grandparents learn to behave respectfully to grown children, while "only yesterday" we were changing their diapers? Most

Solid relationships are built on a foundation of respect.

When you let your grandchildren lead you, you may learn something valuable along the way.

19

"Out of the mouths of babes . . ." Before you jump to the defense, remember tact is a learned social behavior your grandchild may not yet have acquired.

adults have already learned to do this well with their offspring, and that respect given, earns respect in turn. Respect for each other is likely the mainstay in all healthy family relationships, and is seen in families that truly like each other and enjoy spending time together. For these people, it is quite natural to behave similarly with their grandchildren. Those who are still perfecting this skill may find some of these guidelines helpful:

- Try to be "in touch" with what you are saying and with how it is being said.
- Listen to yourself as you talk to your grandchildren to hear if you are criticizing, reprimanding, threatening, coercing, or invoking guilt.
- Envision your grandchild as an adult. What would you say to him if he was your neighbor? Your co-worker? Your friend?
- Be alert to your giving unasked for advice. Try to avoid this wherever possible.

The second quality on my list concerns the grandparent's ability to be open and non-defensive in her relationships with her grandchildren. This may be difficult for many of us who have learned to hide our vulnerability behind a facade of protective defensiveness. When we are confronted with unpleasantness, with anger, with hostility, it is much easier to try to defend ourselves against the assault. A young child who says, "Grandma, I don't like you because you didn't buy me bubblegum," may strike right to the heart of a grandmother who has just plunked down forty dollars for a new pair of shoes for school. The tempting response is to reproach, to invoke guilt, to turn defensiveness into offense:

"What an ungrateful boy you are! I just bought you those beautiful new shoes and that's all the thanks I get!"

It is much harder to put yourself in the child's place and appreciate his disappointment. Sure, he *should* be grateful; but he is also disappointed and his disappointment is more largely felt than the gratitude.

An open, non-defensive response might offer:

"I know you're disappointed about not getting any gum. In all my concern for getting your shoes, I forgot about the gum altogether. I really feel bad that you're *so* angry with me."

Grandparents can learn to be increasingly open and non-defensive by tuning in to the feelings that a grandchild is expressing, and by being more genuine about expressing their own. None of this is quite as easy as it sounds, but knowing about *how* to do this is the first step in perfecting the skill.

The third quality that I would list is for grandparents to retain, in so far as they are able, their sense of playfulness. Here, I'm not referring to "playing toys and games" with the grandchildren. I am suggesting maintaining some sense of the "child" within you. Be more spontaneous, playful, inventive, imaginative, and not so serious all the time! Nowhere is it writ that gray hair and bifocals mean the end of a playful spirit, of comic invention, or of a giving up of a sense of the absurd.

I would love to see more grandmothers who have fun with their grandchildren; who have a flair for the ridiculous, and who invoke all those childish games and pranks we used to play as children. We do have limited wind at our age, but as far as possible we can learn to be more playful and less serious with our grandchildren. I realize this is asking a lot—but if we can learn to keep that playful spirit within us, allowing our own "inner child" to surface spontaneously, we will be able to bring to the relationship with our grandchildren a zest and quality of fun that will add immeasurably to the pleasure in our respective lives.

When you look at the world through your grandchild's eyes—you may see something you haven't seen before.

Step only between the cracks in the pavement, talk to flowers, wear a funny hat and sip soda through a curly straw—have fun with your grandchildren.

# 3

# Keeping the Connection

*"My ideal grandma would have time for me."*

WE LIVE IN A consumer-driven, disposable world, in which to buy, to use up and to throw away is the driving force of the economy. Products are rarely made to endure, and it's the odd one that does. We are continually enticed by the new and are subtly reinforced in the belief that "old is worthless" and that it should be discarded as junk at the earliest possible moment, to be replaced by the newer, shinier, more up-to-date model. This cultural programming is so pervasive, it reaches into virtually every aspect of our lives—from the clothes we wear, to the food we eat, to the technology we use to make our lives ever more comfortable. Not only do we crave the "new" in our search for products, we also seek the new in terms of our experiences. "We've done Mexico," heard from holiday-minded adults, suggests that their two-week Mexican sojourn has totally satisfied their curiosity and exhausted their interest in that multi-faceted country, and that the vacationers are now ready for something different, something new.

In the recent past, in our western culture, people, too—like products and experiences—were implicitly considered to be rejects once they had passed their prime. Of course, we would never openly admit our intolerance and disdain for old folk—for to do that would be tantamount to admitting that we were uncaring, uncharitable villains. Yet, in our day-to-day behavior, in our subtle and not-so-subtle treatment of "seniors," we clearly communicated to them that we had very little regard for their ideas, that we did not want them around, that we did not value what they had to offer.

Such attitudes toward the elderly in our society are, happily, beginning to turn around. Perhaps this is because advances in science, in medical and other health technologies, have made it possible for many of us to live longer and to maintain not only our good health, but also our intellectual powers well past our fortieth birthdays. Perhaps it is because the seniors group has grown so large and represents so many potential votes that it can no longer be summarily dismissed. Perhaps it is because, in a funny attitude reversal that is completely contrary to other recent cultural trends, more young people are finding merit in the experiences and learned wisdom of their seniors. Perhaps it is none of these factors, or a combination. Whatever the roots of this painfully slow turn-around of the "out with the trash" attitude toward seniors, it is a welcome development. The rejection of the over-60 generation as useless, worthless and discardable is not only cruel and inhuman, it is folly. More than ever before we desperately need the rich traditions that our elders transmit through the generations down to our newest babes; for without such transmission of culture and tradition we cut ourselves off from a vital life force, from our roots, from ourselves. We end by being disconnected, alienated, and separated from our humanity.

## Wisdom and Traditions

In the poignant and affecting play (and later, the film) *Fiddler on the Roof,* Tevye, father to five daughters, sings of "tradition"—the unseen and sometimes unspoken set of conditions that shapes the culture, that models for us the values and the rules which bring order,

Grandparents bring the traditions of the past to the young, giving grandchildren a feeling for their past.

Traditions are the threads that weave one generation to another.

purpose, and meaning to our lives. Sometimes, the reasons for such rules are unclear. "Why do we do this?" sings one of the daughters.

"I don't know," responds Tevye, shrugging his shoulders, his hands extended with palms upward. "It's a tradition."

The reasons may not be clear to Tevye, but what he is offering is a rich accumulation of wisdom, the combined experiences of humankind that have brought us to the freedom of choice and possibilities we enjoy today. Through the handing down of culture we can remain connected, one to the other, generation to generation, to the human network. Traditions give coherence to our lives. They establish guidelines for responsible behavior and they help us develop our values. Traditions that have lost their relevance are likely to be reframed and reshaped, over time, as a result of changing times and changing values. But they cannot be tossed away, or walked away from, without breaking important, human connections. People who abandon their traditions are in danger of abandoning the meaning and the continuity of their lives.

It is, of course, our grandparents who are instrumental in handing down the culture, in transmitting the traditions down to the new generation. We may love and value them for many reasons—for their own boundless loving and cherishing of the grandchildren, for their generosity of spirit and pocketbook, for their help and support, for their encouragement, for their fried chicken, apple pie or home-made jam. But beyond all these things, when we give them the space, the time, and the freedom to share with us the sum total of their life experiences—their knowledge, wisdom, and values—we are the richer for it. And so, our present generation becomes connected to our past and we are all one.

When grandparents live close to their children, and where visits are regular and frequent, such cultural transmission is a normal part of family life. It happens subtly, without planning and usually without awareness, simply through *behaving*—in the ways we talk to each other, the questions we ask, the advice we give, the stories we tell. From these scenarios, over time, traditions are established and values made clear. We know what the "rules" are and we know when we break them. We know the penalties.

When grandparents are hundreds or thousands of miles away, there must be other ways of making these connections. Otherwise our grandchildren are bereft, and may start their lives without important ties to the past. This is a major and significant role in grandparenting.

## The Gift of Boundless Love

There is another. Unless grandparents live with their offspring, and are called upon to parent as well as to grandparent the little ones, they enjoy a freedom from the obligations of "behavior management"—a responsibility that parents cannot shirk. In the children's normal, day-to-day growing and learning, parents are the ones who set the limits, reprimand, scold—to protect the children's safety and to teach standards of "civilized" and responsible behavior. While necessary, the teaching of responsible behavior is, for many parents, an arduous task, filled with ambiguities and difficulties in deciding about the "best course of action." It is certainly costly in terms of energy expended, and there is not much joy in having to deal with children when they push at the limits their parents have set. What's more, in early childhood years, the demands on parents for "behavior management" may be unremitting. Grandparents, on the other hand, may safely leave most of it to the parents. If Malcolm gets "out of hand," a grandparent has the freedom to step out of the picture and turn things over to mother—and we often choose to do that. After all, we have already done this work! What's more, it is unseemly for us to step in, usurping the parental role, when parents are on hand. So grandparents have the extraordinary option of loving in a much more liberated and total sense than even the best and most nurturing of parents.

This is a force of great power in the raising of young children, and will contribute to the children's emotional health as well as to their growing ability to like and respect themselves.

When grandparents see their grandchildren on a regular basis, the offering of unlimited love and acceptance is a natural part of their everyday relationship. Young grandchildren, through such contact, learn that they are loved, totally and without bounds, in spite of whatever mischief they may have done. (Sometimes, with their parents, they may not be so sure!) When grandparents are geographically remote, their open, generous, limitless love and acceptance can be offered in other ways. Even at a distance, the power of such a love offering towards the building of emotionally strong and secure children is enormous.

In leaving discipline to the parents, grandparents enjoy the privilege of always being the "good guys."

## The Loving Connection: A Two-Way Street

A friend of many years recently became a grandfather. I always thought of him as a particularly reserved man, very quiet and certainly not given to excessive emotional display. But when he talked about his new grandson, I saw his face light up in new ways, and as he described his relationship with the boy, I heard words of love and utter happiness that, in my twenty year friendship with him, I had never heard before.

As a grandfather, he seemed able to release a flood of feelings that, while they might have been inside of him, were never expressed so openly before. As a grandfather, he could, without constraints, experience the full pleasures of a loving relationship. His happiness knew no bounds.

Grandparents may be very important in the lives of grandchildren, but the joys and pleasures that they themselves experience are exhilarating. Many experience this intensity of feeling from the earliest days of their grandchild's life, and the love, joy, and pleasure in the relationship seem to grow over time. There are no rational ways of describing this to others, either. The feelings are huge, and even though we loved our children enormously, what we feel for our grandchildren surpasses even that.

When the grandchildren are tiny, we take pleasure in each new stage of their development, delighting at the first tooth, the first coherent sound (mamamamamammmmm), the first smile. We are eager, hungry for any and all news, no matter how trivial, that lets us in on any new development, and we must take special pains not to brag about these developments to our neighbors lest we appear too foolish. Only other grandparents can understand and readily enter into a passionate discussion about their respective grandchildren's latest accomplishment. I have the feeling that such a discourse is really about giving each one a turn to talk; listening to what the other is saying is a mere courtesy. ("Do you know, he can already sit up by himself!") We dare not tell of these events to others who are not in the grandparent fraternity; they do not understand what the fuss is all about or why grown men and women would want to spend any time discussing such non-events. You have to be a grandparent to know.

As the children grow into toddlers, they are able to respond much more to our expressions of love and to express their love to us. Stepping out of the doorway of the plane, I hear Arlo shout, in a piercing yell that penetrates to the furthest corners of the airport: "Graaaaaannnddmmmmmaaaaaaaaa!" And I know I am loved and wanted by this curly haired, freckle-nosed cherub, and my life is strangely complete. When on the telephone, I say, "I love you," and he says, without coaching from any adult, "I love you, too, grandma," I am rich. Their gifts of love—wet, undisciplined kisses, small, strong arms that wreak havoc with stiff joints, open expressions of devotion in the public marketplace—these fill our hearts as treasures to hoard which breathe life into the cold, hard winter.

Being a grandparent has all the joys of parenting, without the sleepless nights.

With the cares and worries of young parenthood behind them, grandparents can concentrate on giving unconditional love.

Trading the toddler years for the newly emerging "child" who now goes to school brings its special rewards. Children are more articulate and can tell us more about what is happening in their lives. We may now carry on what almost passes for coherent social discourse.

\* \* \*

*Grandma:* Is there anything you'd like to tell me about school?

*Simon:* We made leprechauns. For St. Patrick's Day, you know.

*Grandma:* What's a leprechaun?

*Simon:* Oh, grandma. You know. It's one of those elf guys, those tiny guys that live in the woods. They're Irish.

\* \* \*

*Simon:* When you come to my house, I have a big surprise for you.

*Grandma:* I wonder what it could be?

*Simon:* I'll tell you that it starts with a "t." (giggles)

*Grandma:* Could it be a top? (No) Could it be a toy? (No) A tom-tom? (No) A kite?

*Simon:* Grandma, kite doesn't start with a "t."

*Grandma:* I give up then. I can't guess.

*Simon:* (Giggles) You'll see it when you come. You'll be soooooooooo surprised.

*Grandma:* Will you ever tell me? Can't you give any hints?

*Simon:* You'll have to wait until you see it. Otherwise the surprise will be spoiled.

\* \* \*

Why is this such fun for a grandmother or a grandfather? Why do grandmothers and grandfathers take delight in repeating these inane telephone conversations to each other, when during most other times we converse adult-to-adult on matters of much greater consequence? It's hard to know why, and perhaps the more important question is not even "why" at all, but how to find ways to experience more of it. It always feels so warm and good. If we mourn the end of the toddler years, and are unsure of what pleasures the school-age child will bring, we can know with certainty that there are many new joys to come.

Pre-adolescence brings other gifts. Now entering their middle years, children are more sophisticated, more knowledgeable, more socialized. They are far more mobile and independent, and can travel by themselves to visit grandparents in far-off cities. They use the telephone frequently to tell you their troubles, and what they'd like you to bring them when you next visit! "My mother doesn't know I'm calling you, grandma, so please don't tell her." The cunning of their learned interpersonal skills may be a constant challenge, placing you in the awkward ethical position of having to choose between respecting your grandchild's request, or letting her parents know that she is doing something about which they would not approve.

Most pre-teens are now computer literate. They have access to computers in most school programs, and can find their way around the Internet as easily as their grandparents do around the golf course. If both grandchildren and grandparents are connected on the Internet, pre-teens will send their own e-mail messages, without instruction or advice from their parents.

Pre-teens can visit grandma and grandpa for extended stays, without waking at night to say how much they are missing home. There are new experiences that you can share—new trips to take, new projects to enjoy together. Pre-adolescence brings an emerging maturity and sophistication that is enjoyable on new and different levels, even though their urgent requests and demands may sorely try your own ethical values! During visits grandchildren are now "mates." They walk with us in the woods or at the beach without getting tired, and take delight in spotting birds. They help with washing the car. They want to see movies that are interesting for us as well. We can count on them in ways that are just not possible in the younger set, like helping

Each generation changes. Your grandchildren will be different again from their parents.

to carry the groceries or threading a needle. Not only can we count on them, but they take pleasure in their ability to be there, in helping ways for us.

Grandchildren who are teens are now young adults. For those with whom we have carried on ongoing, intimate relationships since they were little, the fun is just about to begin! These teens are now devoted members of the inner circle of family, in our golden years. Our special relationships have not diminished; they have rather increased in affection. They come to visit on their own, picking up the phone, and announcing their imminent arrival. That they *want* to come, *choosing* to spend time with us, is a mark of how soundly we have built that relationship. If both grandchild and grandparents are connected on the Internet, e-mail messages will likely be frequent and passionate and will take the place of direct, telephone communication.

"Well, grandma, are we going shopping, or what?" asks Arlo only moments after his arrival. That he enjoys "hanging out" with his grandmother is a gift to me; as we walk the streets, he allows me to ask questions that lead me into the inner sanctum of his life. Although I wish to know everything about his life, I nonetheless try to maintain a healthy respect for his unwillingness to disclose his secrets. He is now planning for his future and tells me about how he sees his life shaping, and what values he holds dear. With each unsolicited disclosure, the privilege I feel is immeasurable.

Shopping has replaced going to Science World, or to the Adventure Playground, or to the Water Park. Like most teens of either sex, both grandsons have a heightened interest in clothes—not only clothes, per se, but what is currently in fashion. Arlo tells me, "Once when I was very small, and we were in a toy store, you told me that one day, when I got to be older, I wouldn't want toys anymore, but I would want clothes instead. I thought to myself, 'My grandma must be crazy. I will ALWAYS want toys!' And now, here I am with you, shopping for clothes! How did you know that, grandma?"

The independence that the boys have as young adults is, at the same

All the different stages of your grandchild's life open up new avenues for sharing experiences and communicating.

time, wonderful and disconcerting. They may choose to stay up late at night when visiting, watching late night movies on TV, my role as the monitor of their bedtime no longer viable. They may choose to go off by themselves, in the evenings, to the movies or to visit friends, as I sit and worry about their safety. Simon, who now drives, has yet to ask to borrow my car—but I'm sure that time is not far off. Yet, when I tell them that I worry about their safety, and that I need them to be home at a certain time, they are respectful of my feelings and allow me to make those demands without any opposition.

The needs and lifestyles of young adults present different challenges to grandparents than those of young children—but the joy and pleasures of these more adult connections are sweeter still. When we went to Simon's high school graduation ceremonies, he was given only two tickets for the special "formal tea" and chose, above all others, to invite his grandparents. Such a reward is only comparable to arriving at the gates of heaven.

We can count on them and they take pleasure in their ability to be there, in helping ways, for us.

Grandchildren who have grown to maturity, and who have had an ongoing, intimate and loving relationship with their grandparents, even across the miles, will be devoted young adults, close members of the inner circle of family, in our golden years. The special relationships seem not to diminish, but rather to increase in affection. When the grandchild is in "full bloom," and when some grandparents may be experiencing physical decline, and the balance of physical strength and personal autonomy tips in the direction of the grandchild, there is much sustained pleasure in knowing that we are loved, cared about, prized—that we are special.

# 4

# The Telephone Connection

*"My ideal grandma would tell me things like 'where space ends.'"*

IN THE DOZEN YEARS since the first edition of this book was published, long distance telephone rates, as compared to other living costs, have markedly *decreased!* Not only are there special long distance "packages" that one can subscribe to, but with telephone companies competing for your business, long distance charges seem almost miniscule, compared to, for example, the price of gasoline! That makes the telephone the simplest, most obvious, and perhaps the most economical way of keeping in touch with long distance grandchildren. Even with special long distance packages, there are still ways to keep costs down, to make the most of precious telephone moments, and to use that cold, indifferent piece of plastic and wire to intensify an emotional contact—even when grandchildren are quite young.

## Long Distance Telephone Costs

Many telephone companies now offer special packages for long distance calling, and if you are going to make serious use of the long distance connection, you might want to check out what your local provider has to offer and what competition there is for your business.

When our grandchildren were very young, we would place our call to them before eight. The little ones were generally awake by 7:00, and probably getting ready for, or in the process of having breakfast. Pre–eight o'clock rates allowed us to talk for twenty or thirty minutes, and both boys had a chance to talk to each of us, with some time reserved to talk to our daughter as well. The bill for such an extended chat usually amounted to less than $10—considerably less than the cost of a tank of gas! Using the long distance telephone allowed us to "visit" with our grandchildren regularly.

## Calling By Arrangement

In using the telephone connection, there are some quite important considerations to take into account if the calls are to be welcome and welcoming, rather than intrusive. In the very first instance, there ought to be an explicit agreement with your offspring about the time at which you call. If the early morning call awakens her each time, the cumulative effect of calling is very likely to be intrusive. If the call comes at the only time she has to share a relaxed breakfast with her husband, then it is also likely to be intrusive. If you are a retired grandmother, with lots of leisure time to spend, it may be hard to remember that your offspring's schedule is quite different from your own. Your son or daughter may not be so readily available to share the time that you may have so freely at your disposal. Much difficulty about this can be avoided if you make a prior agreement with them about the most appropriate time for your visiting call. (To be respectful of and sensitive to your own child's time frame and needs is, I believe, indispensable to a healthy adult-to-adult relationship.)

There is a second consideration. I am always mindful that, even if my call comes at the agreed-upon time, it may at that particular moment be a "bad time." If the children are cranky; if they are fussing and require mother's attention; if they are "otherwise engaged" and unable to come to the phone; if the toast is burning; if there was some marital blowup—there might be a hundred different reasons that your call came at the worst possible time of the day! You will want to develop a sensitivity for these occasions. Even though you have been looking forward to this "visit" with great anticipation; even though your own need to be in touch is great—once more, to be respectful of and sensitive to the situation at the other end of the line is imperative. If it is a bad time, tell your son or daughter, "I'm sorry, sweetheart. I'll call again another time. Will that be okay? Is there anything I can do?" Or, alternately, "It's okay, babe. I understand. Call me back when you can and let me know how things turned out. I love you." Then, with all the self-discipline you can muster, hang up.

No matter how good our intentions, we can, without sensitivity to our children's need for a life of their own choice and style, become more nuisance than loving parent. That is why it is so important to maintain, in so far as possible, that respectful regard—even on the telephone.

## Connecting with Six-Month-Old Children

While to some adults this may sound silly, I began my telephone connection with our boys when they were very young—somewhere around six to eight months old. I would ask my daughter to put the receiver to the child's ear, and I would talk to him in much the same way as I might if I were standing right there, in person, in front of him: "Oh, Arlo. Is that my beautiful Arlo?"

"Where is your nose, Arlo?"

"Where are your pretty little eyes?"

"Where are your sweet little toes, Arlo?"

In these very first telephone visits, my daughter would tell me that the telephone voice slipping into the child's ear would produce a widening of the eyes; an expression of listening. I made sure to use

Children respond to sound and voices long before they learn to speak.

words that were already part of the child's listening vocabulary. His name—used over and over. References to parts of himself—eyes, nose, mouth, ears, toes. There was some assurance that he could begin to comprehend something of what I was saying. More important, he would sense the voice quality and tone—soft, reassuring, gentle; never strident or shrill. What you say, and how you say it, should be inviting, not demanding.

In later months, but still before Arlo was even a year old, using these same words would produce most gratifying responses.

"Is that my beautiful Arlo?"

"Arlo. . ."

"Where is your nose, Arlo?"

"Nose. . ."

"Where are your pretty little eyes?"

"Eyes. . ."

The words are sweeter to your ears than music. And sometimes, when you say, "I'm going to kiss those little toes. Kiss, kiss, kiss," you may hear the most delicious, delightful, delectable giggle of pleasure that will sing in your ears and warm your heart (as Arlo came to say it) "for all day."

The habit of the telephone connection soon becomes a pattern in the life of the long distance grandmother and grandchild. When the grandchild begins really to talk, there is a wealth of material to be mined.

When the boys were toddlers, grandma's call had become an eagerly anticipated morning event.

"It's grandma!" Simon would shout and rush to the phone.

"Hello," he would say softly, still unsure.

"Is that my beautiful Simon?"

"Yeh! Heh! Heh! Heh!"

"I'm so happy to hear your voice."

"Me, too."

"Have you had your breakfast yet?"

On the telephone, try to be inviting rather than commanding.

Scheduling a time to call may avoid friction with your children.

"Yeh."

"Did you have cereal?"

"I had cereal and yogurt."

"With milk on the top?"

"No. Milk was on the bottom."

"Was it good?"

"Mmmmmm…"

"What will you do after breakfast?"

"Watch TB." (!)

"Is it Sesame Street?"

"I don't know. Maybe."

"Is it snowing there yet?"

"Wait. I'll look. (Pause.) No. Not snowing yet."

"Maybe you'll play outside, later."

"Yeh. Maybe."

"I love you, Simon."

"I love you, too, grandma."

"Can Arlo have a turn now?"

"Arlo! Come and have a turn now."

"Goodbye, my dearest Simon." (Kiss, kiss, kiss)

"Goodbye, grandma." (Kiss, kiss, kiss)

## Telephoning to Little Children

There are, as you can see, very many questions and accessible answers. I learned, for example, that when I asked too many broad, open-ended questions, like "What are you going to do today?"—even Simon, at age four-and-a-half, was not able to deal with them. He would say, churlishly, "I don't know," with sufficient inflection to tell me that I asked something more of him than he had data for. Perhaps it made him a little angry. Maybe I had put him on the spot. Maybe it made him feel a little inadequate. Perhaps I was reading too much into his response, but the way he said it, with the "I" stretched out—"I-I-I-I

More direct questions can elicit more productive answers.

don't know"—sounded suspiciously near stress. And that's not what the telephone visit is about.

So I learned to keep the questions as direct, as specific and concrete as possible—so that the communication between us kept flowing. And since "littles" do not yet have the experience of making "small talk," I always assumed full responsibility for keeping the conversation moving.

In talking to young grandchildren it may be helpful to arm yourself with a few good questions in advance. For example, if you ask about the weather, about what they had for breakfast, about the toys they are playing with, you are likely to get a conversation going. With older grandchildren, the options about what you may ask expand enormously. Whatever questions you choose, try them out, and if they bear fruit, use them again and again. What's great about young children (and some older children as well) is that they love and thrive on repetition. It gives them feelings of security. So if you find yourself repeating the same questions time after time, you don't have to worry about being boring.

There was another vital dimension to telephone visits with my grandsons when they were very young—the explicit and open expression of love. I believe this to be far more important than the number or types of questions I asked. In every telephone connection, I tried to convey as much as possible of what I was feeling for them, putting it in words directly and without self-consciousness.

"Is that my beautiful Arlo?"

"I just love you to pieces!"

"I just can't wait to see you!"

"I have been thinking about you all day!"

"I couldn't wait to hear your voice!"

"When I see those goo-goo eyes of yours, they just make me go crazy!"

"I wish I could put my arms around you and give you a big, big hug!"

> Try to have some questions ready before you pick up the phone.

I feel all these feelings for the boys; and I want to be unashamed about expressing them. From very early on, both boys were quite remarkably open about responding in kind:

"I just can't wait to see you!"

"Me, too."

"I love you, Simon."

"I love you too, grandma."

"I love you to pieces!"

"I know," he would say, melting my heart.

Such open and extravagant expressions of affection to my grandsons has always been important to me. It gives me an outlet for what I feel and would have expressed even more, in non-verbal ways, if the boys were closer and I saw them more often. Because there were fewer opportunities for hugging and cuddling and other person-to-person touching, I wanted to ensure that I expressed that love verbally.

There is more. My open show of affection has taught the boys, implicitly, that to express love freely is not only okay, it is welcome, appreciated, and a significant aspect of close relationships. Now, even as young adults, when my grandsons continue to tell me, "I love you too, grandma," it nurtures me and keeps me going until we talk again.

Not every grandparent can show affection openly. Not every grandparent expresses love effusively. Some show love in more subtle ways—in voice inflections that express tenderness and caring, in ways of speaking that communicate regard, in a warmth that is shown even through the wires. Showing interest in what the child is telling you— and it may be a long and complicated tale—will certainly indicate your caring. Being a good listener, not interrupting, being uncritical—all communicate regard, affection, prizing. Instead of gushing kisses, a grandparent may be equally loving with messages such as:

"I really miss you, you know."

"Tell me some more about what you did today."

"I was so happy to get the pictures you sent me. I hung them up

Children learn by example. Open expressions of affection make it easier for children to respond in kind. "I love you too, grandma" will keep you going until the next call.

right here in the kitchen, so I can see them every day. And when I see them, I think of you."

"I remember the good times we had when you were here."

"I am so happy to talk to you. And grandpa wants to have a turn to talk too."

## Telephoning Older Grandchildren

Telephone visits with older grandchildren are naturally quite different again. First, and obviously, they allow for a much greater range of discourse. Also, for whatever reason, older children may be less comfortable with an effusive display of affection—especially on the telephone. We may need to be sensitive to that, and not respond in ways that might embarrass the pre-adolescent and/or teenage boy or girl. Reading the "signals" that the child sends, in the form of how he or she responds to open displays of affection, will tell us if this is embarrassing. Such signals then tell us the extent to which we may allow ourselves to be extravagantly loving.

With older children, there will be much opportunity to talk about school, about their friends, about after-school activities, about weekend experiences, about main events (like birthdays, trips, holidays). If you feel comfortable about it, and if it doesn't seem as if you are prying into matters of a more personal nature, you might want to allow your grandchild a chance to talk about matters of deeper concern—difficulties he might be having at school, or interpersonally. A grandparent who is able to *listen,* and to listen respectfully, and attend thoughtfully and sensitively to a grandchild's feelings is not only a devoted and loving relative, but an emotionally supportive adult as well. Many grandparents who live close enough to the grandchildren to allow for regular and frequent visits are often the "sounding boards" for a variety of complaints. For example:

"My father won't let me go to Billy's house after school."

Older children, particularly teenagers, can be quite self-conscious about expressing sentiments and feelings on the phone.

In the circumscribed world of a child a quarrel with a friend or a run-in with a teacher may have monumental significance.

"My mother thinks I'm still too young to ride my bicycle in the road."

"I don't *want* to take piano lessons. I don't *want* to practice the piano."

"Marsha didn't invite me to her birthday party and all the other girls got to go."

"I have nobody to play with."

"My teacher was mean to me. She made me stay after school."

"I miss my daddy."

After all, grandparents have more time to listen, and they are often more apt to be "on the child's side." Such emotional support is very important for the growing child, and can also be generously given over the telephone.

## Guidelines for a Good Telephone Relationship

In offering this support, there are some important guidelines to keep in mind, so that you are helpful, rather than adding to the problem, and so that you make the most of your telephone time.

- Be a good listener. Let the child have his say. Let him get the problem out, and "off his chest."
- Be attentive to the problem he is describing and to the feelings he is expressing. (His problem may not seem like a huge problem to you, but it may be very important to him.)
- Express your understanding of what your grandchild is saying and feeling. (For example, "I understand how very much you wanted to go to that party, and how hurt you were when you weren't invited.")
- Be respectful to your grandchild as he tells about the situation. Be on his side.
- Allow him the time to talk it out. (If you are on a tight telephone budget and there is not enough time for this, it may be better not to open up this line of discussion, rather than cut him off.)

In remembering what to say, you will also want to remember what to avoid:

- Don't interrupt.
- Don't make light of his feelings or of the problem he is facing. (E.g., "Oh, that's not so bad." Or, "Don't feel bad.")
- Don't try to "fix" the problem for him. ("This is what I think you should do.")
- Don't be critical or judgmental. ("What did *you* do to her that might have caused her not to invite you?") Don't invoke guilt. Don't preach a sermon about the "right thing to do."
- Don't interrogate and make it sound like you are an inquisitor. Do not pry.
- Don't change the subject.
- Don't tell your grandchild how you dealt with similar problems when you were his age.
- Don't cut him off before he has had a chance to finish.
- Avoid criticizing, even implicitly, one or the other of the child's parents. This is a very sure way of driving a wedge between parents-grandparents-children. It will subtract from, rather than build, a good relationship.

It may not sound like a very helpful and supportive strategy to "merely" be a good and attentive listener, and to "merely" communicate that you understand. After all, shouldn't grandparents "take charge" of the problem, and do something magic to fix it, or make it disappear? If you have ever been a supportive listener to another adult, you will be quick to realize that those who wrestle with life problems are considerably helped by a chance to talk these problems out. What they want and need most of all is a chance to get the problem expressed, to talk about their feelings, and to be listened to respectfully. They really don't *want* our advice; and most of the time, giving it is entirely inappropriate. (How can we really know what other people *should* do?) By listening, by responding in a way that

People—children and adults alike—don't want their problems "fixed," they just want someone to listen.

communicates "I understand," you allow the person to gain perspective on the problem for himself. You also communicate your support and your understanding. To receive such understanding and respect is a powerful force for good in most relationships. And when we have even one person in our lives who can do this for us, we are very lucky.

You can, if you choose, be that understanding grandparent for your growing grandchildren. You can communicate, even on the long distance telephone, that you listen, you care, you understand. With teenage grandchildren going through their rebellious years, who are constantly at odds with parents, such listening, caring, and understanding from grandparents can be their primary source of empathy. One of the concerns frequently expressed by teenagers is that "nobody understands me." Grandparents can listen; they can understand. And through that understanding and acceptance we can contribute immeasurably to the self-confidence, self-esteem and self respect of our loved ones.

The key to all of this is: If you choose. Some grandparents may feel unequipped to carry out such a discourse. Some may wish (understandably) to retreat from such emotional discussions. Some of us may feel uncomfortable doing this on the telephone. Some may feel it is better and wiser to leave such discussions in the parents' domain. We are, of course, "in charge" of whatever topics we want to deal with on the long distance telephone. And, since discretion is the better part of valor, it is probably much wiser for all concerned that whatever topics are opened, they feel both natural and comfortable to us.

If you do choose to talk to your grandchild, hearing her out about her anger, disappointment, frustration, anxiety, fear—or whatever is troubling her heart, the sample dialogue that follows may be helpful. Note particularly how grandma listens, and communicates her understanding. Note, too, how this response encourages her grandchild to talk out her feelings.

*Andy:* I wanted to have a sleepover at Emily's house this weekend, but my dad said I couldn't go.

If your grandchild raises a question that is too uncomfortable or disturbing for you, gently steer the conversation to safer ground. Abruptly changing the subject may appear a rejection.

*Grandma:* You were disappointed. This was important to you.

*Andy:* Yeh. Barbara and Susan are going too. Now, I'm the only one who's not going.

*Grandma:* You feel left out of all the fun. They're going to have a great time and you'll be missing it.

*Andy:* Yeh. I don't know why my dad has to be so mean to me.

*Grandma:* You're angry with your dad. You feel he's being unreasonable by not letting you go.

*Andy:* Well, he thinks I'm too young for it. The girls stay up all night and watch TV, you know.

*Grandma:* Your dad doesn't want you to stay up and watch those late programs all night.

*Andy:* Yeh. I'm getting old enough to do that, you know, grandma.

*Grandma:* You're disappointed that your dad doesn't think so.

*Andy:* He thinks I'm still a baby.

*Grandma:* You feel very grown up, and you'd like him to know that you are growing up, too.

*Andy:* Grandma, how come you understand me? It feels so good to talk to you.

*Grandma:* It feels good to me to talk with you, too, darling. I hope we can talk again soon.

Grandma does not try to fix Andy's problem. She doesn't tell her "not to feel bad." Nor does she give advice or sermonize. Grandma is not judgmental, neither does she ask questions. She "merely" listens, attends to what is being said, and responds in a way that shows that she understands. And this kind of response not only helps Andy to feel better; she also has an increased perspective on the situation. She knows too that grandma is on her side and that she has, in grandma, a "listening ear"—a person to turn to when things get rough. While grandparents can and do offer such support and emotional sustenance "in the flesh," the powerful impact of a grandparent who understands is not diminished in the long distance connection.

There will, of course, be those times when you telephone, and your

Having their feelings validated by an adult builds children's confidence and self-esteem.

Insisting your grand-
children pay you
respect and show you
love is likely to back-
fire. Respect must be
given to be gotten and
love cultivated like
prize roses.

grandchild, older or younger, will not wish to talk. He may be "too busy" or involved in an activity that he does not wish to leave at that moment. He may be wrestling with his own demons; he may be late for football practice with his friends. If the principle of respect is in operation—respect for your grandchild's right to make that choice— then your response to it is clear. You will be disappointed, even hurt at what may appear to be a slight. You may feel that he is being disre-spectful of you. You may have to "manage" your own needs to talk to him and put them aside in deference to his needs. In your heart, you may wish that his mother would insist that he drop everything and come to the telephone.

You, of course, will have to decide how to play this one out, remem-bering all the while that there is no "free choice." If you coerce, or in-sist; if you allow your own needs to take precedence over the child's; if you invoke guilt—you are paying a big price for a moment's conversa-tion. And only you can decide if it's worth it. Too many of these insis-tences are likely to make a larger dent in your grandparent-grandchild "bank account" than all the long distance telephone calls put together.

There are many ways to communicate to your grandchildren that you love them. The way you do it must be your own way—not forced, not according to someone else's formula—but genuinely yours. In the telephone connection, it is the communication of love that is the key. And if the telephone visit is the best we can have, let us make the most of it. Heart to heart.

# 5

# The Postal Connection

*"My ideal grandma would have time for me. We
would do puzzles together."*

NOW MOCKED as "snail mail" by those who have learned to use other,
more high-tech modes of written communication, like the fax machine, overnight express delivery services, and of course, the ubiqui-
tous e-mail, the postal connection still endures as an important
means of reaching out and making contact with long distance grandchildren. In an era when the art of letter writing is losing ground, it
may be considered archaic to write; but, in fact, there is nothing quite
like getting a real letter from someone you love.

From the time that our grandchildren were about two, I began to
develop the "postal connection." Letters from home, and letters and
postcards from travels were the two main vehicles, and more about
each is written below. But first, a few words about the age at which to
begin, and about the potential side benefits far beyond those of the
connection itself.

## When to Begin

The age of two seems a good time to begin writing letters to your
grandchild. It is at about two that most children begin to use language more fluently. At this age they can understand sophisticated

45

Letter writing should be approached with the idea of communicating—to reach out and touch—not motivated by a desire to push grandchildren to read and write earlier than their natural development allows.

thoughts and directions far beyond their ability to express their own ideas in words. But their use of language and understanding of meanings is definitely in full bloom. Before two, in my experience, children cannot make much meaning of what the mail might bring in the form of letters—other than as something to taste, chew, or use to pat the dog. At about two, somehow, magically, a bridge is crossed. The way we communicate our thoughts and feelings through spoken and written language is now much more clearly understood. Of course, how and when this occurs has a great deal to do with the language experiences a child has at home (how much reading is done with him, how he is talked to and encouraged to talk, by his parents).

Of course, the age of two is not some kind of magic number, and a bridge is not crossed the moment children reach their second birthday; it's a "ballpark" estimate. Children who reach this stage earlier, or even much later, are neither more gifted, nor more backward. They simply have made their crossings earlier or later, for reasons we do not as yet understand. We used to believe that the timing of a child's developmental stages had everything to do with genetic ability. We believed that we could make fairly accurate predictions about overall intelligence and future abilities based on such things as early language development. A child who spoke early was "obviously gifted," and clearly headed for high academic achievement and a successful future as a literary giant. Children who lagged behind were "developmentally slow," and perhaps signalling problems with intelligence, lower potential for future scholastic performance, and who knew what other difficulties as an adult.

We have learned that nothing could be further from the truth, and know now that such predictions are folly. Even worse, they set up wrongful expectations that can do serious damage to the way children see themselves and greatly limit their opportunities to grow at their own comfortable developmental pace. In fact, there is evidence that children who are slow to speak may, as adults, show extreme intelligence, even genius (Albert Einstein, for example). On the other hand, children who speak very early may as adults show no other remarkable talent. Children can be, and often are, greatly harmed by subtle, even unvoiced, adult expectations, and we grandparents must be extremely cautious about communicating such expectations either to parents or to grandchildren.

Assume the age of two, then, as a general reference point, not as a figure writ in stone and handed down from the oracle. Writing to your grandchild before the age of two will certainly do no harm, but letters that come at two or later probably will have a greater chance of intensifying that grandparent-grandchild connection.

Writing letters and postcards to very young (and older) grandchildren has many potential benefits which give the postal connection great power above and beyond the mere contact itself. First, and most obviously, it communicates to your grandchildren that they are important. Important enough to have their very own letters. Think of how we feel when someone of significance takes the time to write to us. Think of how we feel when we see, in our own mailbox, that special letter from a special person. Those very same feelings of being esteemed, that same joy in receiving an important letter of one's own, can be clearly seen in young children as well. Having your very own letter is far more consequential than having a mere sentence devoted to you tacked on to someone else's letter. So, for the sense of importance they give, such letters are very significant.

There is, of course, much more. Through the spoken word, very young children learn that this is one way we humans can convey our ideas and feelings. Learning that they may be communicated via the written word as well is the next major stage in acquiring literacy. To be able to record thoughts is one of the more important attributes that distinguish humans from other species. It is one of our most precious gifts, for once we can read and write, worlds hitherto unknown and unexpected are opened for us.

Receiving their very own letters with their names on the envelope makes grandchildren feel important, thereby building self-esteem.

Writing letters and postcards to our very small grandchildren teaches them that what we want to tell them may be transmitted to them via pencil and paper. This is a powerful and profound message. They are learning, in a natural way, that written words carry meanings. Our letters will generate a desire to take meanings from these written words, and will create a strong motivation for reading and writing. What's more, personal letters will teach your grandchildren respect for the written word. So writing to grandchildren is a very powerful and important contribution to their growth.

During my academic life, I had to travel frequently, and on those journeys it took very little effort to select, from among the picture postcards at the airport or the hotel, a card that I thought would have special appeal for one or the other of our boys. If I happened to be in San Francisco, for example, I might choose a picture of a cable car, or the sea lions sunning themselves at the edge of the Pacific Ocean. The message that I would write to our preschool-age grandchildren would be simple, describing where I was, and what the picture on the postcard had to do with my travels. Each grandchild got his very own postcard. And if the picture on each of the cards was the same, my message for each boy would be different—a special message for each special boy.

My dearest Arlo: I hope you like this picture of a cable car. I can see it here on the street, in San Francisco. I love you. G.

My dearest Simon: Can you see this cable car? It runs up and down the big, big hills here in San Francisco. It has a big, loud bell. Clang! Clang! (The bell says, "Watch out, everybody! Here I come!") I love you. G.

Dear Jane:
This building
looks like it is
going to fall over.
It is called the
Leaning Tower
of Pisa. GRAN
x n x

If you are a frequent traveler, picture postcards are fun as well as a lesson in geography.

48

If I found myself in a less interesting place, there was always a picture postcard of an airplane that I could send. Both boys were keen on airplanes—and I tried to capitalize on their interests. But it's also possible to include pictures that might extend their interests into other, virgin territories. For example, from London:

My dearest Betsy: This is a picture of a big bridge in London. You can see the towers. The boats go under it. When you grow up, maybe we can go together to see this bridge. I love you, Betsy. Grandma.

Or, for example, from Victoria:

My dearest Franklin: Whew! Can you see all those flowers in that market? This place is full of flowers. Flowers everywhere! And the flowers smell like perfume. Victoria is beautiful, but I miss you. I love you. Grandma.

Your grandchild may have other interests and there are so many cards to choose from:

Dear Sean: I thought you would like this picture of a whale. It is such a beautiful animal, and so smart, too. There are two whales like this in the aquarium here. I hope you like this picture of the whale.

Dear Franny: The birds come to eat the crumbs of bread right from our table. We like to sit here in the morning and watch the birds have their breakfast with us. I'll bet you can put some crumbs out for your birds at home.

Dearest Maggie: Did you ever see such huge blueberries? They look good enough to eat, right off this card! Wouldn't you just love a big piece of blueberry pie with vanilla ice cream on top? I wish we could grow blueberries like this in our backyard.

Perhaps you have a grandchild who loves cars. Postcards of classic models could carry messages such as "Grandad used to drive a car like this one—only it wasn't pink. Don't you think that's very cool?"

Dear Polly: Here's a picture of our hotel. Isn't it big? I think it looks like a castle where a fairy princess might live. I wonder if there are any fairy princesses that still live here?

Grandmothers don't have to be travelers to use the postcard connection. There are picture postcards on the racks of your local greeting card shop, supermarket, and drugstore with intriguing alternatives that capitalize on the best of what your home territory has to offer:

Dearest Jason: When spring comes, our park is full of spring flowers. The colors are so beautiful. Here is what the flowers look like when they are all in bloom. Don't you just love those colors!

My dearest Ellen: This is a picture of the ferryboat that takes the cars over to the island. You can drive your car right onto the boat and get a ride across the river. I wonder how people got their cars across to the island before ferryboats were invented?

Hello, my sweetheart: This man was fishing in the lake and he caught this big carp. I guess they took this picture right after it happened. He looks quite happy, doesn't he? Do you suppose he is going to cook it for his supper? He'll be eating fish every day for a week!

While postcards can and should be sent to young grandchildren, you will want to send them to the school-age grandchild and teenagers as well. To be especially remembered with your own post-card message is important for grandchildren of all ages. Through this gesture, they will feel esteemed and valued. For young school-age children, the postcard will also give them practice in reading and deciphering handwriting (printing is probably a good idea), as well as expanding their sense of geography and place. It may also stimulate their interests in history, in new flora and fauna, in art. Teenagers who are more sophisticated may enjoy postcards because the photographs are aesthetically appealing, or because they present a "flavor" of a place that is more attractive than what they will find in a textbook. They may even enjoy collecting the stamps!

Dearest David: When I read about King Henry VIII in my history books, I never realized his size! Here's a picture of the armor he wore when he went into battle. Whew! He was huge! I thought about the poor horse that had to hold both him and this huge, metal suit! Love from London.

Dearest Johanna: When the train rounded the bend and I got my first glance at the Canadian Rockies, they just took my breath away! For a moment, I hardly believed that I was still on earth! Love from Calgary.

Dearest Jim: We've settled down into our RV campground for the night and before going to bed, I want to write this card to you about cactus! My word! Those are strange and wonderful plants, of the most unusual shapes. They say that some parts of them are good to eat. But what about the bristles? Love from Santa Fe.

Dearest Peggy: Grandpa and I took a trip downtown yesterday to see the St. Patrick's Day Parade. I have never seen it before. What fun! All the marchers *and* all the watchers in green! A great day for the Irish. Love.

## You Don't Have To Be a Writer

Taking on the letter connection requires no special talent. You don't have to be a "writer" to do this. Letters to young grandchildren can and should come more frequently than postcards—perhaps as often as twice a month—depending upon the amount of free time you have, and upon how important the connection is for you. Letters, unlike postcards, can be longer and fuller in detail. They can and should bring special messages of love, as well as some other messages you want to tell. And even if you live a perfectly serene life, in which "nothing much happens"—there's generally more to write about than you might believe.

Letters do not have to be profound. They do not have to be witty, or even wise. They do not have to be original, or acts of depth and significant creativity. They need merely be your thoughts, transformed onto paper with pen or pencil.

Dearest Jon-O (To a "little"): I am so happy to be writing this letter to you. I have been thinking about you. I wish you were here with me right now. If you were, I would give you a hundred kisses—some on your nose and some on your toes and some on your fingers, too. And some right on your belly button, where it tickles! I am sending you these kisses and hugs in this letter. Kiss, kiss, kiss. OOOXXX from Grandma.

In writing to our young boys, I liked also to send them messages about events in our lives. These were actually quite simple stories, told in letter form. The events were far from spectacular, and quite the garden-variety type. Of course, when there is a spectacular event, make capital of it!

Dearest Arlo: Hello, my little love. I went out to the garden today and guess what! I saw the first crocus of spring. There it was, all by itself, right in the middle of the garden. A beautiful, golden

Children are not art critics. Stick figures and representational drawings will evoke as much pleasure as more accomplished creations.

crocus. Maybe it will be spring soon. I hope so. You will be able to go and play outside in the springtime without those heavy boots and snowsuit. Will you like that? I will make a picture of it for you. Love, Grandma.

(Drawing pictures is *not* my cup of tea, and I feel as clumsy with a drawing pen as a rhino in a flower garden. But the stick figures I did, no matter how inept, seemed nevertheless to delight our boys, and their enthusiasm for my "pictures" encouraged me to keep sending them.)

Dearest Simon: It was grandpa's birthday yesterday. Did you know that? His birthday comes right after yours—sixteen days after. Sixteen ones. We had a little party for grandpa. No balloons, though. He had a big, big birthday cake, with lots of chocolate. Is that your favorite, too? There were lots of candles on grandpa's cake. So many candles! I'm making a picture of grandpa's cake, so you can see it. I love you, dearest Simon. Grandma.

You can see that a grandparent does not need to be a literary giant to write letters to grandchildren. Perhaps such expertise is even more of a handicap than an asset! All that is required is the expression of thoughts and feelings—the kinds of things you would say if your grandchild were there, sharing the experience with you.

## Things to Write About

What might be included in letters to grandchildren? What should be avoided? Though there are no hard and fast rules, here are some guidelines and ideas that come from my own experiences with children, and from my own grandparenting trials and errors:

- Experiences from your own home, garden, street, shopping, recreational activities.
- Experiences you have had with your grandchild that you want him or her to think about and remember.

Always keep in mind that in writing a letter you are giving something to your grandchild—a story, a past or present experience, an expression of your love.

- Experiences from your own childhood which are similar to and/or different from your grandchild's.
- Experiences about a pet and/or other animals.
- Experiences the child has had that you have learned about from the parent. For example:

Dearest David: When I spoke to your mommy last night, she told me you had a new tooth! Oh, boy! How many teeth now? Lots! You are getting to be such a big boy! Do you think I will recognize you when I see you? I love you, Grandma.

- Anticipation of happy events. For example:

Dearest Melissa: Guess what! I am coming to visit your house. I am coming with grandpa, on the airplane. In two weeks! I can't wait! Will you come to the airport to meet me? Then you can see the plane land. What a big noise it makes! What will we do together when I get there? Get your hugs and kisses ready. Here I come! I love you. Grandma.

## What Not to Write About

As a matter of personal preference I avoid letters about TV programs and letters about "What should I buy for you?" Topics I consider harmful and best avoided include:

- Letters that ask for skills beyond the child's capability. (For example, "Can you count to 16 yet?")
- Letters that exert subtle pressure. (For example, "I wish you could come and stay with me at my house.")
- Letters that invoke guilt or are subtly punitive. (For example, "I was sorry to hear that you were a bad boy.")
- Letters with a disciplinary tone which set up expectations for certain behavior. (For example, "I hope you are being a good boy, and that you are helping your mother with chores.")

"This is a picture of grandpa's birthday cake. Look at all that delicious chocolate icing and all those candles."

- Letters that dwell on tragedy.
- Letters that divide the child's loyalties. (For example, "Do you love me best of all?")

These are, of course, my opinions. I believe that children have sufficient exposure to TV, and much of what they see is not worth watching, let alone writing about. Nor would I dwell on the purchase of new toys, as I do not wish to exploit the "grandmother-is-for-buying-toys" association. I also believe that exerting subtle performance expectations ("Can you count yet?") may make the child feel stressed. If so, he or she will certainly not look forward to your letters or to the messages they bring. The same is true of messages that invoke guilt or disciplinary and behavioral standards. Surely in every normal family children get abundant doses of these things, without adding more of the same via long distance.

For a rule of thumb on what to include and what to avoid, try to put yourself in the child's place. What would you love to hear? What would make you feel unhappy? Upset? Tense? Use that as a simple guideline and start writing. And be open to what your son or daughter tells you about how your grandchild feels when he or she gets your letter, and make adjustments accordingly.

## The Rewards

In the early childhood years, keeping up the postal connection may seem like casting bread on the waters, with little likelihood of a return. But when it finally comes, it is sweet: "Hi Mom. Simon goes down to the mailbox every morning to see if there are 'any grandma's.'" (Aaaaahh!) And in a telephone visit: "Grandma! I got your letter!" And when I hear that the children ask to have the letters read several times, and that they ask to keep them in some special place with other cherished mementos, I know that my efforts have borne fruit.

Eventually, in the mail one morning, will come the first reply. Perhaps a gaggle of red, blue, black and yellow chicken scratches on a

piece of paper. We treat it as a historical document. It is a grandchild's first attempt at reciprocating in the postal connection. It matters not one fig that we have no comprehension of the scratching. But what is of monumental significance is that the child is making the breakthrough into literacy. Think of how such a powerful awareness is now likely to blossom.

## Writing Letters to Older Grandchildren

At first blush, writing letters to the older grandchild may seem a little more intimidating. Today, even at the elementary grade years, children are much more sophisticated than when I was in school. Their lives include a wider range of options and their experiences, even in the seven to ten year-old group, are extensive. Would they be at all interested in anything we had to say? Would they be critical about our spelling? Our handwriting? The experiences of our lives?

The power of a personal letter to a child is, first of all, not to be underestimated. It will not matter if she has every new advertised toy, or if her idea of a field trip is two weeks in London. If you write to her, a letter for her alone, you make her feel special. And whenever you can evoke these feelings of being special, you enrich the emotional connection between you. Besides making the child feel special, a personal letter has other benefits. It allows us to tell our grandchildren more about ourselves and our lives, and in that way, it helps them to know more about us: Who we are and what we do and how we feel. It allows them to know us from many perspectives. We reveal much more of who we are through our letters. And, if we choose to be very open, it allows them to know us intimately. Of course, they would know us better if we lived close by, but the letter connection bridges that gap, and allows intimacy to develop at long distance. Why do people save letters for years? It is not only because of what they are about, the letter itself is the treasure and so is the connection it makes. What's

Children are naturally curious. Writing personal letters about your life can fill in the blanks for long distance grandchildren, allowing them to feel closer, by knowing you better.

more, the postal connection with older grandchildren goes two ways, helping to build the habit of letter writing.

Letters may also become part of the family history, documenting relationships with our children and the children of our children, forming a diary of our lives to be treasured and passed down through subsequent generations.

In writing, we should not set ourselves impossible standards or expectations about *what* to write—for if we did that, we would avoid writing altogether. To write and tell about ourselves and our day-to-day lives and to write as naturally as talking is the key. If writing is difficult for you, keep the first letters short. Like anything else we do, writing letters gets easier to do the more we do it. Think, too, of a letter of yours found in a family album eighty years from now. What a treasure it will be for the family members who find it to learn about you, in this time and place!

## Some Letters to Older Grandchildren

My dear Ruthie,

It's hard to believe the winter is finally over. Everyone here breathed a sigh of relief when the clouds brought rain, instead of another snow. It was a hard winter and the ice storm in February was a climax! While beautiful in a bizarre sort of way, it did a lot of damage. We had to go without electricity for several days. The ice lay heavily on the wires and many of them just snapped, like dried-out branches breaking off the trees. Not only was this inconvenient, it became downright dangerous to be outside. Naturally, we were without heat and grandma and I had to keep the fireplace going all the time, and we huddled around it, like a scene out of the 1880's! Driving was impossible and walking, especially for these old and shaky legs, to be avoided if at all possible! Fortunately (you know your grandmother!)

"It is not because things are difficult that we do not dare; it is because we do not dare that they are difficult."
SENECA

57

there was enough food in the pantry to keep us going. Losing the refrigerator was no problem. We had the whole of the outdoors for cold storage. I shan't forget that experience too soon. Our neighbors, the Martins, came over every day to see if we were all right, and I thought that was especially nice of them. When the ice finally melted and we could go outside again, neighbors gathered up and down the road to talk about how the experience had been for them. It was like we had all lived through this disaster! Sometimes I think it would be nice to live in a milder climate and I know your dad talks to us often about moving south. Yet, in spite of the cold, harsh winter, we do feel so much that we belong here. After all, both grandma and I grew up in this town and it would be very hard to leave here now, at this age.

This morning, I saw the cardinal in the yard and I knew we could expect warm weather soon. We are anxious to hear about school and what your plans are for this summer. Grandma and I would love to have you come to visit, so let us know if that's a possibility. Love from your Grandad.

My dear Steven,

Your mother has just written about your team's winning the soccer championship. She says that you made two goals in the final game. Golly, you must have been very proud and very excited to have been the best team in your district. You must have to practice very hard to be that good. What do you have to learn in order to play soccer? Can you describe it for me?

Last night I dreamed that it was your birthday, though I know that's rushing things a bit. You will soon be ten, and I am wondering if you are growing really tall! Do you have any birthday plans? Will you be going camping with your dad? I know that's your favorite thing and I hope it works out for you.

When I went to the market, I saw that the local strawberries

A much anticipated moment in a long distance grandparent's life is opening your grandchild's first letter to you.

were in, so I bought several quarts to make some jam—your favorite kind—and I'll send you some for your birthday. Then, each morning when you have your breakfast, you will think of me thinking of you. Your loving Grandma.

My dear Janey,

You will never recognize this house when you come to visit again! Grandma and I have changed just about everything about it. First, we painted the outside, from roof to cellar. Can you imagine the two of us on ladders, painting this whole house? What a job! And we were covered in paint, from hair to toes. It took very nearly two weeks to get that job done. We were both quite tired from it, but it looks so nice. Instead of that old gray color, we now have gold, with a brown trim. You will hardly recognize it.

We changed a bit on the inside too. Remember the room you stay in when you come? I built a new table and there is a new carpet on the floor. Grandma made some curtains, very gay, with flowers, for the window. As you can see, we have been busy.

This weekend, I hope to go fishing. Grandma isn't sure that she wants to come. I don't think that cleaning fish is her idea of a good time. I know if you were here, honey, you would surely choose fishing with grandpa! In that way, we both are very alike. Love from your Grandpa.

Dearest Robby,

I have had your letters. Thank you. I appreciate them very much. With my new reading glasses I can read the handscript with no trouble.

I've had some hard times this year, but I'm happier now that I can read. I also have distance glasses and can see every pebble on the beach on the other side of the island. Both glasses give me brilliant child-like sight but both wipe out my distance and

balance and that remains a problem for me. I go to the doctor next Tuesday. But the miracle remains that I can see, dearest, and never mind if I can't drive the car.

Yesterday I began on a crash diet program for two weeks for gross overweight. It's lovely, really. All salads and eggs and grapefruit. James took me out on Wednesday and we found some low-cal beer which is at least acceptable. I think this diet might influence the arthritis which I've never admitted to any-one, and which I think is all in my mind anyway, and as I am much calmer in mind now I believe will recede. I think of you with much love. Me.

## What? Me Write! No Way!

In spite of the ease with which some of us take pen or pencil in hand and whip off a letter to grandchildren, there are bound to be grand-mothers or grandfathers "out there" who are convinced, utterly con-vinced, that they cannot write letters. The obstacle seems formidable and alternatives to letter writing may have greater appeal for keeping up the postal connection.

## Alternatives to Letter-Writing

If writing is "not your thing," there are other resources to draw upon in exploiting the long distance postal connection. Some grandparents may have artistic talents. Instead of writing letters, can you draw? Paint? Sketch? Can you caricature? Can you cartoon? Think of how special your grandchild would feel if he or she received a drawing from you on a regular basis! I know one grandfather who has created a comic strip especially for his granddaughter, and he sends one strip out to her every month. And if you do not draw, pictures cut out from newspapers or magazines would also work to tell a picture-story. Or you may wish to engage in a long distance game. (This would be better with older grandchildren.) Tic-tac-toe (naughts and crosses) could be played for a few rounds. Scrambled words could be sent back and forth:

Dear Philip: Here is a word for you to unscramble. It's a hard one, this time. Send me your answer if you can unscramble it. Then, send me a scrambled word for me to unscramble.

E  B  E  V  T  E  A  G  L  S

Hah! Love from Grandpa. (VEGETABLES)

Riddles could be exchanged, and there are probably a dozen riddle books in the children's section of the library. (This riddle comes from *THE ELEPHANT BOOK* (Price/ Stern/Sloan) 1963.)

Dear Aaron:
How do you know if an elephant's standing near you in the elevator?
You can give up if you can't guess and look inside the sealed envelope for the answer.
(BY THE SMELL OF PEANUTS ON HIS BREATH)
Do you have a riddle to send me? Love from Grandpa.

You could write limericks together:

Dear Patsy:
I'll start this limerick this time. Add one line and send it back to me:

THERE ONCE WAS A MONSTER NAMED MARCUS

Games with numbers could be fun:

Dear Martha: How many squares can you make with 24 toothpicks? Draw a picture of the squares you made. Then send me a problem to do with toothpicks, too. Love from Grandma.

Cartoons cut from local newspapers can be fun in themselves. Remove the captions and invite your grandchildren to invent their own.

Dear Martha: How do you measure a duck? Got any ideas? Write me your ideas and send me a problem to do with measuring. Love from Grandma.

While the letter-writing habit is likely to be the more satisfying over time, the postal connection could endure in different forms as well. In addition to the games, riddles, puzzles, and drawings suggested here as alternatives to letters, the next chapter opens up another set of options that also makes use of the mails.

# 6

# The "Playful" Gift Connection

*"We would go to the store and buy sunglasses."*

GRANDPARENTS ARE notorious in their reputations for largesse toward grandchildren. Look at any group of travelers—at the bus depot, the train station, the airport—and you will be able to pick out the grandmother at a single glance. She is the one loaded down with one, two, three shopping bags full of presents, in addition to all of her other luggage. When I am ready to make a trip to see the boys, a coworker who shares with me a membership in the department's "grandmother club" jokes: "I'll phone the airline and tell them to put on an extra section." She knows that I will be carrying presents for the boys. This is what grandparents do—whether they live near or far. We love to give, whenever we can, whatever we can—sometimes to excess. Our desire to give knows no bounds, no constraints. Grandparents are toy stores' best customers. (We are an economic force!)

There is, however, another kind of gift giving quite different from what is normally done at Christmas or birthdays or visiting times—and that's what this chapter is about. Here, what the gift *does* for the connection between grandmother and grandchild is more important than the gift itself. I call these gifts "playful" because they need to be

Some gifts are playful, and can also stimulate a healthy interest in science and nature.

chosen with some imagination and are intended to be used creatively. "Playful" gifts are always small and inexpensive, and are often used in some special, constructive way. They may be sent frequently—but not more than once a month, lest the joy of the experience becomes burdened by having to invent something new too often. These gifts are always accompanied by a small note, suggesting how the child might use the gift. This connection could begin at about age two and one half, but you are likely to be the best judge of how to match the gift to the child's age and his or her ability to enjoy it.

## Choosing What's Appropriate

For example, if the gift requires the child to do cutting and pasting, or sewing, or use of tools, or winding a top, you will want to make sure that his small fingers are up to the demands of these tasks. If it involves a messy activity that might create dirt on mother's immaculate kitchen floor (like papier maché, finger paint, or water play) you will want to know in advance that such an activity is acceptable to the parents and that your grandchild is capable of helping with the clean up. If these gifts set up expectations that are impossible for the child to achieve they can become despised, rather than enjoyed. If unsure about how your small grandchild will be able to handle a gift and the demands it makes, a consultation with mom or dad will help.

Here is a small list of "playful" gifts with messages suggesting ways they can be used. You will surely be able to think of dozens more.

## Ideas for Very Young Children (3 to 6)

A very small, hand-held magnifying glass. (Found in stationery and variety stores.)

*Message:* This is a magnifying glass. If you hold it up to your eye, you'll see that it makes things look bigger. Take it into the garden.

Look at a little flower. Does it look bigger? Look at a little bug. Does the bug look bigger? Look at a little leaf. Does the leaf look bigger? Look at a little stone. Does it look bigger? Look at your dad's nose. Does it look bigger? What else can you see with your glass?

Two balloons.

*Message:* I found these balloons in the store and I thought you'd like them. Blow some air into them. Then, let the air out and feel it on your face. Blow some more air in. Then let the air out and feel it on your hand. Blow some more air in. Then, let it out and see if you can push a piece of paper with the air. Does it work? Can you do a balloon dance? What else can you do with the balloons?

Small horseshoe magnet. (Found in stationery, variety, hardware stores.)

*Message:* Do you know about magnets? Well, now you can find out. Try to see what this magnet will stick to. It will stick to some things. But it won't stick to other things. You'll have fun finding out.

Box of crayons or non-toxic, felt pens.

*Message:* Here are some crayons/felt pens for you to make some pictures. You can make whatever you like. I hope you'll send me a picture some day.

A small pocket flashlight.

*Message:* Do you have a flashlight yet? A flashlight of your own? Here is one for you, all for yourself. You can make it shine in the dark. You can play with it in the dark and see how the light shines. You can shine it behind a door and see how the light creeps through the cracks.

It doesn't have to be expensive to be fun.

You can use it to make shadows on the wall. Can you make some shadows with your flashlight?

A pennywhistle or harmonica. (Found in chidren's toy stores, variety stores, music stores.)

*Message:* You'll like this pennywhistle/harmonica. You can play some tunes with it. Try to make a loud song. Try to make a soft song. Try to make a song that goes doodlidoodlidoodlidoodlidoo.

A packet of flower seeds.

*Message:* Do you want to grow some flowers—all for yourself? You'll need a little can, or the bottom part of a milk container. Maybe your mommy can give you one. You'll need to put some dirt in the can. Put some seeds in the dirt and then put a little water in. Watch it every day and see if a flower will grow. I hope you'll have a beautiful flower.

A box of plastic straws.

*Message:* Straws are fun to play with. You can blow through a straw and make air come out. You can feel the air on your hand when you blow. You can use the straw and blow through it to push a piece of paper around the table. Try it. What else can you push? You can use the straw to suck up some milk or juice. You can suck up the air and use the straw to hold a piece of paper. Try it. What else can you suck up with your straw?

A box of face decorating pastels. (These can be found in some specialty toy stores, in shops where theatrical make-up is sold, and in some well-stocked stationery stores.)

*Message:* You can use these make-up crayons to make a mask right on your face. You can make a happy face. You can make a sad face. You can make a scary face. When you put make-up on your face, you can be anything you want! A cowboy! A princess! The king of the castle! A monster! I hope you have a good time with this face make-up.

A finger or hand puppet. (Found in children's toy stores, and in some department stores carrying toys. Grandparents may also make and send puppets.)

*Message:* This puppet's name is King (or Queen) of the Castle. He (she) is the boss. When you put your hand inside the puppet, you can make him (her) move and talk. See what he (she) will say and do.

A packet of plasticine. (Found in most toy stores, and in art and craft supply shops.)

*Message:* This plasticine can be kneaded and molded. You can make any shape with it. A pancake! A hot dog! A ball! You can stick it on your nose and make a big, long, crooked nose for your nose. See what you can do!

A plastic eyedropper. (Found in "superdrugstores" and pharmacies.)

*Message:* Here's an eyedropper all for yourself. See how you can fill it up with water. See how you can make the drops come out. You can make the drops come out fast or slow. I hope you like it.

A bottle of bubble solution and one or two bubble pipes.

*Message:* You'll love making bubbles. Can you make some big, big bubbles? Can you make some tiny, tiny bubbles? Have fun making bubbles.

Young children are extremely inquisitive and will relish gifts that stimulate their curiosity.

A cassette tape of children's songs/games.

*Message:* Here are some songs for you to listen to. I hope you like them. Maybe you can sing and dance too.

A pinwheel.

*Message:* Watch how the wind makes this pinwheel go! Watch it go outside! You can make it spin inside the house, too, by blowing on it. It can go fast or slow. I hope you like it.

A box of old discarded clothes, eg. worn or out-of-fashion hats, shoes, ties, handbags, jewelry. (Every grandmother has, somewhere in the dark recesses of a closet, or attic, or basement, a box of old clothing—dresses, hats, shoes, handbags—clothes that were once favorites, but have gone out of style, or that we have "outgrown.") We have kept them because they are still in good condition and it offends our sense of economy to throw them away. Some can become very attractive and delightful dress-up outfits for your grandchildren. Send only those that you are happy to part with, and don't send family heirlooms! They are unlikely to be in a returnable state after dozens of dress-up plays.

Playing dress-up is a favorite game for many children. Sending your old clothing and asking mom and dad to send you a snapshot can create new opportunities for learning about the past.

A word of caution: There are, of course, "costumes" or "outfits" that may be purchased for dress-up as cowboys, or firemen, or ballet dancers. I urge against these for several reasons. First and most important, they are artificial and phony; they don't inspire the kind of imaginative play that comes from "real life" clothing worn by real people. Second, higher quality costumes are costly and this is not what the "playful" gift connection is about. (And the cheaper costumes are tacky and aesthetically unattractive.) Grandma's old hat with veil, a memento from her femme fatale days, is likely to give her granddaughter far more pleasure and far more creative play opportunities than any store-bought costume.

*Message:* This box of stuff is for when you want to play dress-up. Do you like to play dress-up? When you play dress-up, you can be anything you want. A fireman! A prince! The King of the Castle! A shopkeeper! The mailman! You can make up stories with your dress-up clothes. I hope you have fun.

Face masks. (These are found in toy shops, but may be more easily made from pieces of felt, with elastic bands. Cut out holes for eyes and decorate imaginatively with other scraps of fabric, buttons, beads, etc.)

*Message:* These face masks are for you to put on and play with. You can play pretend monsters. You can be scary. You can play ghosts and goblins. Boo! Watch out for the scary masks.

A packet of multi-colored construction paper.

*Message:* Here's some colored paper for you to play with. You can make shapes—circles, and squares, and triangles. You can make pretty designs with your shapes. You can make spirals. You may want to use a pair of scissors to do this or you may want to tear out your shapes. I hope you have fun with these colored papers.

A tape of grandpa's songs. (Some grandparents are amateur (or professional) musicians. Making a tape recording of songs, unaccompanied or accompanied by guitar or violin or piano, would make a wonderful "playful" gift for grandchildren of all ages.)

*Message:* I'm sending these songs especially for you. I hope you like them. Do you like to sing? Maybe you can sing along with me.

A tape of rhythms and rhymes, especially good for very young grandchildren. (If we were closer, we would do these rhythms and rhymes in

Part of the fun of playing dress-up is wearing hugely over-sized clothes.

Origami requires a certain level of dexterity but you could include instructions for simpler bend and fold projects.

person. At distance, we can do these on tape, and make the tapes a part of our "playful" gift connection. Here are some suggestions that go right back to our own childhood days.)

Pat-a-cake; Ring-a-round-a-rosie; Jack-be-nimble; Peas-por-ridge hot; Row-row-row your boat; Baa-baa black sheep; Hey diddle-diddle; Hickory-dickory-dock; London Bridge;
Sing a song of sixpence; Twinkle-twinkle; Humpty-dumpty;
Farmer in the dell; Jack and Jill; Did you ever see a Lassie?; Little Boy Blue; Loopy loo; Mary had a little lamb; The muffin man;
Pop goes the weasel; Here we go round the mulberry bush;
Three blind mice; Tisket-a-tasket.

*Message:* Here are some songs and rhymes I made especially for you. If I was there with you, we could sing them together. But maybe you can sing along with me, on this tape. I hope you like these songs.

## Ideas For Children 4 to 7

Marbles. (Found in most toy shops and "superdrug-stores.")

Do you have a children's song or rhyme from your homeland or cultural/ethnic heritage? Send it on tape with the promise you'll teach your grandchildren the words and their meaning next time you meet.

*Message:* Do you like to play with marbles? Here are lots for you and there are two shooters, too. When I come to your house we can play marbles together. Did you know that I was the marble champion of my block when I was a boy? Do you think you can beat me? Hah!

Pipe cleaners. (Try the tobacco shop or the "superdrugstore.")

*Message:* These pipe cleaners can be twisted and turned and made into all kinds of shapes—circles, squares, triangles, and free forms. You can twist several of them together and make figures of all kinds.

Will you send me something you have made out of these pipe cleaners?

Wool scraps. (Grandmothers who knit will have lots of wool scraps to send. Or wool can be bought inexpensively at the supermarket. Heavy wool is better for this. Cut the wool into long, even strips, and secure them so that they don't get tangled in the mail.)

*Message:* Here's some wool with many different colors. See what kinds of designs you can make with these strands. Then, maybe you can paste your designs on a piece of paper. When I come to your house, maybe you'll show me what designs you made with this wool.

Cloth book. (For grandmothers who like to sew! Cut 5 or 6 pieces of unprinted, colored cloth into 12" × 16" rectangles. Arrange them evenly, one on top of the other, and sew a seam down the center, to bind them together. You may want to pink the edges so they won't fray. Write your grandchild's name, in crayon or felt pen, on the cover.)

*Message:* I made this book for you. You can write or draw in it, and make anything you like. You can use crayons or felt pens. Have fun with your book. When you've filled up this book, I can make you another one.

Special boxes. (Sometimes I get a gift wrapped in an unusually attractive and sturdy box—good for keeping lots of little treasures in. I don't know why these "treasure boxes" have such appeal for children, but they do.)

*Message:* I found this box and I thought of you. Would you like to have it? You can keep all sorts of things in it—all your treasures. It's a special box, and you are special to me.

> The more equipment and instructions a game or activity requires, the less room for spontaneity and invention.

> Children quickly tire of things they have "figured out." Think of gifts that are more open-ended in their use and application.

## For Grandchildren Eight Years and Over

Every child is an artist. The problem is how to remain an artist once he grows up.
PABLO PICASSO

Stamps, from near and far.

Baseball cards.

Discarded small appliances to take apart (like clocks, can openers, and old radios).

Tape measure.

Hobby and craft activity cards. (Book shops, hobby shops, craft shops are all good sources. "Superdrugstores" and large supermarkets may also carry a stock of crafts books.) Instead of purchasing entire hobby and crafts books, and sending out reams of these in a steady flow, purchase only one book, then tear out pages to send, one at a time. Mount them on a card to reinforce them. They may even be laminated, if the activity is worth saving and doing repeatedly.

Recipes. (Include dishes easy for the child to make with a minimum of adult supervision.)

Cloth, needles, and thread.

Mobile-making activity. (Four or five ¼" wood dowels, cut into lengths of 3" to 12"; colored cardboard shapes; a roll of magic tape; string.)

In encouraging playfulness in your grandchildren you'll be nurturing that same quality in yourself.

Instructions for a card trick.

Instructions for a magic trick.

72

This list of "playful" gifts barely scratches the surface of what is possible. It does, however, provide some ideas about how many different kinds of things can be sent that will encourage creativity, imagination, and a child's investigative play that will bring grandparent and grandchild closer. In adding to the list of possibilities, you will want to keep your eyes peeled, not in toy stores that trade in tanks, trucks, designer dolls and their wardrobes, battery operated robots, and toy machine guns, but in shops that emphasize arts and crafts materials, construction materials, hobby shops, hardware shops, cookware shops, stationery stores, museum gift shops, aquarium gift shops—even the neighborhood junk shop and flea market. Once you have developed the "playful" gift habit of searching for possibilities, there will be no end to the imaginative options you will find.

"Playful" gifts send messages of love—much more so than the toys that cost a month's retirement benefits. They say to your grandchild: "Hey, sweetie. I am thinking about you. I found this and thought you might have a few moments of pleasure with it." They do not depend upon a special occasion. They come from the connection, from the desire to be close and make an intimate contact. They are tokens of love, rather than symbols of material acquisition. And many grandchildren will want to reciprocate in kind.

"Grandma!" says Arlo with his heartfelt gift of love, "when I grow up, I gonna give you a big, big gum, all for YOURSELF. For all day."

A few hours spent digging around in your attic or basement can yield an Aladdin's cave of treasures for your grandchildren.

# 7

# The Lens and Shutter Connection

*"My ideal grandma would explain things like why birdies don't need a raincoat."*

IS THERE A GRANDMOTHER in the house who does not keep and cherish an album of photographs of the children? Does the grandmother exist who does not return to these photographs again and again, savouring yet another glance at Arlo in the tub with his hair still so curly, or Simon for the first time on skis, standing alone? What is there about photographs that feeds our hungers, that allows us to satisfy three-dimensional needs in a two-dimensional plane? Long distance grandmothers depend upon photographs to bridge the gap between flesh-and-blood visits.

Interestingly enough, photographs appear to have equal power for children as well. You may have seen this in your own grandchildren. Even in the very early years, from one to two, for example, children will show interest in the photos you have framed and mounted around the house. Later, from about two on, children will want to study photos, and tell stories about them. They are interested in photos of themselves as infants, as they are in photos of their parents, brothers, and sisters. And the interest they show does not wane after one viewing. They are as happy to see the photographs for the fifth time as they were for the first—perhaps even more so. One of the

boys' favorite activities, when visiting us, is to take out the family albums and study the photos—again and again and again. Children in
the elementary school years may seem to lose interest in photographs,
but this loss is temporary. Their interest is renewed in their teens,
when they study family albums for more mature reasons—to trace
their roots, to compare family members with themselves at the same
ages, to study the family history, in time, place, and in relationships.

## Photos' Special Appeal

It's not altogether certain why photographs have such personal appeal for the younger child. Children are, of course, attracted to artful
illustrations in picture books. I have seen even very young children
much absorbed by the clever children's book artistry of Maurice
Sendak and Brian Wildsmith, for example. Children seem to use illustrations to help their understanding of not only shapes and colors,
but of content, as well. They also use illustrations to help them come
to terms with their own powerful feelings. Such illustrated books for
young children as Wildsmith's *Where the Wild Things Are,* and
Sendak's *In the Night Kitchen* help children give vent to their fears of
"things in the night," bringing them into the daylight and making
them less frightening and more manageable.

Photographs may do even more. They are, after all, a documentary
of children's personal histories. They provide an opportunity to revisit significant events, and, I believe, they help children make a powerful personal connection with how they see themselves in relation to
their families.

## Captioned Photos

The lens and shutter connection as a bridge between distant grandparents and grandchildren has many rich advantages. For one, photos
are accessible. We all have stacks of them, tracing grandchildren back

Photographs can open a child's world to his family history and cultural background.

to their first days, if not first hours. For another, they are easily captioned. It does not take wondrous creative talent to write a line or two about what is happening in the photo. But captioning photos has other attractive benefits. It can provide not only the children but all of the family with a documented, photographic history of the lives of all the members of the family. Photos of parents, as children, and the children themselves can be shown in comparison. Perhaps there are family resemblances? Photos of grandparents as children, or in earlier years may reveal much about history, culture, and change.

Captioned photos also provide young children with pre-reading and early reading experiences. When they hear these captions they can make the connection between spoken and written language—and with stories that have immediate, personal, and tremendous psychological appeal. There is something wonderful in reading a "story" about oneself—a story in which the grandchild is the key character, in which the illustration documents that starring role.

Older grandchildren may find the captions reveal much about their parents that they want to know, allowing them glimpses into the past:

"This is your dad when he joined the Cub Scouts."

"Here's your mom when she and your dad were dating."

"This is your mom when she was three years old and that's her favorite doll."

"We all lived in this house."

"Here's grandpa on his way to work. That's his lunchbucket. I used to make a lunch for him every day."

"We used to like to go on picnics every Sunday to Cunningham Park."

"Your mom liked to climb this tree in the backyard. Everyone called her a tomboy."

The photos and captions give reality to past experience, and they invite our grandchildren to reach back into that past. Perhaps that is why the film *Back to the Future* had such widespread appeal to teenagers. In the movie, through the kind of time travel that only Hollywood can give us, the hero becomes a part of his parents' past lives. Maybe the fascination of old photographs is that we all secretly long to be in a different time .

There are many ways to use photographs in building a long distance connection, from the very straightforward to the very imaginative, and my examples are intended as guidelines rather than as procedures to be rigorously followed. Once you have dipped into your own photos, and re-examined them for the lens and shutter connection, their captions will become very clear, and will be very much your own.

Oh, yes. One more thing. You may not be enthusiastic about giving up your precious family photos to the grandchildren—no matter how noble the endeavor. Not to worry. Modern technology saves the day! Photos can be photocopied, cheaply, and with excellent fidelity. And most local libraries and post office stations have photocopiers available for public use.

Some very straightforward photo captions—particularly suitable for children who don't yet read, and for those who are just beginning to read:

- Arlo is in the tub. You can see that he is happy.
- It is Simon's birthday. He's got a birthday hat on and he had his favorite supper: Spaghetti! Do you remember?
- Arlo is in his swing and Simon is helping him. Did you like to do that?
- Momma is hugging Arlo. Momma loves Arlo.
- Momma is reading a story to Simon and Arlo. Look at Arlo's face. I think he likes that story.
- Can you guess who this is? This is your Momma. When she was a little girl.

Family photographs are not the only option. Perhaps your grandchildren love animals, flowers, cars, unusual road or shop signs.

When your parents were small they didn't have computers and video games so they often made up their own games.

- Here's grandma and Simon. Simon is biting his teddy bear. Does it taste good?
- Did you know it was grandpa? When he was a little boy?
- Simon is in the pool. It was a hot, hot day.
- Simon is skiing with Momma. She is holding him very tight—so he won't fall.

Some more complex photo-story arrangements:

- This is Simon when he was just born. And this is Arlo when he was just born. Can you see how different you look?
- I found this picture of Momma when she was just a little girl. You can see that she's playing with Nixie, the little dog that lived next door. Your Momma loved dogs even then. Do you love dogs too?
- When Momma was a little girl, we took her on a trip to Disneyland. She was afraid of the tigers. Are you afraid of tigers?
- Here's grandma when she was little. And this is grandma's poppa. You can't remember him, but he was very tall. Who does he look like, I wonder?
- When grandpa was a little boy, he lived in a different place. He wore different clothes. Would you like to have clothes like that?
- Do you remember when Arlo was born? Your Momma had to go to the hospital. And when she came home, there was Arlo. He was crying.
- Can you remember when you were a little bitty tiny baby? You used to sleep in this cradle. Can you remember anything about when you were very little?
- Here's your Momma when she was a little baby, and here's *her* grandpa! Her grandpa is hugging her, because he loves her, too.

For older and more mature grandchildren, captions may be more sophisticated, with more about time, place, event, and relationships:

- Here's Uncle Ted. You can see that he wore quite thick glasses even when he was sixteen.
- You never knew your other grandpa. But you can see what he looked like in this photo. Tall and thin. And what about those knickers! Can you believe those fashions!
- Aunt Blanche was quite a femme fatale in her day. The boys chased her all the time, and she could have had her pick of them.
- When Aunt Margaret came, we used to clean the apartment for days! What heavy weather she used to make about a spot of dust!
- Cousin Barney was Aunt Bea's boy. He was the first one in the family to get his own car. Boy, was he smug about it, too.
- Your mom's hair was long—down to her waist. I couldn't see why she wanted to put up with the fuss of taking care of it!
- Your great grandpa, my dad, found this little dog. She was a stray, all skinny and dirty and quite starved. When he brought her home for me to keep, I thought I would die of joy.
- When grandpa and I were just married, we lived in this little house in the suburbs. It had four little rooms and a little backyard. We lived here when your mom was born.
- Your dad's folks came from Ireland. When they arrived in the United States, all they had was $25, and their personal belongings. Can you think of how frightening and exciting it must have been for them?

## Some Practical Guidelines

In exploiting the lens and shutter connection, there are no rules to follow, and few guidelines. Go to your storage place of tenderly kept family photos and sort through them, putting into a special category those that you are prepared to part with, and those to be photocopied. If you choose to send the actual photo away, consider the possibility that you may not see it again, and choose selectively. There is no logical order for captioning and sending. Just put down what comes to

Captioned photographs are, like picture storybooks, engaging to leaf through.

GRANDPA BUSTER

JOEY, AL AND ME AT GRANDPA'S FARM

mind when you look at the photo, and write "long" or "short," as you please.

Mount your photo or photos on a folded piece of 8½" × 11" white or colored paper. This is certainly not essential; it's just a tad more elegant to present it as a booklet. (You may have other, even more creative ideas for presentation. Try them. Your grandchildren will be so appreciative.)

Particularly with young children, use "people" photos rather than "place" photos. Snow scenes from Aspen or the beach at Waikiki, no matter how beautiful, are less likely to be appreciated than the people who are most important in the children's lives.

Write at least a sentence for the photo caption, rather than a single word or phrase. Mention both the person in the photo and the context. Additional sentences might extend the "story," or pose questions for the children to think about.

There are no wrong ways to caption these photos. Whichever ones you use, whatever you write will be welcomed and appreciated. Through them, you provide your grandchildren with a window into their past, so they may know a little more about the people who have given them a family.

# 8

# The Audio-Tape Connection

*"My ideal grandma would read to me."*

ON SIMON'S FIRST extended solo visit, when he was four years old, I took him to the local public library, where he chose about a dozen books for "bedtime stories." Each evening at bedtime he would choose a book and the two of us would snuggle together on his home-away-from-home bed for the last activity of the day—storytime. I am a compulsive reader, so it is natural that I would want to share this joyous and major experience with my grandchildren. Storytime is more than just the reading of a wonderful and delightful tale, as any parent knows. It is a time of tight togetherness—an intensely powerful shared experience. It is a time for transporting ourselves into fantasy and adventure, when joy, laughter, whimsey, sadness, tears, and wonderment are encouraged to surface. It is also a time for growing and learning, for stories are rich in their potential to teach. Through good stories, we know the power of the written word to enchant, to delight, to bemuse, to scare, to worry, to help our worlds unfold. Storytime is magic. And it is made sweeter with the intimacy of touch.

Because of my own deep longing to read to our grandchildren, and the impossibility of doing this often, I began to think of how stories might be read at long distance. The audio-tape connection seemed like an attractive option.

## How to Record Stories on Tape for Young Children

I invested $49.95 in a good quality tape recorder with rechargeable batteries, and one dozen blank cassette tapes. Naturally, one does not need to use a particular brand to make this connection work. Any good tape recorder will do.

Our local library has a particularly fine children's section with thousands of picture storybooks for young children, and my adult card will permit me to borrow a dozen books at a time. For my first trial run, I tried to choose books that did not rely heavily on pictures to make the story come alive.

On a rainy Saturday morning, I girded my loins and sat down with four of the books, one blank tape, and my own recorder that comes with a built-in microphone. I was nervous. I am not a good oral reader, and my voice lacks both the elegance of Katharine Hepburn and the resonance of Richard Burton. (I thought of Burton's recorded reading of *A Child's Christmas in Wales* and almost gave up the idea altogether!) What is it about talking into a tape machine that is so intimidating? Haltingly, my voice stumbling over the words, I began talking to no one.

"Hello, dearest Simon. Hello dearest Arlo. I'm going to read you some stories. You can listen to one story at a time, or you can hear them all at once. You can listen to them as many times as you want. I am making these stories for you. The first story is called *Rumplestilt-skin*. So sit down in a nice comfy chair, tuck yourself in, settle down, and get ready to listen. Here we go. Once upon a time, there was an old miller . . . "

When I had finished the story, I asked if they had enjoyed it. I also said that they could turn off the tape now and rest, or listen to the next one, which was to be *Snow White*.

One way children grow to love reading is by being read to.

With further experience in reading to "no one" my voice got stronger and more confident. I began to change the written text, to editorialize. I added comments about the illustrations, and I became more "dramatic," changing my tone of voice for the different characters. I now felt confident that even if the telephone did ring, or if I was discontented in some way with the way I had read the story, I could erase and redo any part quite easily. After the first few stories, I began to feel I had mastered the technique. What's more, I even began to enjoy it, with fantasies of myself as a "radio days storyteller" for children.

The question was, would the boys enjoy these tape-recorded stories? Without actual books and their fine illustrations would they be totally uninterested? After all, today's children are very much visually programmed by TV. Had I spent sixty-five hard earned dollars on an idea that would be useless? Or even worse, would I be ridiculed for my naiveté about what would be enjoyed and appreciated?

When I was a child, long before television was a thought, let alone a reality, the radio was a vital presence in my life. As children today have programs like "Sesame Street" and "Mr. Rogers' Neighborhood," I had mine: "Tom Mix," "Little Orphan Annie," "The Green Hornet"—fifteen-minute radio serials that entertained me every afternoon. I was addicted to these as any contemporary adult the night time soaps! My most precious program, though, and one I would not miss under any circumstances, came on Saturday mornings at ten o'clock: "Let's Pretend." Each week, a group of repertory players performed a classic fairy tale like *Cinderella, Snow White and Rose Red, Jack and the Beanstalk, Rumplestiltskin, The Little Match Girl, Sleeping Beauty*—every story that haunts our early childhood years. It didn't matter how many times the stories were repeated. I loved those Saturday mornings with my ear glued to the radio. And as I listened, my imagination created the scenes, costumes, castles, faces, the scenery. It was a wonderfully rich mental exercise, one that today's television generation rarely experiences, let alone enjoys. How would Simon and Arlo respond to the tapes?

You can personalize some stories by substituting your grandchild's name for that of the hero or heroine.

I had the full report via telephone from my daughter in two days. Having their very own tape recorder, which they were allowed to operate under adult supervision at first, was a "big deal," and contributed substantially to the children's sense of independence. Now here was a really "grown-up" machine which they could operate for themselves. Second, grandma's voice reading stories seemed to have great meaning for both boys. They listened together, then they listened individually, and taking turns had to be worked out. They took the tape recorder and the stories to listen to at bedtime. The fact that there were no illustrations in no way diminished their pleasure. I quickly set about making more taped stories.

These days, you can go to any bookstore and see that this small idea has come into its own. For $9.95 a grandparent can purchase a plastic packet containing the tape recorded story and a cheap paperback book. And on these tapes you will find some expert and entertaining storytellers: Meryl Streep reading *The Velveteen Rabbit,* Cher reading *The Ugly Duckling.* But while these fine actresses have dramatic skill and elegance of diction, their voices are those of strangers, with no personal connection to your grandchildren. If you wanted to carry this idea to its elegant extreme, you might consider becoming a private entrepreneur in this market. For Christmas, Hanukkah, birthdays, other events or non-occasions, consider buying a book *and* a blank tape, and making your own package. While more amateurish and less glamorous than the commercial product with the glitzy wrapper, it will be more meaningful, and will have considerably more personal appeal.

Stories on tape read by you can be played over and over again.

Well, that's fine for younger children. It's a treat to snuggle down in an easy chair on a rainy afternoon and "turn grandma on" with tales of *Peter Rabbit,* and *Winnie the Pooh* and *Alexander and the Terrible, Horrible, No Good, Very Bad Day.* But what about the older grandchild? Would the audio-tape connection be appropriate for the eight-to eleven year-olds?

The answer is: "It depends." But the chances are good, and I base this on having seen teachers in classrooms reading to large groups of very interested children, at all ages and all levels of the elementary grades. Most children love to be read to, providing the books are interesting to them. When the story is a carefully chosen one, with dramatic power and humor or tragedy or excitement—children will be interested and will listen. When the story is read by grandmother or grandfather, the interest is likely to be even greater.

## Recording Stories on Tape for Older Children

You will want to be thoughtful about the books you choose for your older grandchildren. It may be a good idea to search for stories that appeal to the child's particular interest, whether it is fantasy, or sports, or animals (or specifically horses), or mysteries. It may not matter if she already knows the story. Some children enjoy reading and hearing favorite stories over and over again.

Books for children in this age group tend to be quite lengthy, so you may have to do the recording chapter by chapter, in several sittings. One book is likely to consume an entire tape, both sides. But the variety of what is available for children is extensive, and in addition to the public library, you will find moderate cost paperbacks available in most bookshops and the more comprehensive "superdrugstores."

If you are serious about making packages of books and tapes to give as gifts, you will find unbelievable bargains in used book shops that carry a section of juvenile fiction. Depending on the shop and its location, you may find books in perfect condition for as little as ten and twenty-five cents. You will certainly find many between one and two dollars. If the shop is local, it's a good idea to make a friend of the owner. He or she may telephone you when the next good supply of juvenile stock comes in and you can get first pick. These stocks change from month to month, and frequent trips may net very good results.

Sending stories on tape may be a real help for your own children, giving them a few extra minutes to catch up on the housework or take care of business.

Consider taking incidents from your own children's lives and sending them as fictionalized stories on tape.

Even if you do not want to send the books away, you can build up a small home library, for those times your grandchildren come to visit, and they tell you they have "nothing, nothing, nothing to do."

If you are at all in doubt about what book to choose, you might consult with your grandchildren. One of the nice things about older children is that they *know* what they like. You can ask them directly: "I want to send you a story that I will read on a tape. What kinds of stories are your favorites? Tell me, so I can be sure to pick something that you'll like." If she asks for a book that you have doubts about, best to check with mom first.

Some grandparents are "natural" story tellers. They delight in making up yarns as fanciful and rich as any found on the library shelves. If you are an inventive story teller, you will have your own creative imagination to draw from in making tape recorded stories for your grandchildren. Grandparents with other talents that can be transcribed and sent on an audio-tape (e.g., singing, playing a musical instrument) can extend the audio-tape connection as far as individual creativity allows.

Of course, the audio-tape connection does not take the place of the living, breathing grandparent, snuggled together with grandchild, sharing a bedtime story. But it is the best way to bring storytime, books, fantasy and dramatic play between grandparent and grandchildren together across the miles.

# 9

# Stories for Young Children

*"My ideal grandma would tell me stories."*

GRANDPARENTS WHO themselves love books and reading have already found their way into their local bookshops and scoured the children's sections for books that would be appropriate for even their youngest grandchildren. If you are in this group, you will have discovered there are vast numbers of books available for young children, with hundreds of new ones coming out each year. Some bookshops carry the most lamentably meager and mediocre books for children, while others contain substantial collections that cover topics from A to Z. If you value books and reading as I do, you will no doubt by now have contributed to your grandchildren's collection a substantial number of beautifully illustrated and delightful books to mark every special occasion. If your grandchildren are treated to books and reading as a regular event in their lives, they will have learned from very early years to take pleasure in stories, to find enchantment, delight, and wonder in the tales they relate.

There are very important reasons that we would want to help open up the world of books to young children. Of course, we want them to become literate. We want them to know that books can give them in-

In writing books for your grandchildren you'll not only be helping them to develop their appreciation of the written word, but also helping yourself by demystifying the act of writing. Remember: Rule #1, sit down at a table. Rule #2, pick up a pen...or turn on the computer...

formation about the past and present, and speculations about the future, information about the world in which we live, the creatures that inhabit it, and information about what and how other people think. Books do more. They make us feel less lonely, they help us appreciate others' lives, they give us things to think about. Books also set standards. They provide us with guidelines about "what is right" and "what is wrong" in human behavior. Books stimulate our imagination, and extend what we know, as well as entertaining us in the process. We must never underestimate the role of books and stories in the lives of children. In today's world of TV and computer games, the value of books and reading for the developmental health of children is more critical than ever. If anyone doubts the role that books still play in children's lives, think of the extraordinary success of the Harry Potter series in turning kids onto reading.

With such a range of books available—books that come from writers with considerable style and imagination, beautifully and colorfully illustrated, with attractive and visually seductive designs, and bindings that make them less vulnerable to toddler-attack—why would a grandmother even think of herself writing books and stories for the children? What reasons make such efforts not only worthwhile, but something you should think seriously of doing?

## Why Write Stories for Grandchildren?

Let me say straightaway that I do not see personally written stories for grandchildren as a substitute for buying books. I think that both published stories and personally written stories can co-exist on children's bookshelves, each with its own particular, but not mutually exclusive, set of merits. Though published books are wonderful and we should give them with as much generosity as we can afford, here is what personally written stories can do that store-bought books do not. Personally written stories are drawn from real events in the child's life. Because they are about the child and his own experiences, they have much meaning for him. While it is delightful for a child to read store-

If your grandchild has had her first trip to the airport, you might write what you know of that experience.

bought books, it is a wondrous experience to have a personal event written about that places him in the centre as the "hero," while describing activities that he has lived.

As you compose your stories, think of how you would say these words to your grandchild if he or she were sitting right there with you. Here are some guidelines that might be helpful:

- Keep the language simple—well within his or her ability to understand.
- Don't put too many sentences on a single page. Too much text may give the child "information overload." One or two sentences a page seems comfortable.
- More ideas about layout, book construction, printing, etc. are found later on in this chapter.

These stories may be aimed at your grandchild's particular developmental level. So, for example, if you know that your grandson is just learning to brush his teeth, a small story might be created that would not only tell about it, but would also describe some of the difficulties he must face.

Or, if your grandchild has had her first trip to the airport, you might write what you know of that experience.

Personally written books and stories have other advantages. Through them we can teach our grandchildren about events and experiences and values that we think important. And, of course, they will help develop our grandchild's literary awareness in personally meaningful ways. And what's more, the price is right.

## Writer's Block?

"But I can't write," you shudder, as you retreat from the very thought of such an undertaking.

If you believe this, truly and deeply, from your toes up through the roots of your hair, and if you are paralyzed by feelings of underconfidence in the "written word department," then that is that. Case closed.

Identification with a protagonist or character in a book is one of the key reasons people turn pages.

## Some Sample Stories

ARLO
CAN BRUSH
HIS TEETH
by Grandma

Arlo has a new toothbrush.
He brushes his teeth in the morning.
But he is too short to reach the sink.

1

So he has to stand on a chair.
Sometimes the water spills on his shirt, or on the floor.
Uh, oh.

2

His favorite toothpaste tastes like...bubble gum!
He doesn't like the kind that tastes like peppermint.
Ugh. It's yukky stuff!

3

He brushes up and down.
And don't forget those teeth in the back, too.

4

Rinse, rinse.
Now climb up on the sink and look in the mirror.

5

Teeth all sparkly white?
Arlo can brush all by himself.

6

SARAH'S AIRPLANE

Do you remember? Your Momma said, "Today's the day we go, Sarah."
So she put on your boots and your warm coat and hat and mittens.

1

And Poppa took you in the car to the airport.

You saw the plane come out of the sky. It made a loud, roaring noise. You put your hands over your ears. Too noisy!

3

When the plane was in the sky, it looked like it was a very little airplane.

But when it came down to the ground, it was very big. Bigger than a car. Bigger than a truck. Bigger even than your house. Big as anything!

5

4

Hey! Here comes Aunt Helen, right off the plane.
Aunt Helen came to see you.

In the airplane. Flying in the sky. From her house, far away, to yours.
How do planes get up in the sky?

6

7

91

Step-by-step instructions for making pancakes, or flying a kite lend themselves easily to this format.

There is likely nothing I can write here that will persuade you otherwise. But if there is somewhere within you a trace, a glimmer, a spark of "Hey, this sounds intriguing! I'm no Mark Twain, but I'd sure like to try this"—then what follows in this chapter may help. If you are still anxious at the idea of putting pencil to paper, remember that your grandchildren are not critics who will condemn your work for what you believe is an amateurish effort. On the contrary. They are more likely to appreciate what you have done, and to ask to have it read to them again and again. Through these stories, you can make a vital, long distance connection to your growing, learning grandchildren, sharing together through the written word.

In combatting the defeatist "I can't write" obstacle, try these strategies:

- Sit down at your table and pick up a pencil or turn on your computer. Once you have mastered this first step, you are more than halfway there. For most people who are bogged down in the "I can't write" syndrome, it is often the act of sitting down that is the most difficult.
- Be alert to certain strategies you may be using to avoid this first step. For example, "But I have to do the ironing now."

## What to Write About

- In trying to decide about what to write, think of the very last conversation you had with your son or daughter. What did he or she tell you about the children? Is there a new toy? A new pet? Was there a trip? A new tooth? A visitor to the house? Did the washing machine break down? Was there mischief afoot? Now imagine that your dear grandchild is sitting across the table from you, and you are going to be talking to him or her about that event. Keep the idea of talking in your head, but instead of talking across the table, write what you would say.

92

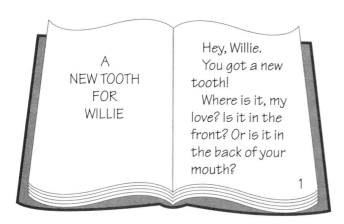

A
NEW TOOTH
FOR
WILLIE

Hey, Willie.
You got a new tooth!
Where is it, my love? Is it in the front? Or is it in the back of your mouth?

1

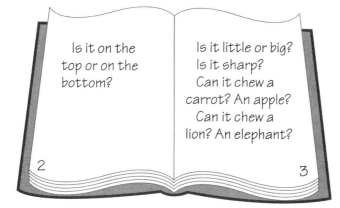

Is it on the top or on the bottom?

Is it little or big?
Is it sharp?
Can it chew a carrot? An apple?
Can it chew a lion? An elephant?

2

3

How many teeth now, all together?
Count them with your tongue.

Now, count them with your finger.
One? Two? Four? Ten?

4

5

While you're not aiming to write award-winning fiction, it does help to remember the words of Brenda Veland: "Everybody is talented, original and has something important to say."
*If You Want To Write*

Children are acutely aware of all changes in their bodies. Heights are marked on walls, missing teeth proudly displayed to shopkeepers and playmates alike.

POOR
HELEN

She had to go
to the doctor.
For a shot.
So she wouldn't
get the measles.

1

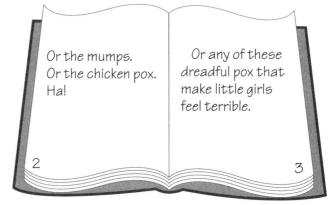

Or the mumps.
Or the chicken pox.
Ha!

Or any of these
dreadful pox that
make little girls
feel terrible.

2                                               3

But it was no
fun to go to the
doctor either.
  "Roll up your
sleeve, Helen," he
said.

"This isn't going
to hurt a bit."
  But it did. And
he lied. And you
had to cry.
  Just a little bit.

4                                               5

- Use the pencil or your computer and write the words that you would say. Write them just as they come out of your mouth. Do not monitor or censor the words. Just write.
- When the thoughts have been written down, when they are there on the page, this is the time for editing. Use the eraser, the delete key, or scratch out what you don't like or want to change, fine-tuning what you have written to your liking.
- Liberate yourself from worries about good grammar or sentence structure. Use the written word to represent, as closely as you can, your spoken words. The more your story resembles the way you speak, the more charming and the more natural it is likely to be.

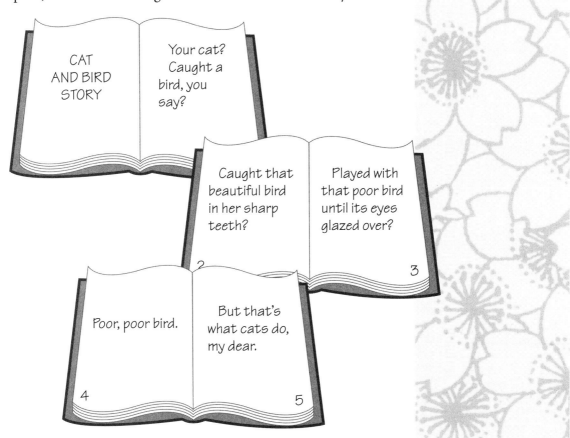

- Give yourself no more than ten minutes to do this. You are not writing *Gone With the Wind*. If you labor too long over this story, you are likely making too much of it. What's more, if you turn it into a chore, it is unlikely that you will want to do it again. Remember, your grandchild is NOT a literary critic. Your story will not be judged. It will be appreciated, cherished, and likely even stored away as your grandchild's personal treasure.

## Assembling the Book: The Materials

You will need some very simple tools and materials for your books: some newsprint or other blank paper sheets, cardboard or tagboard for a cover; a stapler; scissors; non-toxic felt pens. Of course, you may play variations on any one of these items.

Children with pets will enjoy stories about their animal's skills and quirky habits.

The kinds of paper available for the pages of your book are impressive. Newsprint is perhaps the cheapest, and comes in large sheets that need to be cut to size. Newsprint is available in most well equipped stationery stores or office supply stores. Bond paper is the easiest to get hold of, but more expensive. Looseleaf filler and white pad paper are all available in the large drug stores. Get what's easiest for you to acquire and what suits your budget. No matter what quality of paper you choose, your book is likely to have a very short shelf life. Home-made books are consumable. They may be as handily chewed as read, and if they disappear like popcorn, as many do, they have still served their main purpose.

In any stationery shop or art supply store, you are bound to find a package of multi-colored 8½" × 11" construction paper. These sheets are heavy enough to serve as covers for your book, yet still pliable enough to bend, staple, and punch holes through without an electric drill. Covers of different colors add interest and variety. Or, instead of colored cover sheets, try using wrapping paper, cut-up cardboard boxes, paper bags. Wallpaper sample books are fun for covers too, and if you have fabric remnants at home, these can make attractive and interestingly textured covers. Fabric can be edged with pinking shears, so no sewing is necessary, and fabric covers will endure longer than paper.

## The Size and Shape

For the pages, fold the sheets of paper in half, so that the folded edge becomes the *outside* edge of the paper. You will have somewhat more durable pages of double-thickness this way. Putting the folded edge at the outside makes the whole book more sturdy and longer-lasting, too. Place the cut edges into the inner fold of the cover sheet and staple. (You can, of course, punch holes instead, and use colored wool to fasten with rings, loose-leaf style, or sew with colored wool, the way real books are bound.) When you've got the hang of positioning the sheets into the cover and stapling, you can begin to think of alternate sizes and shapes for your book.

If you are working with 8½" × 11" sheets (standard typewriter size) the doubled sheets will produce a standard-sized, home-made book of 8½" × 5½". But there's no reason in the world that you can't be more imaginative with both size and shape. A round book? A semicircle? A long, narrow book? A tiny 2" × 2" square? A book in the shape of a banana? Why not?!

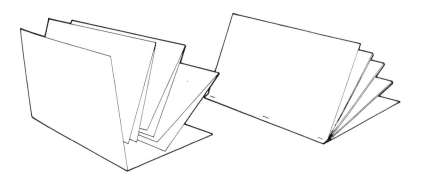

First fold, then staple the folded pages into the cover.

Make the outside cover bright and cheerful— inviting the reader inside.

If you go overboard with your presentation you may end up with a book your grandchild is afraid to touch or open.

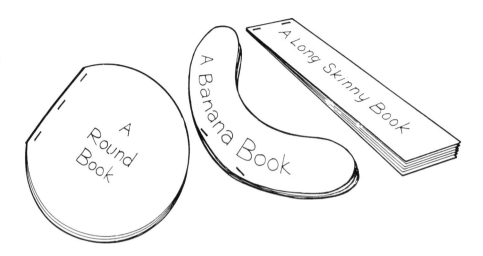

Books can be made in any number of shapes and sizes.

## Illustrating the Books

Illustrations. Ah, my nemesis! As some of you may feel about putting words down on paper, I feel about my adequacy with a drawing pencil. For whatever reason, the skill of drawing or illustrating anything at all eludes me completely. I've come to the point in my life when I no longer fight it; I'm reconciled that illustration is not my strong suit. Be that as it may, I have other resources if I choose to illustrate my books for the boys. I am a klutz with stick figures, and even when I try, they look like the products of a troubled six-year-old. No matter—I use them, and the boys think they are just swell! I am equally maladept at copying pictures, but will copy from illustrations that I have seen if convinced they are needed. I cut and paste pictures from magazines or newspapers, and have taken to keeping a clipping file of illustrations which might be handy for some future book. There are some very talented grandparents who are able to take pen in hand, and with a few quick strokes make a cat out of the air, an elephant in a hat, a sled. If you are one of these grandparents, you have the happy possibility of creating some magical, personal drawings that will add much to your stories. How I envy that talent!

There is, of course, nothing writ in stone that insists that the personally written stories *must* be illustrated. Some are even more powerful without illustrations; and you will want to decide if a stick drawing is likely to add to your story or diminish it. Whatever you choose, remember that this experience is supposed to be fun for you and make your choice accordingly.

The stories I have sent to our boys over the years (between the ages of two and five) describe some of the events in their lives. These events did not have to be milestones in order to create a story, and as you will see in the following examples, they may be very ordinary.

The stories may also reflect the children's feelings. Even small children have strong likes and dislikes. They have fears—both vague and concrete. They also get angry. So stories that give expression to these feelings can be very important, not only by acknowledging them, but also by helping the child deal with them in healthful ways.

In some instances, stories help children to understand more about abstract ideas—for example, stories about up and down, counting things, colors, mechanical functions. I would not shy away from writing such stories as long as they are about the child's day-to-day real life experiences, and as long as they do not ask the child to understand (or to "give answers") at levels beyond his capabilities. Nor would I worry about occasionally using words that might require the child to reach beyond his own level. It is, after all, through hearing new words that children learn.

Writing personal stories for your grandchildren has considerable benefits. The very fact that *you* are doing the creating for them, that the stories come from *you,* brings you closer together, and does so in a rich and most advantageous way. Personal stories also help build your

While published books abide by certain rules and formats, you are free to invent different shapes and sizes— maybe a book in the shape of a banana.

As generations of teachers have discovered, a stick figure here, a few squares and circles there, both inform and amuse.

grandchild's self-esteem. Think of how valued they will feel when they find stories about themselves, about their lives, about their experiences, and in which they are the leading characters. Such stories also teach about feelings. They expand horizons. They build vocabulary. They provide opportunities to revisit experiences and to examine them from new perspectives—to discuss them and to find new meaning in them. Indirectly, personal stories teach about right and wrong, about the values of the family. As if all that were not enough, they also work just like published books, to develop children's sense of the written word, showing how thoughts and experiences can be translated into written language.

## Examples of Stories

In the following pages, I have included many examples of the kinds of stories that may be written. These stories are for ages two to five, and are meant for very young children who can't read. (The ideas in Chapter 11, on the other hand, are more appropriate when writing for grandchildren who are able to read on their own.) They are intended to be read to the children and the books then turned over to them. If they are then "loved to death," so be it. There are lots more where they came from!

Many stories represent real events in the life of a child. In some, I emphasized the child's feelings. In others, I have included some abstract concepts that the children may be learning about: big and little; many and few; up and down; time and place.

Some stories give expression to the "bigger" feelings, like fear, anger, and revenge. These stories are likely the most difficult to write, so avoid them if you aren't sure you'd like to wander into this highly emotional territory. A few stories here depart from reality altogether, capitalizing on children's delight with fantasy and wild exaggeration. There are many stories to tell, and what your young grandchild can enjoy covers a vast range of possibilities.

## Guidelines: What/How to Write for Young Children

- Stories that discuss events in the child's life are more meaningful and have more "personal power."
- Whenever possible, make your grandchild the "star" and central character of the story. Use his or her own name.
- Involve others that are important in the child's life—mother, father, siblings, pets—as they have played parts in the event.
- When appropriate include feelings related to the event.
- Sometimes include things about what the child is learning, and work these into the story.
- Make up stories of fantasy and imagination, if you enjoy telling purely fictitious and delightfully exaggerated tales.
- Keep the writing simple and natural. And try to write as you and the children would speak.
- Avoid stories about TV programs. While children may spend a lot of time watching them, they lack the attraction of real-life events.
- Avoid stories that are subtly coercive or manipulative. ("You will be a good boy from now on, won't you?") They will diminish the child's pleasure and subtly invoke guilt.
- Avoid stories that set up expectations that may worry the child. ("Max can count to five. Can you count to five yet, Steven?")
- Avoid excessively moralistic stories. ("If you don't behave, you will be punished.")
- Avoid stories with promises that can't be delivered. ("If you eat all your carrots, you will get big, strong muscles.")
- Avoid stories that emphasize the horrible and the morbid—stories about guns, war, terror.
- Avoid stories that threaten the child's security. ("If you don't behave, the rat that lives in the sewer will come and chew you up.")
- Avoid stories that emphasize what is phony and that communicate phony sentiments. ("Girls don't play with trucks.")

Remember that what you can offer is unique. You are not trying to compete with commercially produced, store-bought books.

## Getting Started

How can you say you can't do something unless you've honestly given it your best shot?

For those grandparents who are unaccustomed to writing, just getting started may be the single, most difficult obstacle to overcome. Coming to terms with our own inner critic—the voice inside of us whispering, "It's not going to be good enough!" seems like going to war. For many of us, dealing with those inner critics may present greater problems than the actual work of writing. Yet, as with other things we have done in the past, the more we do something, the easier it becomes to do, and this is as true for making pie crusts, driving a golf ball, and playing bridge as it is for writing stories for grandchildren. The more we do, the more skilled we become. You may feel it to be a stiff and awkward process at first, but the more comfortable you become with yourself in the process, the more you shed your own unrealistic expectations for yourself, the more you are likely to write—and even enjoy it!

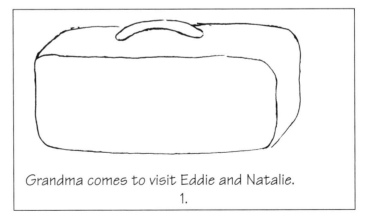

WHEN GRANDMA COMES TO VISIT

If you can't draw a scene, abstract it: a heart with names for love, lips for kisses, a mouth and upturned tongue for delicious, or a bat and ball for baseball.

Grandma comes to visit Eddie and Natalie.
1.

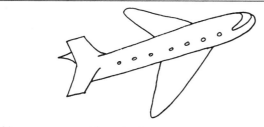

She comes on the airplane.

2.

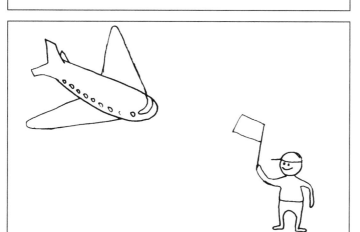

Eddie and Natalie go to the airport with Momma.
They wait for the plane to land.

3.

"I see Grandma," says Eddie.
"Where?" asks Natalie.

4.

Send a pencil and a pad of blank paper. Ask your grandchild to make some illustrations for the book.

Write for ten minutes without stopping. Put down anything and everything that comes into your head. Now read it back—you'll be surprised.

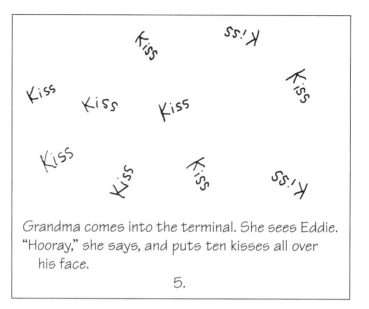

Grandma comes into the terminal. She sees Eddie. "Hooray," she says, and puts ten kisses all over his face.

5.

Momma is holding Natalie in her arms. Grandma wants to give Natalie kisses, but Natalie hides her face in Momma's neck. Natalie is hiding.

6.

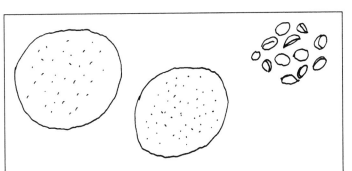

Grandma has cookies from the airplane.
One for Natalie.
One for Eddie.
Grandma has peanuts too. To eat in the car on
    the way home.

7.

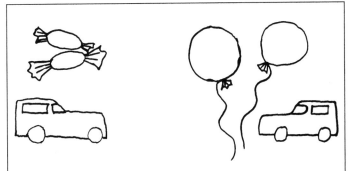

When we get to Nelson, we have to go to the
    store. When Momma does her marketing,
    Grandma can get some balloons and bubble-
    gum for the children. She gets a little truck
    for Eddie and one for Natalie.

8.

If you want to illustrate but feel woefully inadequate to the task you can always cut out pictures from magazines.

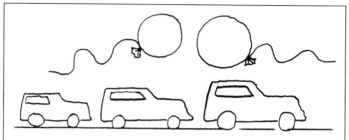

At Eddie's and Natalie's house we play some games.
Balloon games.
Truck games.
Hockey games.
Abracadabra games.
And kissing games, of course.

9.

Natalie's a sweet kisser. Sweet, smoochy kisses.
Eddie's a delicious kisser. Kisses! Delicious,
    smoochy kisses.
Grandma loves those kisses! Grandma loves
    Eddie and Natalie.
Yeh! Yeh! Yeh!

10.

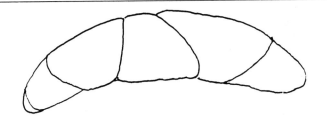

On Sunday we have brunch. Natalie and Eddie eat
    lots of croissants. They're making big muscles.
    For skiing.

11.

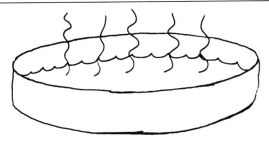

Then John takes everybody to the hot tub for a
    good time.

12.

Children need to know that emotions like anger and frustration are valid.

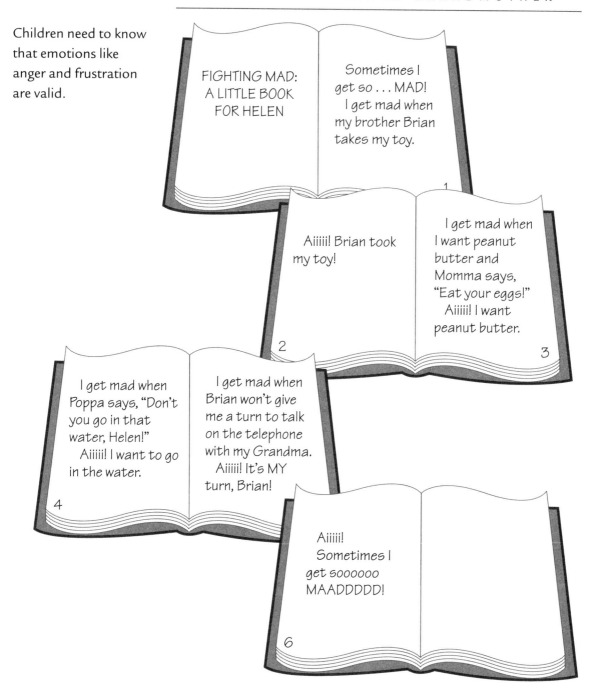

FIGHTING MAD: A LITTLE BOOK FOR HELEN

Sometimes I get so . . . MAD! I get mad when my brother Brian takes my toy.

1

Aiiiii! Brian took my toy!

I get mad when I want peanut butter and Momma says, "Eat your eggs!" Aiiiii! I want peanut butter.

2

3

I get mad when Poppa says, "Don't you go in that water, Helen!" Aiiiii! I want to go in the water.

I get mad when Brian won't give me a turn to talk on the telephone with my Grandma. Aiiiii! It's MY turn, Brian!

4

Aiiiii! Sometimes I get soooooo MAADDDDD!

6

FIGHTING MAD: A LITTLE BOOK FOR BRIAN

Sometimes I get so mad! I get mad when my sister Helen takes my toys.

HELEN! Don't you take my truck! Grrrrrr! Aaaaarrrrr gggghhhhh!

2

I get mad when Momma says, "No more cookies, Brian," and I want another cookie. Aaaaarrrr gggggghhhhh! I get SO MAD!

3

I get mad when I'm playing and Poppa says, "You have to come home now, Brian."

I want to stay outside and play! Aaaaaaarrrrr gggggghhhhh! I get SO MAD!

4

I get mad when I want to talk on the telephone and it has to be Helen's turn.

I get SO MAD! Grrrr! Growl! Harrumph!

6

7

Stories that don't provide a solution to dealing with anger or fear or other strong emotions can pave the way to a discussion with mom or dad.

Indulge in some silliness. Too much of life is taken up in serious matters.

**RUTHIE CAN MAKE FACES**

Ruthie can make faces.
   Scrunch up your nose, Ruthie.
   Make a funny face.

1

Roll up your eyes, Ruthie.
   Make a funny face.

Pull your cheeks out, Ruthie.
   Make a silly face.

3

Stick your tongue up on your nose, Ruthie.
   Make a ridiculous face.

Open your eyes wide, Ruthie.
   Make a surprised face.

4

Pull your cheeks down, Ruthie.
   Make an ugly face.

Get the little mirror, Ruthie.
   Look into it and see your beautiful face.

6

7

HARRIET
COMES TO VISIT
GRANDMA AND
GRANDPA'S
HOUSE

Harriet comes to visit Grandma and Grandpa.
She comes on the airplane. With Lin.

"Hooray! Here's Harriet," says Grandma. "At last."
Hugs and kisses are everywhere.

Harriet and Grandma have many treats.
They go to the aquarium to see the whales.
The white whales and the killer whales.

2

3

The whale swims to the window of the tank.
He puts his eye near the window. He looks at Harriet. I think he likes Harriet.

Harriet and Grandma go to the movies. It's Lady and the Tramp. With Siamese cats. They're rascally. Harriet eats a whole bag of popcorn all for herself.

Harriet and Grandpa go swimming. Look at that Harriet swim! Wow! Oboy! What a good swimmer.

Grandpa goes to the library and brings home a movie on tape for Harriet. There's Sleeping Beauty and the Magic Kiss. And Babar.

4

5

6

7

And every morning Grandpa puts the cereals in a circle around Harriet's cereal bowl. So Harriet can choose.

When Harriet comes to visit Grandma and Grandpa it's such fun!

8

9

That precious visit can turn an ordinary event into an extraordinary one.

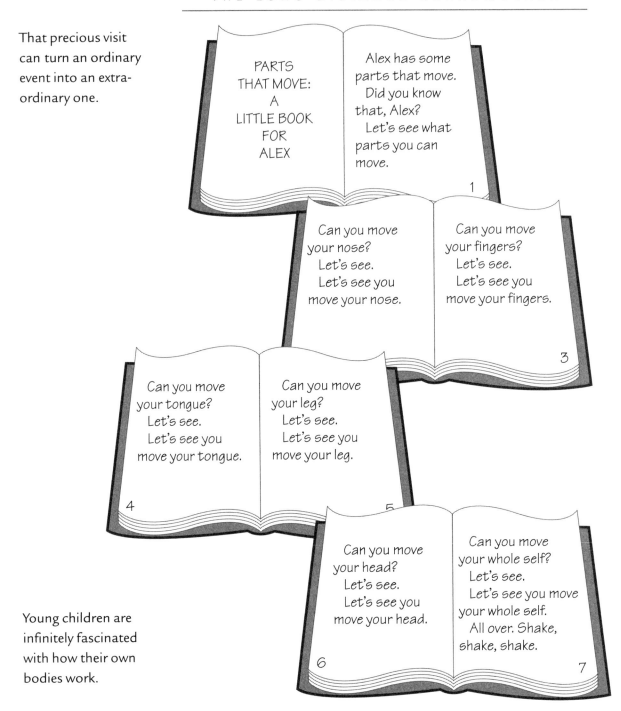

PARTS
THAT MOVE:
A
LITTLE BOOK
FOR
ALEX

Alex has some parts that move. Did you know that, Alex?
Let's see what parts you can move.

1

Can you move your nose?
Let's see.
Let's see you move your nose.

Can you move your fingers?
Let's see.
Let's see you move your fingers.

3

Can you move your tongue?
Let's see.
Let's see you move your tongue.

Can you move your leg?
Let's see.
Let's see you move your leg.

4

5

Can you move your head?
Let's see.
Let's see you move your head.

Can you move your whole self?
Let's see.
Let's see you move your whole self.
All over. Shake, shake, shake.

6

7

Young children are infinitely fascinated with how their own bodies work.

112

Familiar objects can be used to learn about unfamiliar concepts.

RACHEL'S
BOOK
OF
UP AND DOWN

Rachel's bed is up.
Nancy's bed is down.

Momma's bedroom is upstairs.
Rachel and Nancy's bedroom is downstairs.

2

The plant is up there hanging on the hook.
The carpet is down—down there on the floor.

The cat jumps up—up there on the shelf.
The cat jumps down—down to eat her food.

4

The moon is up—up there in the sky.
The car is down—down there on the road.

5

Poppa goes up—way up to the top of the mountain with his skis on.
Poppa skis down—down to the bottom of the mountain.

6

The ball bounces up and down. Up and down.
Rachel jumps up and down. Up and down.

Stand on your head, Rachel.
Are you up?
Are you down?

8

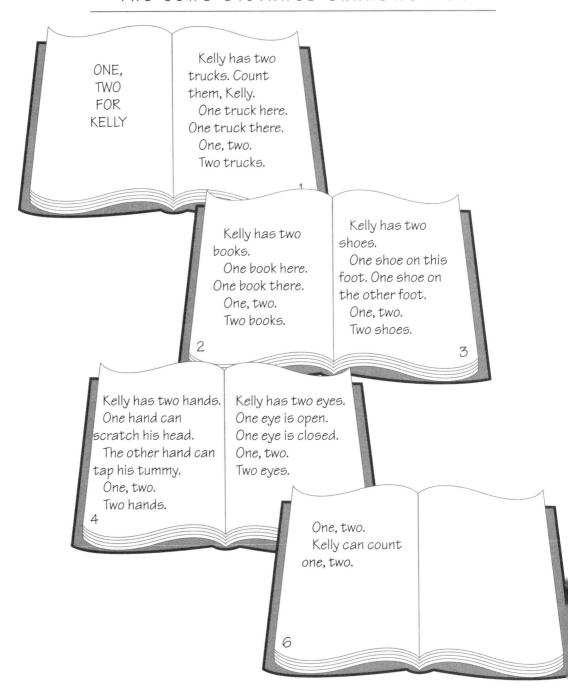

ONE,
TWO
FOR
KELLY

Kelly has two trucks. Count them, Kelly.
One truck here.
One truck there.
One, two.
Two trucks.

1

Kelly has two books.
One book here.
One book there.
One, two.
Two books.

2

Kelly has two shoes.
One shoe on this foot. One shoe on the other foot.
One, two.
Two shoes.

3

Kelly has two hands.
One hand can scratch his head.
The other hand can tap his tummy.
One, two.
Two hands.

4

Kelly has two eyes.
One eye is open.
One eye is closed.
One, two.
Two eyes.

One, two.
Kelly can count one, two.

6

114

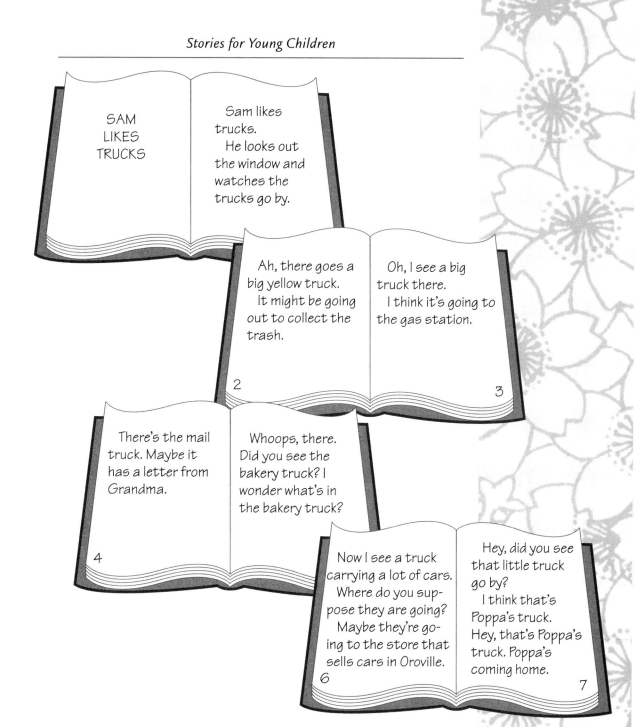

SAM
LIKES
TRUCKS

Sam likes trucks.
He looks out the window and watches the trucks go by.

Ah, there goes a big yellow truck.
It might be going out to collect the trash.

2

Oh, I see a big truck there.
I think it's going to the gas station.

3

There's the mail truck. Maybe it has a letter from Grandma.

4

Whoops, there. Did you see the bakery truck? I wonder what's in the bakery truck?

Now I see a truck carrying a lot of cars. Where do you suppose they are going? Maybe they're going to the store that sells cars in Oroville.

6

Hey, did you see that little truck go by?
I think that's Poppa's truck. Hey, that's Poppa's truck. Poppa's coming home.

7

I GET SCARED: A LITTLE BOOK FOR ARLO

I got scared when Simon hid behind the door and jumped and said, "Boo! Arlo!"

I got scared when I couldn't find my Momma in the store.

I got scared when Simon said, "There's a ghost under your bed, Arlo!"

3

I got scared when I saw the snake in the garden. Do snakes eat people?

I got scared when the doctor gave me a shot.

4

5

I got very scared when I heard the loud, loud noise of the thunder.

When I get scared, I go to my Momma and she takes me in her arms and says, "There, there, Arlo." And all the scares go right away.

6

7

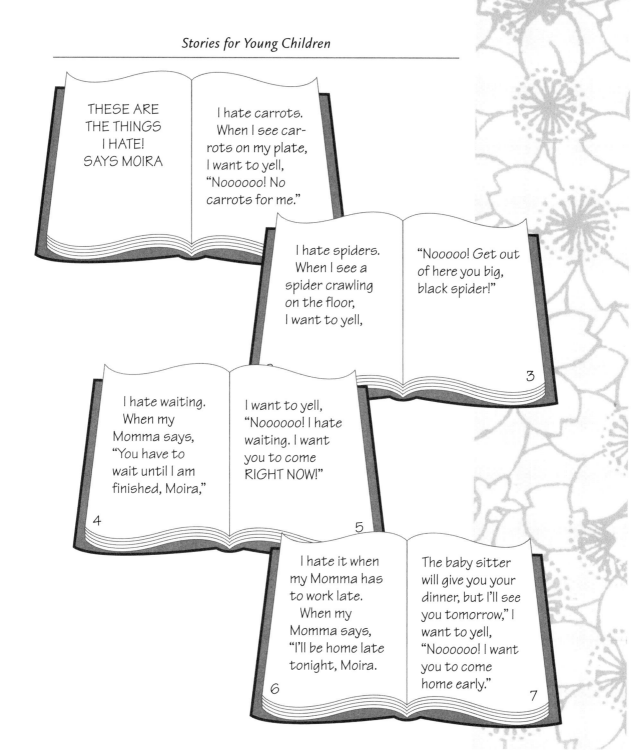

THESE ARE
THE THINGS
I HATE!
SAYS MOIRA

I hate carrots.
When I see car-
rots on my plate,
I want to yell,
"Noooooo! No
carrots for me."

I hate spiders.
When I see a
spider crawling
on the floor,
I want to yell,

"Nooooo! Get out
of here you big,
black spider!"

3

I hate waiting.
When my
Momma says,
"You have to
wait until I am
finished, Moira,"

4

I want to yell,
"Noooooo! I hate
waiting. I want
you to come
RIGHT NOW!"

5

I hate it when
my Momma has
to work late.
When my
Momma says,
"I'll be home late
tonight, Moira.

6

The baby sitter
will give you your
dinner, but I'll see
you tomorrow," I
want to yell,
"Noooooo! I want
you to come
home early."

7

I hate to wear my big boots. When it's raining hard and Momma says, "Get your boots

8

on Moira," I want to yell, "Noooooo! I hate those boots!"

9

"Oh, I see a big truck. I think that's Poppa's truck.

I wish I didn't have to eat carrots, see spiders, wait, wear my big boots. I wish my

10

Momma could come home early every day.

11

118

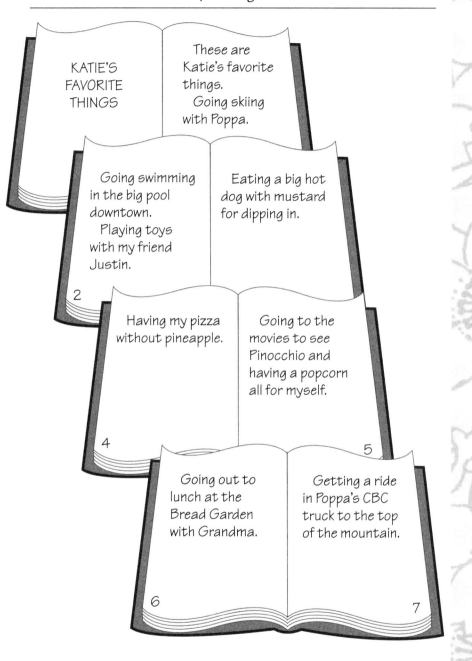

KATIE'S
FAVORITE
THINGS

These are Katie's favorite things.
Going skiing with Poppa.

Going swimming in the big pool downtown.
Playing toys with my friend Justin.

Eating a big hot dog with mustard for dipping in.

2

Having my pizza without pineapple.

Going to the movies to see Pinocchio and having a popcorn all for myself.

4

5

Going out to lunch at the Bread Garden with Grandma.

Getting a ride in Poppa's CBC truck to the top of the mountain.

6

7

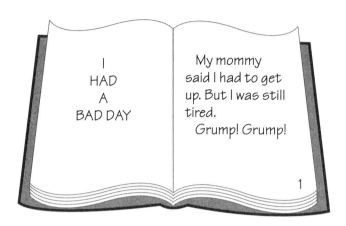

I
HAD
A
BAD DAY

My mommy said I had to get up. But I was still tired.
Grump! Grump!

1

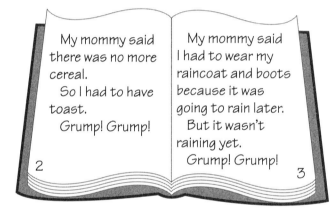

My mommy said there was no more cereal.
So I had to have toast.
Grump! Grump!

2

My mommy said I had to wear my raincoat and boots because it was going to rain later.
But it wasn't raining yet.
Grump! Grump!

3

My mommy said I had to sit in the shopping cart when she did her grocery shopping.
Grump! Grump! Grump!

4

My mommy said, "No treats. You'll spoil your lunch." What's the good of going to the market if you can't get any treats?
Grump! Grump! Grump!

5

My mommy said, "You'd better have a nap this afternoon." I'm too old for naps now.
Grump! Grump! Grump!

6

My mommy said, "Pick up your toys! Your room is a mess!"
Grump! Grump! Grump!

7

My mommy said, "Eat your vegetables."
I'd rather have spaghetti.
Grump! Grump! Grump!

8

My mommy said, "Goodnight my little sweetheart. I love you. Sweet dreams."
But I had a bad day anyhow.

9

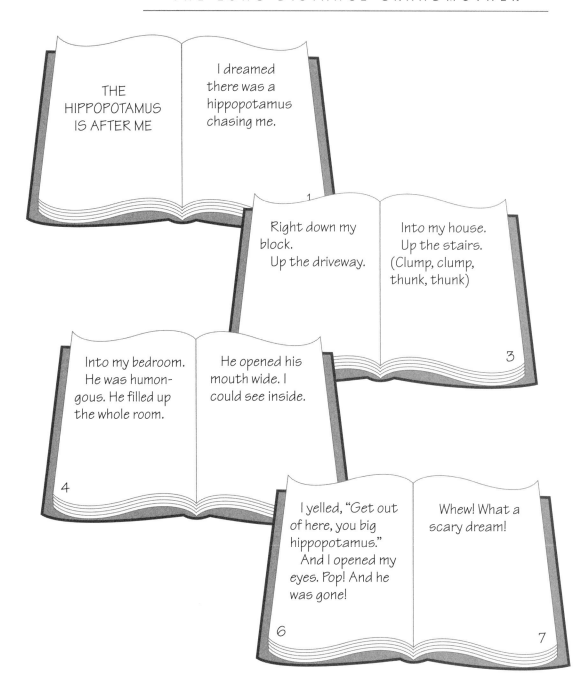

THE HIPPOPOTAMUS IS AFTER ME

I dreamed there was a hippopotamus chasing me.

1

Right down my block.
Up the driveway.

Into my house.
Up the stairs.
(Clump, clump, thunk, thunk)

3

Into my bedroom. He was humongous. He filled up the whole room.

He opened his mouth wide. I could see inside.

4

I yelled, "Get out of here, you big hippopotamus." And I opened my eyes. Pop! And he was gone!

Whew! What a scary dream!

6

7

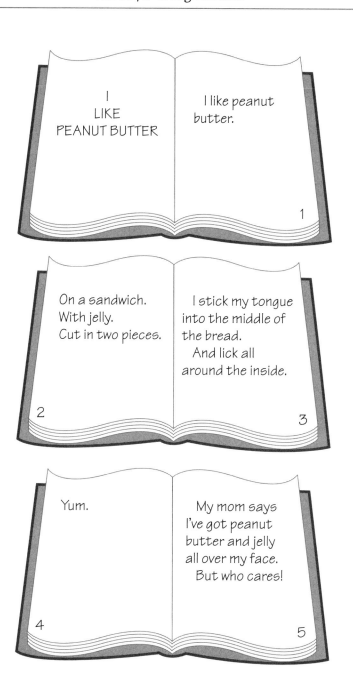

I
LIKE
PEANUT BUTTER

I like peanut butter.

1

On a sandwich.
With jelly.
Cut in two pieces.

I stick my tongue into the middle of the bread.
And lick all around the inside.

2

3

Yum.

My mom says I've got peanut butter and jelly all over my face.
But who cares!

4

5

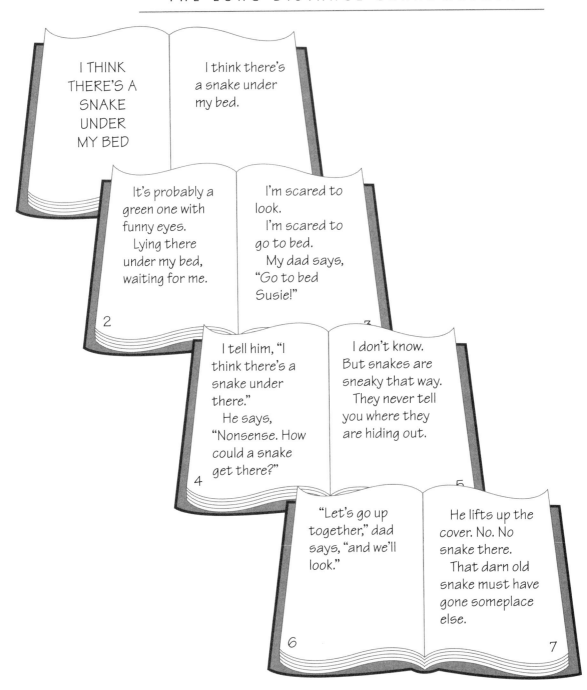

I THINK THERE'S A SNAKE UNDER MY BED

I think there's a snake under my bed.

It's probably a green one with funny eyes. Lying there under my bed, waiting for me.

I'm scared to look.
I'm scared to go to bed.
My dad says, "Go to bed Susie!"

2

I tell him, "I think there's a snake under there."
He says, "Nonsense. How could a snake get there?"

I don't know. But snakes are sneaky that way. They never tell you where they are hiding out.

4

"Let's go up together," dad says, "and we'll look."

He lifts up the cover. No. No snake there.
That darn old snake must have gone someplace else.

6

7

124

SIMON GOES TO SCHOOL

Simon is five years old. That means he can go to school now.

In the hot summer days, Simon went to the beach. He went swimming.

He went to visit Grandma and Grandpa at their house.

2

Grandma said, "When the summer is over, you'll go to school."

"When is that?" Simon asked. "In September," Grandma said.

4

5

"When is September? How many sleeps?" They count the sleeps. It's still a lot to wait.

Simon has to wait a long time. But finally it's time for school.

6

7

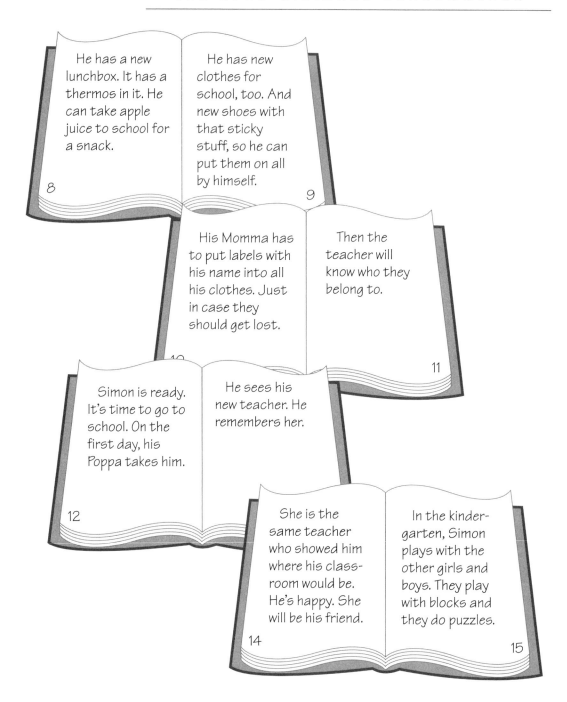

He has a new lunchbox. It has a thermos in it. He can take apple juice to school for a snack.

8

He has new clothes for school, too. And new shoes with that sticky stuff, so he can put them on all by himself.

9

His Momma has to put labels with his name into all his clothes. Just in case they should get lost.

10

Then the teacher will know who they belong to.

11

Simon is ready. It's time to go to school. On the first day, his Poppa takes him.

12

He sees his new teacher. He remembers her.

She is the same teacher who showed him where his classroom would be. He's happy. She will be his friend.

14

In the kindergarten, Simon plays with the other girls and boys. They play with blocks and they do puzzles.

15

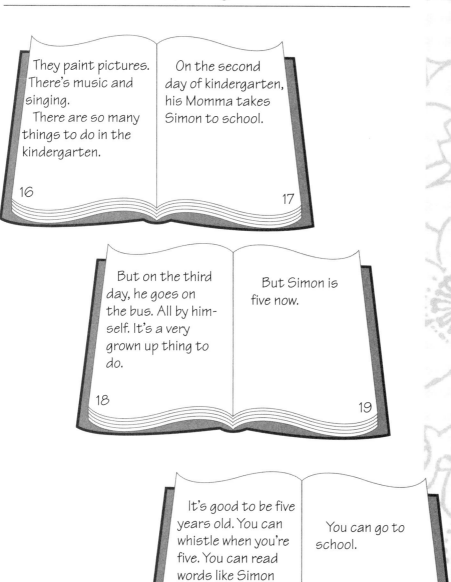

They paint pictures. There's music and singing.
  There are so many things to do in the kindergarten.

16

On the second day of kindergarten, his Momma takes Simon to school.

17

But on the third day, he goes on the bus. All by himself. It's a very grown up thing to do.

18

But Simon is five now.

19

It's good to be five years old. You can whistle when you're five. You can read words like Simon and Momma and Poppa.

20

You can go to school.

21

MARY BETH
VISITS
GRANDMA
AND
GRANDPA'S
HOUSE

When Mary Beth came to visit Grandma and Grandpa's house, she came in John's car. With Momma and John. It was a long, long ride. For all day.

It was night time when they got there. Grandma and Grandpa were sleeping. But a little bed for Mary Beth was ready.

2

And she could skootch down into it, warm and snuggly, under the big red quilt. She had the whole room all for herself, too.

3

In the morning, Grandma and Grandpa were waiting to see Mary Beth. Oh, there were SO many kisses. "I

4

am SO happy to see you, Mary Beth," said Grandpa. Grandma said, "Now we can go out to play."

5

Mary Beth had cereal for breakfast—just the kind she likes. With yogurt and milk and a little brown sugar sprinkled on the top.
　　Then, it was time

6

to go and play. Grandma took Mary Beth to the SeaBus. It went across the water. We could see all the other boats and big ships in the harbor.

7

Then, Mary Beth and Grandma went on the Sky-Train. It was a long ride. It went underground, in the tunnel. Then it

8

went high up, on the tracks. But not as high as an airplane. Only a little high.

9

When we got off the SkyTrain, Mary Beth had a ride on the carousel. She rode on the horse that went up and down.

10

We went back home on the SkyTrain and SeaBus too.

11

And had a ride on the escalator. And on the elevator. And to the Ball Room.
Mary Beth went down the slide and covered herself all over with balls. Then

12

we went to the toy store and Mary Beth chose a jet ball for herself.
At Grandma's house, Mary Beth had a movie for a treat. It was the Magic Pony.

13

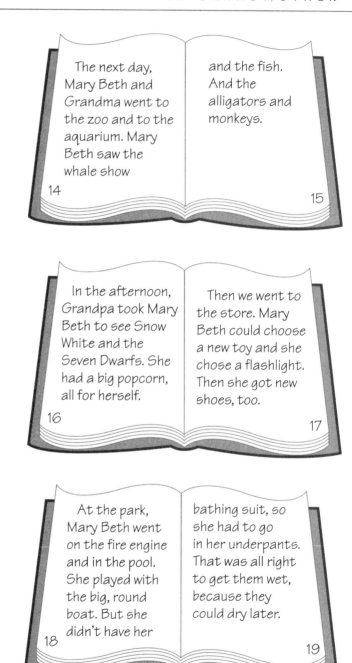

The next day, Mary Beth and Grandma went to the zoo and to the aquarium. Mary Beth saw the whale show

14

and the fish. And the alligators and monkeys.

15

In the afternoon, Grandpa took Mary Beth to see Snow White and the Seven Dwarfs. She had a big popcorn, all for herself.

16

Then we went to the store. Mary Beth could choose a new toy and she chose a flashlight. Then she got new shoes, too.

17

At the park, Mary Beth went on the fire engine and in the pool. She played with the big, round boat. But she didn't have her

18

bathing suit, so she had to go in her underpants. That was all right to get them wet, because they could dry later.

19

On Saturday, Grandma and Grandpa took Mary Beth to the airport. We all went on a little airplane,

20

with propellers. The lady in the airplane gave Mary Beth apple juice and nuts, all for herself.

21

When we got off the plane, Momma was waiting for us. She said, "You got new shoes, Mary Beth."

"Did you have a

22

good time at Grandma and Grandpa's house, Mary Beth?" Momma wanted to know. "What were your favorite things?"

23

What were your favorite things, Mary Beth? What did you like best at Grandma and Grandpa's house?

24

Sympathy for your grandchild's accident goes a long way.

ALBERT
IS
FOUR

"Wake up, Albert," said Mommy.
"It's your birthday!"

Albert opened his eyes and looked around his room. That's funny. Everything looked the same as it did yesterday.

2

"You can wear your new corduroy jeans and your new red shirt that grandpa sent you," said Mommy. "For your birthday."

3

Albert put his clothes on all by himself. He was four now. He only needed some help getting his shoelaces tied.

4

For his breakfast, Albert had his favorite things. Pancakes! Mommy made them specially for a birthday treat.

5

Grandpa telephoned to sing "Happy Birthday to Albert."
"Are you four?" asked Grandpa.
"Yeh," said Albert.

6

"How does it feel to be four?" asked Grandpa.
"Good," said Albert.

7

"Let's see," said Grandpa. "Now that you are four, is there anything different about you that I should know about?"

"What?" said Albert.

8

"Well," said Grandpa. "Did you grow a beard yet?"

Albert laughed. "No, not yet."

9

"Hm," said Grandpa. "Does your face look the same now that you're four?"

"I don't know," said Albert.

10

"Better look in the mirror and tell me," said Grandpa.

11

Albert went to look at his face in the mirror. Hey, it looked just the same. He ran back to the telephone and told Grandpa.

"It looks the same, Grandpa."

12

"Whew! Thank goodness, Albert. I just wanted to be sure that I'd still recognize you when I see you, now that you are four years old."

13

133

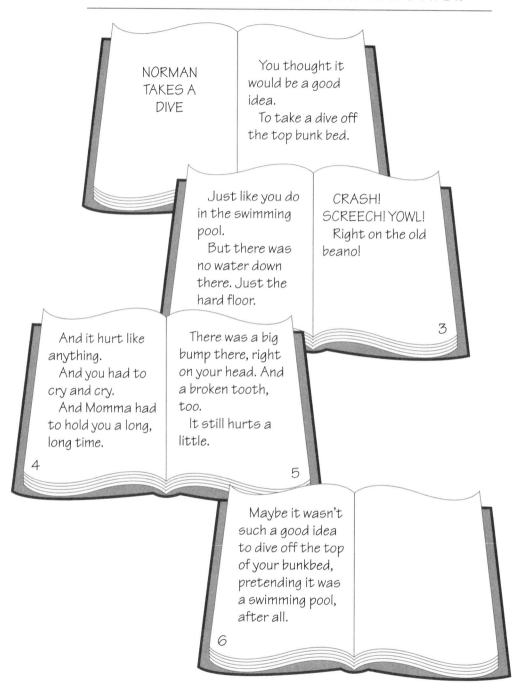

NORMAN TAKES A DIVE

You thought it would be a good idea.
To take a dive off the top bunk bed.

Just like you do in the swimming pool.
But there was no water down there. Just the hard floor.

CRASH! SCREECH! YOWL!
Right on the old beano!

3

And it hurt like anything.
And you had to cry and cry.
And Momma had to hold you a long, long time.

There was a big bump there, right on your head. And a broken tooth, too.
It still hurts a little.

4

5

Maybe it wasn't such a good idea to dive off the top of your bunkbed, pretending it was a swimming pool, after all.

6

## Dear Grandma and Grandpa

This holiday season, a small miracle occurred at our house. A parcel arrived with a set of pictures and stories that the boys made for us. They have taken the first giant steps of transforming their thoughts into written language to send. Of course, Momma does the writing-down, but the written communication of ideas has begun.

Dear Grandma and Grandpa,

I love you and I'm giving you a lot of presents. Four pictures for grandma and four pictures for grandpa. We're having a lot of fun at Mum's house and Dad's house. And someday we would bring you here for a tea party. And if you forget my teacher's name I'm going to tell you it. It's Mrs. Doerfler. We have a new art cupboard and our beds are down. It's snowing here but I'll bet it's not snowing at grandma and grandpa's house. We're doing stuff that's really nice. Love from Simon.

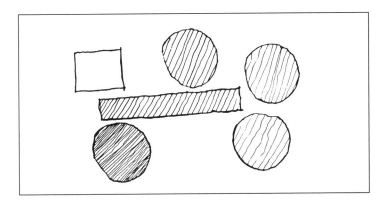

This is a truck with a box on the back and it has no engine and it has no window and it has no gate to open. Simon loves Grandma and Grandpa.

Imagine how it feels to receive a parcel of stories and pictures put together by your grandchildren.

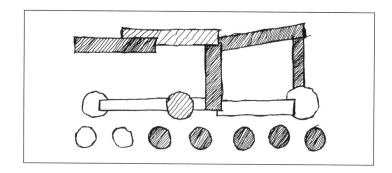

This is a toot-toot train going. From Arlo.

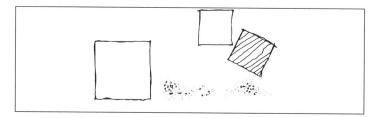

This is a picture that might glow in the dark, even the little and big squares. This picture is made from a lot of stuff but I don't remember what the sparkly things are. From Simon.

On one of the boys' visits to our home, Arlo, now in his mid-teens, became suddenly reflective. "Remember," he asked me, "those books you used to write for us when we were little?"

Surprised that he would remember, I said that I did remember those books quite well.

"You know, I've been saving them. I don't have them all, because some of them got wrecked, but the ones that I have—I'm going to keep them for my own children."

Could there ever have been a Pulitzer Prize winner that felt more gratified by such an acknowledgment of her work?

# 10

# The Grandchild's Personal Words

THERE WILL COME a time in your young grandchild's life—a magic moment—when he or she will begin to take notice of the written word.

"Mommy, what does *this* say?" says Benny, pointing to the word *milk* on the carton.

"It says 'milk,' sweetheart," says Mum.

"And what does *this* say?" says Benny, now pointing to the word *tea* on the box.

Different children come to these magic moments at different times. Whether they come to them earlier or later is not a sign of either brilliance or backwardness, but it is a moment that signals the child has now taken his or her first steps into the world of written language. Some children may do this earlier, some later. When it happens, it is a time of celebration, and the world of books and reading may now begin to unfold.

Writing and sending stories to your grandchildren is one way of cultivating these interests. And store-bought books do this as well.

## Making Personal Word Books

Personal word books capture those words that have powerful meanings. The "stories" are the words themselves.

There is another form of book I used that does not fit into the category of stories. Instead these little books are books of *words*. They have another style, another format, another purpose in the long distance connection. I call these books "personal word books." (They evolve from the work of writer Sylvia Ashton-Warner, whose book *Teacher* tells about the power of personal words in making the bridge to reading.) Instead of telling a story, these books use only single words—and these words must be of great personal significance in the life of the child for the books to have meaning. These words represent the child's strongest feelings: what he loves and what he hates; what he is afraid of, and what upsets him. *Mommy, Daddy, Arlo* (siblings), *ghosts, sharks, bears, monsters, new tooth, baby, Justin* (friends), *pancakes*—whatever you have discovered about his life that has very great personal meaning. In writing these words, we must not choose words *we think he ought to find important*. We must choose only those words that are important to *him*.

These books are, in some ways, much easier to write than personal story books. They do not even require that a tale be told, or that there is some coherent whole to the book. And more important, according to their inventor, they do not require illustrations. On the contrary, illustrations are banned, because they tend to detract from the power of the personal word.

The age to begin writing personal word books is not fixed in stone. About the middle of the third year seems a good starting point, if your grandchild has already had lots of books and stories in his life. I would not send a personal word book as his *first* book. Let the personal story books described in chapter nine pave the way. There should be no rush into personal word books. Generally, later is better than earlier. But, of course, once the child is a fluent reader, these books will have lost their potential appeal.

The word I would start with is, for obvious reasons, the child's first name. There is no other word that has more power. And a whole four-page book can be built around this word. (Read Chapter Nine for suggestions on how to put together a book.) Be innovative about the covers (cloth, cardboard, colorful paper bags and/or gift wrap), and about the shape of the book, as well.

The act of reading begins with sight recognition—the power of the word rather than individual letters.

Page 1

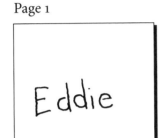

Page 2

Page 3

Page 4

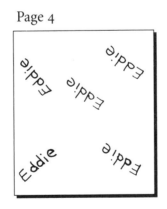

Of course, the words should be *printed*, preferably in manuscript letters. (The Sources section at the end of the book shows how to make easy-to-read manuscript letter forms.) Rather than to be avoided, repetition is encouraged. Don't overcrowd the page. (Less is more!) The designs you make in the ways you arrange the words on the page supply variety and allow you to use the same words again and again.

Other "first" personal words will likely include "Mommy" (or "Mamma," or whatever the child calls his mother); "Poppa" (or "Daddy" or "Dad"); names of brothers and sisters; names of pets; grandparents; special babysitters or nannies. Choose the words in the forms that the child uses. If he, for example, calls his father "Poppa," that is the form that should be used.

Keep the personal word books short—four to six pages at most. As a general rule, repeat the same words and do not include more than three different words in one book, or you may be in danger of overkill. Don't try to make stories with these words, and don't ask for assurances that the child can read them.

Perhaps you could write one personal word book per month for your grandchild until he or she is five. Then, you might try linking his or her words together, into phrases of two or three words, and writing phrase books. If you are on the telephone together, you might expand these words by asking your grandchild what word he or she would like you to send next. It's a good idea to keep a list of words that you have been sending, so that you will have an easily accessible record of what you have used, and what is new. But whatever words you choose to send, stay with those with a powerful emotional connection, since these are the ones which will bring the most pleasure, while also building bridges into reading and writing.

# Examples of Personal Word Books

Page 1

Page 2

Page 3

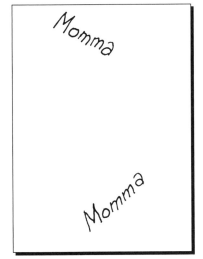

Page 4

Page 1

Page 2

Page 3

Page 4

Page 5

Page 6

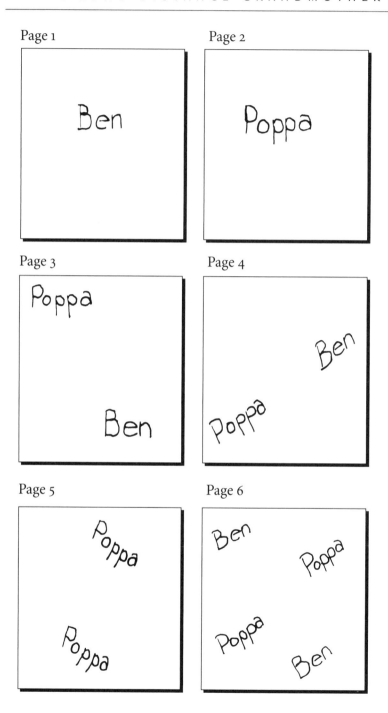

Page 1

Lenny

Page 2

Stefi

Page 3

Stefi
Stefi
Stefi
Stefi

Page 4

Stefi

Lenny

Page 5

Lenny

Stefi

Lenny

Page 6

Stefi
Lenny
Stefi
Lenny

Page 1

Jimmy

Page 2

Momma

Momma

Jimmy

Page 3

Poppa

Jimmy

Poppa

Page 4

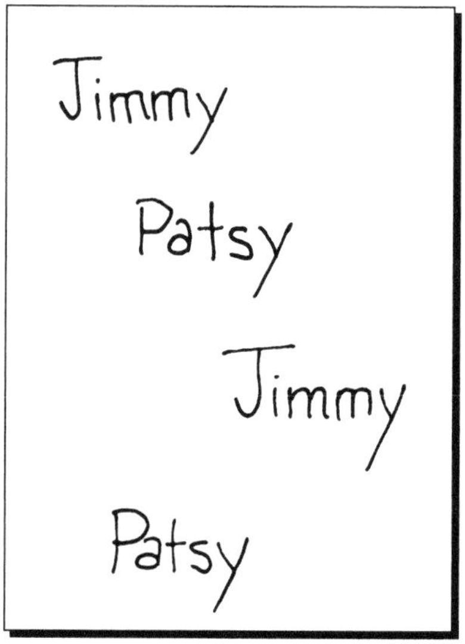

Jimmy

Patsy

Jimmy

Patsy

Page 1

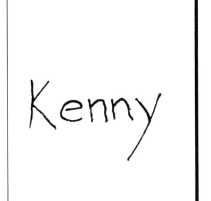

Page 2

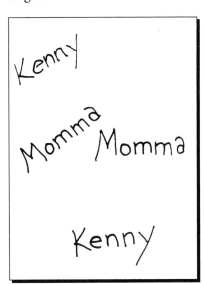

Page 3

Page 4

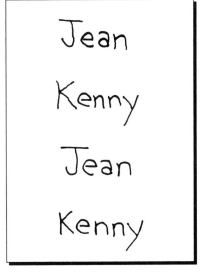

Page 1

Poppa

Jay

Poppa and Jay

Page 2

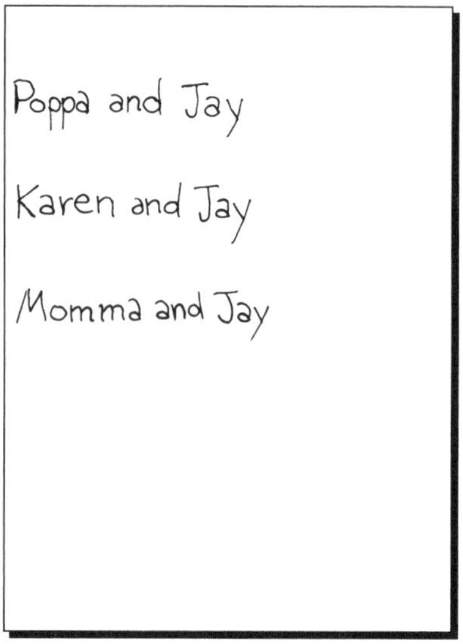

Poppa and Jay

Karen and Jay

Momma and Jay

Page 3

Grandma

Grandma

Grandma

Page 4

Grandma

and

Jay

# 11

# Writing Stories for Grandchildren Who Can Read

*"My ideal grandma would have time to explain to me, and tell about her life."*

## My Grandmother's Story

My own grandmother was in many ways an extraordinary woman. Like many other immigrant women of her era, she found her way from the tiny shtetl in Poland, where she had been born and where she had lived the cloistered life of an orthodox Jewish daughter, across a continent, onto a ship, across an ocean, and onto a new land. This she did with a baby in her arms, unaccompanied by friend, relative or spouse, at the tender age of—who knows?—because her birth had never been properly recorded. She had never before ventured beyond the tiny enclosure that was her village; nor was she able to speak in a language that would help her to make her urgent needs or wants known to the officials that guarded the gates of passage. She made this trip without adequate funds, without maturity or worldliness, and with the fears that came from having grown up in terror of the "outsider"—those who lived outside the walls of the shtetl and who might, for whatever reason, bring rape and plunder and violence and villainy to the village without provocation. Her story (and the stories of others like herself) was good enough to have become a successful

There is something both familiar and exotic about stories of family history.

The cataclysmic world events of the twentieth century have touched every family to some degree.

and long-running play. Later it became a movie: *Fiddler on the Roof.* My grandmother was one of the many who moved to and settled into the Lower East Side of New York City.

What an adventure that must have been for her! What experiences she must have had! I cannot imagine what it must have been like for her to cross the ocean with her infant son, on her own, in steerage! And what it must have been like for her to have my grandfather waiting for her as she came through Immigration. My grandfather took her to their first apartment—a fourth floor, "cold-water" walk-up flat, with a shed in the yard—the single toilet for all the tenants. When they walked past the push carts to get home, he bought her a banana (because she had never seen one in her life), to see if she would eat it with the skin on, and have a joke at her expense. But she robbed him of the comedy, peeled it and ate it, much to his pride in her. Obviously, this tough woman was going to make it in the New World!

As a child, I never tired of hearing such stories from my grandparents, and I would listen to the same ones again and again, always begging for more:

"Grandma, tell me about the time you came in the ship."

"Grandma, tell me about when you moved to Brooklyn."

"Grandma, tell me about. . ."

She would tire of the telling more quickly than I of the listening. "Again?" she would ask in Yiddish. "You want to hear that again? How many times do you need to hear that!" But she would gather me into her lap and hold me close. I could smell the cinnamon on her apron as I snuggled into the warmth of her, making pictures in my mind of the events as she retold them. Always, her eyes took on a faraway look. She did not look at me, but always at a time long past, as she recreated her stories for me—her history, my history.

My grandmother, for all her many virtues, never learned to read and write, never learned to speak English. Education in the shtetl was for boys only. The girls learned to cook and sew and sweep, so that they might only become good mothers and wives. In the New World, she could make do with Yiddish in the home and in the marketplace. On occasion, she would find use for her Russian or Polish—both of which she spoke fluently—to my great surprise. But they were not her languages of choice. For her they remained the languages of the enemy she had learned to fear, from outside her village.

## The Legacy of Family Chronicles

Even if she had learned to read and write, it is unlikely, given her way of life, that my grandmother would have dreamed of recording her stories, to be passed down from generation to generation. What a legacy to pass down to our children! What a sorrow to lose these oral histories with the passing of the storytellers! I have a friend who began, when her father turned seventy-five, to sit with him in front of a cassette recorder, gathering his family chronicles on tape. She will have these in her family history "books" to pass down through the generations. Such chronicles can hand down our culture through the generations, and become a treasure house of the stories of our lives.

Our contemporary lives are littered with consumer goods, and it is hard for many of us to wade through it all and keep some perspective about what is junk and what is of value. Our grandchildren's lives, too, are inundated with junk—junk food, junk toys, junk TV—and in the midst of it all, they may find it difficult to discover what is important, and what has real meaning for them. When children lose the ability to tell these apart, they have lost much.

Writing your own family stories does even more than teach your grandchildren about their roots. It teaches them about the value of life experiences. It puts value on lives, rather than on products. It helps them to know, with certainty, that grandma and grandpa were young, too; had lives that endured struggle and found joy; had some experiences in common with them and others radically different.

Family chronicles can offer a sense of continuity and connectedness in a world where much is transient and disposable.

Through these stories, our grandchildren come to know us as real people—not just as wallets with wrinkles.

## When to Start

I would begin writing family chronicles for grandchildren at an age when they can grasp the meaning of a story with some understanding and sophistication. Depending on the child's life experience, this might be as early as age six or seven. Waiting until age eight is not a disadvantage. These stories may be read by the parents to the children, or by the children themselves. And, of course, such stories should also be written for our older grandchildren.

## Making Family Chronicle Books

Because these family chronicles have more than a passing interest, what they look like and the materials you use need some consideration. I would expect the shelf-life of a family chronicle to be considerably greater than the life of the personal word books described in Chapter Ten, or the personal stories for toddlers. Because these family chronicles will be treated with respect, they should be made to endure. And they will be cherished just as we cherish photographs of the past.

This is why family chronicle stories are best written in notebooks, or in other suitable blank books. Notebooks of every size, shape, and quality are easily found in the large drug stores that sell school supplies. Beautifully bound blank books can be found in better quality stationery stores. Which you choose will depend on your budget and taste. If you care a lot about this venture, go for the bound books. They have substance and they add a certain class to the undertaking. A soft cover notebook is,

Your story is precious— it should be presented as such.

after all, only a notebook. But a looseleaf binder is the least preferable, because it's not a *Book*. (The pages fall out too easily, and there is no spine.)

You can print your story directly into the book. Printing (hand lettering as shown at the back of the book) is easier to read than cursive writing. In that way, younger children may read the story by themselves. Or, you can type the story on bond paper, and then paste the sheets into the book. If you are "computer-broken," and have a machine, you can avail yourself of a score of type faces, sizes, and even some graphic designs. The importance of *what* you write will not be diminished by the way you choose to transcribe the story. A handwritten story may be more prized, for example, than a neatly put-together, straight-margined computer printout.

## Coping With "Writer's Block"

For too many grandparents, the thought of writing a story is as formidable as climbing Mount Everest. The claim, "I can't write!" is a familiar, self-protective ploy. But the truth is that grandparents *can* write. They may lack experience or practice, they may lack confidence, they may believe that they lack ideas about what to write, they may be afraid of writing—or any combination of the above. But *can't* is different. "Can't" means unable. If you can write a shopping list, you can write a story. If you lack the experience or practice, you will gain them from the very act of writing. If you are at a loss for ideas, there will be lots of suggestions for you to choose from in this chapter—until you discover your own source of ideas. If you lack confidence in yourself as a writer, console yourself with the knowledge that most *great* writers, when confronting the blank page, experience tremendous feelings of anxiety about their ability to write well. (Yes, it's true!) The secret key to dealing with lack of confidence is to sit down to write. *Just write and keep writing.* Confidence grows with expertise, and expertise grows from practice.

> You have more to tell in a story than you think. Putting it on paper takes a little time and practice.

Editing is a separate process from writing. Write first; then edit. Give yourself permission to write freely. You can edit out what you don't want later.

If you are intimidated by the thought of writing, try this approach. Tell your story into a tape recorder. Then, play it back and write it down. Whichever way you begin, you will go through many edited versions, and finally produce a polished draft that can be written into your blank book. Keep in mind that you are not undertaking to write another *War and Peace,* or aiming for the Nobel Prize in Literature. If you had "bad marks" and criticisms from your school teachers about your English compositions, remember they are no longer there to judge you. What's more, their evaluation of your work was not *the truth,* but only one person's opinion.

One way to overcome resistance to writing that is rooted in unnamed fears is to figure out some coping strategies—and each of us has his or her own techniques for doing this. We all face situations in our own lives that present real obstacles to overcome, and somehow we figure out ways to overcome them—from "driving on the wrong side of the road" in England, to leaping off the high board at the community pool. If it's important enough, we take ourselves in hand and find a way. The more we do it, the less difficult it is. And finally, it's not difficult at all. The writing can become as familiar as driving, and we can be as comfortable doing it as we are in making pastry dough.

Before going ahead with ideas for family chronicles, I want to add a few more thoughts about the act of writing. From very early on in school, we have been taught that what we put on paper must be perfect—perfect in spelling, perfect in grammar, perfect in sentence structure, perfect in punctuation. This message has been drilled home with such success that the act of writing has become intimidating. In school, there were prices to pay for less-than-perfect papers: a large C in the top right hand corner of our paper, and red pencil marks throughout the body of the work to point out our errors and imperfections. No wonder so many of us grew up disabled rather than "enabled" as writers!

Every life is marked by triumph and heartache; all are worthy of transcribing for the family history.

Happily for children today, they are having better writing experiences in school. Today many teachers work on the idea of the "process" of writing: We get an idea, then we put the idea on paper. What is important is to get the ideas down, not to get them down perfectly. (To aim for perfection is never to write at all!) What is produced is called a "draft." The draft is a piece of writing that needs work: editing for punctuation, grammar, spelling. We make corrections. The paper goes into a second draft. Then more editing is done. The content, sequence, paragraph breaks, clarity, are all examined, thought about, re-worked. This process of draft-edit-draft-edit till the final story is the way in which all writers work. I do not know of a single writer who uses original draft work as final copy. It may be helpful to remember that the draft of your story is probably going to be shaped, molded and remolded, like a piece of clay. It is pliable, and intended for manipulation, not sacrosanct or hardened in concrete. When is a draft a final copy? When you are content with it! That's the key. When you are happy with what you have done, it is time to put it into final form.

## Ideas for Family Chronicles

Family chronicles could and should be the life stories of the key family members—starting with grandma and grandpa. Write about yourself first.

What were your toddler years like?

Where did you live?

How did you live?

Who were the people in your family?

What did your father do?

What did your mother do?

When did you go to school? Where did you go? What kind of school was it?

What do you remember of your school experiences?

Don't put the chores first—leave them until after the writing is done.

Set aside a time to write. Don't let anything steal that time from writing.

Writing your own story can take you back in time to relive those powerful events . . . like starring in your own movie.

What was the neighborhood like?

Who were your friends?

What did you do for fun?

Did you have a best friend? Best buddies?

What do you remember of your teachers?

What was your family life like?

Did you go on trips together? What trips were important?

Did you have brothers? Sisters? How did you get along with them?

Which people in your family were special to you? What made them special?

What did you love to do as a child? Did you have favorite toys? Games? Pastimes?

What events gave you special pleasure?

What unhappy events do you remember?

Did you have serious illnesses? How did they affect you?

Did you have to move? What were the consequences?

Were you shy? Did you have difficulty making friends? Were you lacking in confidence?

Did other children tease you?

Did you have to wear ugly shoes?

Was your family poor? Wealthy?

Did you live in a time of war? What did this mean in your life?

Was your life in danger? Was your family in danger?

Did you have to leave your country?

Did you experience any severe losses?

Did you always fight with your older brothers or sisters? Did they pick on you and call you names?

Did you have a secret hiding place? Did you go there and pretend you were a princess? Did you invent stories of fantasy in which you were the hero?

Did you do any mischief? Did you get into big trouble? Were you punished?

Did your mother run a boarding house? Did strange people come and go? Did someone give you a nickel for carrying his suitcase?

Any of these questions, by itself, can become the focal point of a story.

Events of importance in the family's history can be another resource for stories. While there is overlap here with personal stories, in the first group *oneself* is central and the events are secondary. In the second group, the *events* are central and the oneself secondary. Many grandparents who are my contemporaries will have the events of World War II as part of their childhood experience, and these events should go on record, as we lived them, in our family chronicles. There are likely dozens of significant events to be remembered in the life experience of every grandparent.

Here are some events that I recall, each of which could be developed into stories:

- The day the Japanese bombed Pearl Harbor.
- The day my father had kidney failure and was taken by ambulance to the hospital.
- Moving to Alabama Avenue because we were so poor, we couldn't afford the rent where we were living.
- The many months my father was out of work in the Depression, and how it felt.
- How the war affected our lives at home.
- When my uncle went to war and how everything changed after that.
- My mother going back to work and how everything changed after that.
- The day my grandmother died and how everything changed after that.
- The day the teacher took us on a field trip to the library—my very first experience in a library—and how I changed after that.
- How I met your grandpa, and. . .
- The day your momma was born, and. . .

## Remembering Past Events

What were some significant events in your life? Sit down, close your eyes, and remember everything you can. Make a list of what you remember. *Don't censor your list*—just write everything as it occurs to you. Your list will give you some rich ideas, and now that you have it, you can play with it, picking and choosing, modifying, discarding, adding. You'll find that you have more than enough ideas here for an abundance of stories.

In remembering past events, it is not important to remember *everything;* nor should we wish to do so. (It would create terrible mental burdens to have immediate recall of all past events.) If you cannot recapture all the details or names of the key players, or exactly how the event unfolded, such lapses hardly matter. Make up what you don't remember! After all, we are not writing factual historical documents, but personal histories which may well profit from exaggeration!

Have a good look at your collection of treasured family photographs, and see if you can find in them some ideas for stories. Go through them and find any that show moments with a particular significance for you. Write the story and use the photo, too.

## Some Sample Stories

These stories may be read aloud to children, or the children may read them themselves.

## I Was a City Child

We lived in the city. On our block, five large apartment houses were attached to each other without so much as a crack between them, making them look like one huge, block-long brick fortress. All the houses were built of the same dark gray brick. The sidewalks were gray, too, and the street was paved with black asphalt. My world was

In revisiting the events of our past we can gain fresh insight and understanding, and perhaps let go of stored-up feelings that we no longer need to hold on to.

colored gray, without a tree or a hedge or a bush to lighten the bleak monotony of the granite cityscape.

Like other city children, I played on the sidewalk. We had our own games. One of our favorites was potsy (also called hopscotch). It consisted of drawing boxes and numbers on the sidewalk, throwing a "potsy" (which could be a bottle top, a skate key, or any other small object that had both the weight and the density to be aimed true) into one of the boxes, and hopping around on one foot from box to box, picking up your potsy on the way.

Then there was jump rope, "single" and "double dutch." And stoop ball. Some of the boys played stick ball in the street, but girls were not invited to play with them. If your friends were not around, you just hung out on the sidewalk, waiting for someone to come out. There was not very much for children to do on the sidewalk in the city.

My mother and father didn't allow me to cross the street by myself until I was seven. I didn't think this was fair, because I felt that I was old enough to watch out for cars and I could cross carefully. I sometimes put my foot in the gutter—to tease them—but they got quite mad at me and I had to go to my room as a punishment. When I was feeling quite naughty I went halfway around the block and crossed the street where I knew no one would know me or report what I had done to my parents. I knew that crossing the street was wrong, and I knew that my parents would be very upset if they found out. But I did it anyway.

In the summertime when the heat was oppressive and school was out, time was the enemy. I sat on the steps of our apartment house trying to figure out what to do. Most days, there was just nothing to do. In the summer, some friends went away with their families to "the country." Some got to go to the beach regularly. I felt as if I were the only one left on our block who had to endure the summer in the city, all by myself. There was nothing so terrible for me as hanging around with nothing to do. I hate the thought of it even now.

One day, quite without warning, my mother told me that we were

Many stories grow richer in the retelling, but this doesn't detract from the story's essential truth.

If you use a lot of unfamiliar or outdated terms you might want to define these in a brief directory at the end of the story.

going to the country. We would be there for the rest of the summer. No more city sidewalks! No more stifling apartments! No more hanging around with nothing to do! I was going to the country. I had never been to the country—and I imagined a paradise, a fantasyland, in which I would be a fairy princess having a wonderful time. I watched my mother packing our things, and she had to scold me many times for getting in her way. But I was too excited to care.

My father borrowed my uncle's car to drive us up to the country. The ride took forever. It was hot in the car and I was squashed in the back seat between my mother and my grandmother, both of whom were quite huge. When I wriggled around, they nudged me to sit still. I found it very hard to sit still in that hot, hot car, for such a long trip. It was dark when we got there and I had fallen asleep. I missed my chance of seeing "the country" that night.

When I woke the next morning, I took a look at my strange new surroundings. We were in a small room with a wood ceiling, uneven wooden floors and wooden walls. There was more wood in that room than I had seen in all my life. The room had two beds, a larger one for my mother and grandmother, and a cot-sized one for me. There was a table in the center, and a small sink on the wall near the door. We were renting this small room, in an old farmhouse in the Catskill Mountains—about ninety miles from my home in the city. To me, it was like being on another planet.

The world outside the farmhouse was a green and blue world— green grass everywhere, trees and leaves as green and bright as my best green crayon in my coloring box. Rolling green hills meeting blue, blue cloudless sky. Not another house anywhere in sight, except for our farmhouse. Not a sidewalk, not a gutter, not a single brick. The color gray had been completely erased from my world.

Children delight in learning that their parents and grand-parents pushed at the boundaries set by their mothers and fathers.

I had breakfast in the communal kitchen that the summer room-renting tenants shared, all exiles from the steaming city. My mother put a bowl of cornflakes down in front of me and poured some milk into it, from a pitcher. At home, at my house in the city, milk came in bottles. The milkman delivered a new set of bottles each morning, picking up the empties, as well. If you were up early enough, you would see him making his rounds, his horse pulling a wagon loaded with jiggling milk bottles.

I dipped my spoon into the cereal and tasted. Ugh! This was not like milk at all! "This is not my milk," I protested to my mother.

"This is milk," she told me. "This milk came directly from the cow. After I unpack, I'll take you to the barn to see the cows."

"I don't want milk from the cow. I want horse's milk. From the Sheffield milkman." (Sheffield was the name of the milk company.)

How could I, a city child, know about where milk came from? To me, it came from the milkman. As far as I knew, he milked his horse every morning before he made his deliveries. And what's more, it tasted swell. This cow's milk had a strange, weird taste and I knew I would never get to love it.

Later that day, my mother took me to the barn to see the cows. I was terrified of these great hulking animals that made large, guttural, rude sounds. The farmer was milking and he offered me a dipperful fresh from the milking pails. It was warm, and foamy, and tasted disgusting. As we walked through the field back to the farmhouse, my mother pointed out a young calf that had been tethered to a telephone pole. No, I didn't want to pet it. No, I didn't want to be near it. I didn't believe you could trust these animals—not for a minute.

The country might be green and blue and smell sweet, but in my heart, I was a city child.

## My Friend Audrey

Audrey lived three houses down the block. She was six months younger than I, and about a head smaller. Her mother and my mother were friends. They said that we should be friends. They said that we had to play nicely. I was four and quite big for my age. Audrey was three and a half, and quite small for her age.

If you can remember an event that took place thirty, forty or fifty years ago as if it were yesterday, then it's worth writing down.

My mother would say, "Go outside and play with Audrey," and, at first, I would go quite happily. I needed help putting on my leggings, which were those long pants that kept our legs warm on cold days. I don't know why they were called leggings, rather than pants. Perhaps in those days it was not good form for girls to be wearing pants. Pants were only for boys in those days.

I got some help taking out my doll and carriage and pushed them down the block to Audrey's house. It wasn't long before she had taken over doll, carriage—the lot. She wouldn't let me push. She wouldn't let me touch the doll or the carriage. She wanted it all for herself. But wait a minute! It was my doll, my carriage. We got into a tussle and she kicked me in the shin. I punched her in the arm. She ran into the house, yelling like anything, and I repossessed my carriage and doll and pushed them indignantly home.

"What happened?" asked my mother.

"Audrey kicked me and I punched her back." I told it all, so that she would know that my aggressive act had been provoked.

"You mustn't fight with your friends," she said. "No hitting and no kicking. You go out there and make up."

I was stubborn and wouldn't do it. "I don't like her," I said. But my mother was having none of it. All day she treated me with utter disgust.

Several days later, the doll and carriage battle behind us and almost, but not entirely, forgotten, my mother told me once again to go out and play with Audrey. Once again I was seduced by the appeal of a playmate. This time, the battle was over my ball. She grabbed it from me, without so much as an if-you-please.

"Gimme back my ball," I shouted at her. For an answer, she spat directly in my face. I was furious. I pummeled her, using the leverage of my size to knock her down. But her smaller size and weight did not disadvantage her. On the contrary. She was wiry and strong and cunning, and she put her teeth into my leg like an angry pup. I yowled. She screamed and ran off to her house. I limped home, crying.

Perhaps you were raised in the countryside, or in a different country. Your first impressions of city life would make for a memorable tale.

My mother was already on the telephone with Audrey's mother, and when she put the phone down, she brought her full anger to bear on me. Audrey was smaller, younger. I was bigger, older. I must know better. I needed to be more responsible. I needed to protect Audrey. She was little and you never hit anyone who was smaller, because that made you a bully. And my mother would not tolerate having a bully for a daughter.

Not only had my mother not taken my side; she stood against me. I was hurt and indignant. But I knew from that moment on that any arguing, any revenge, any fighting back I would do with Audrey would be seen as bully-ish—and that my mother simply would not tolerate this behavior. So I had to swallow my pride.

Audrey, that three-and-a-half-year-old terror, persisted in her aggressive acts towards me. I learned to stay away from her, despite my mother's and Audrey's mother's urging that we play together. When we were forced into togetherness, I allowed her to hit me without hitting her back. For these acts of non-violence I was praised by my mother, who would brag about my "turning the other cheek" to Audrey's aggressions.

It's funny that I should still remember Audrey, even though I have not seen her in over fifty years.

## What About Style?

Before presenting more family chronicles, it seems a good idea to deal very briefly with some questions of form and style.

When I wrote the two stories, "My Friend Audrey" and "I Was A City Child" I kept in mind that I was writing for children. So there was no need to write in the sort of sophisticated, adult style that can be a burden even for quite experienced writers. I tried to use language that stayed close to ordinary speech, and that did not over-use metaphors and other literary devices. Yet neither did I "write down" by making

> "Grandma, did you have fights with you friends, too?"

> Grandchildren will be surprised and delighted to learn that grandparents had similar experiences when they were growing up.

Who cannot relate to the friend we didn't like or the bully who lived down the street?

the language too simplistic. ("This is the cow. See the cow. The cow says moo-moo.") Try to write as if you could hear yourself "speaking the story," and that can help you stay in the middle ground between literary art and simplism. If you want to shift from this middle ground, shift upward. It is better to extend children, to make them reach, to have to explain what they don't understand, and to let them ponder about the unknowns, than it is to trivialize and reduce the content to a simplistic level.

There are important differences between writing simply and writing simplistically. Simple writing reads clearly, crisply and cleanly. Sentences are usually short and to the point. Simple writing sounds natural.

Simplistic writing is artificially simple. It says things in a way that is not natural, either in spoken or written form. Simplistic language is neither how we speak, nor how we write. Here are some admittedly extreme examples:

Simple: I liked the way she wore her hair.

Simplistic: That was her hair. Her hair was long. It was black.

Simple: They stood close to the tracks and waved as the train went by.

Simplistic: We saw the train. We saw the people wave. They were waving at the train.

## Length of the Stories

Some will ask, "How long should the stories be?" and the answer to that is, "It depends." Some stories may want to be quite long; some very short. The guideline here is say what you have to say, and stop writing. These stories do not have to satisfy a 2,000 word-count assignment, in which we write and write and write until we have the required number of words. A good story can be only several paragraphs long. It can be five pages. It can be twenty.

Remember, too, that in the process of editing you can add, delete, and re-shape. If it seems short, perhaps that means that important parts are missing. If it seems long, it may mean that you have over-written and some pruning is required. Above all, try to find your own voice—and this means being your own natural, genuine, unselfconscious self in the writing process—setting down on the page what you think and what you feel, so that those thoughts and feelings are communicated to your family. This is the nature of the task. And if you learn to love it, you will have given yourself a treat even greater than the joy the stories will give to your loved ones.

Use adjectives and adverbs like ornaments—too many burden the story; too few make it barren.

## More Sample Stories
## I Want to Choose My Own Life

*(A grandfather writes for his grandchildren, aged 10 and 13.)*
We lived in a large apartment building, on the third floor. We had no elevators, so that meant walking up and down every time we went out. My mother did her marketing every day and she went out at the same time every day. You could set your clock by the sound of her footsteps going to the door. When she got older, I worried about her climbing those stairs carrying those bags of groceries.

My father worked as a jeweler, in a big jewelry house downtown. He had one of those jeweler's glasses that you stick in one eye. It made him look like a gargoyle when he was working. I used to wonder if that glass made his eyes bug out. He wanted me to be a jeweler, like him. He said the money was good and even in hard times you would always have a job. Especially if you learned how to cut diamonds. The diamond cutters were the top craftsmen. My father was a diamond setter.

All the while I was growing up, he would tell me about the benefits of working as a jeweler. I always listened, because he demanded respect! When I asked him if he *liked* being a jeweler, if he *liked* his work, he got very angry. "Like!" he shouted. "What's like got to do with it. It's work, and it earns you a living."

When I was in high school, I studied about as hard as any boy of my

163

Pretend your grand-
child is sitting next to
you. Tell the story
aloud, as you write
it down.

age who was not headed for college. There were other things that were
more important than school. My grades were never that good; I was
never studious. My one big love was music. I think music was in my
blood from the day I was born. When I was about 16, I finally got up
the nerve to tell my father. I thought he would have a heart attack!

He told me all the reasons I shouldn't be a musician. Terrible working conditions. Poor pay. And, "you'll never know where the next dol-
lar is coming from." I knew he wanted the best for me. He wanted me
to have some security in my life. Playing the guitar was no way to
make a living!

The more he shouted, the quieter I became. Then, for weeks, he
barely spoke to me and the tension in the house you could almost
touch. I felt ashamed. I knew how disappointed he was. But I could
not change what I felt and I could not change who I was. I could not
make my life into what he wanted. It was my life.

I think it was my mother who finally helped me out—but I never
knew for sure. One morning, at breakfast, my father was cracking his
soft boiled egg and he said to me, "Pass the salt." Just like that. "Pass the
salt." Like nothing ever happened between us. I knew then that he had
finally given in. The battle was over. I would play the guitar and my
father would stay in the jewelry business.

## Changes

*(A grandmother writes for grandchildren, aged from 8 to 18.)*
We moved to Alabama Avenue when my father got sick with a kidney
infection, and had to go to the hospital for three months. He was
taken away in an ambulance from our house on Miller Avenue. I remember waving to him as they lifted the stretcher through the rear
door of the van. No one told me that he was ill and that he would be
away for a long time. It was 1933 and I was four. My father's being removed in an ambulance was just another event in the lives of adults
with whom I lived, about which they told me little.

Sometimes starting
a story with a saluta-
tion: "Dear Tommy,"
as if it were a letter, can
dispel some of the fear
and ease you into the
writing process.

Not much changed on the surface of my life during my father's absence. My grandfather went every day to the tailor shop around the corner, to work at some dark table, bent over mysterious black-satin triangles, sewn on two sides. My grandmother continued to keep house for us. She'd make a lunch for my grandfather and we'd walk together, to deliver it to him, and we'd wait while he ate. This was before sandwiches and wax paper were invented, although I doubt very much if such modern conveniences would have persuaded my grandfather to veer from the traditional forms. My mother bobbed in and out. When she was in, she was headachy and tired, and she kept her distance from me. When she was out, I stuck close to my grandmother, which was always more than all right with me. My mother's being away didn't bother me much. I preferred to be with my grandmother, who was always busy doing something wonderful—which I could watch or stick my fingers into.

At the best of times, grandma gossiped with neighbors, in which the most wonderful stories of sinfully wicked relatives were told and retold. In Yiddish, of course, so that I would not understand. When my mother was home her despair and fatigue took the shape of crankiness and impatience with me, and I learned to keep out of her way. Given the situation as I now appraise it, she must have spent hours each day going to visit my father in the hospital, a trip that required three different buses each way, in addition to the stress of the actual hospital visit. Kings County General Hospital, a refuge for the indigent poor of Brooklyn, was not exactly the Ritz.

As for my father's absence, well, that was all right with me too. My father was a giant in my life—not the Jolly Green variety, but more like the kind who chased Jack down the beanstalk. His moodiness, his flash of temper, his overt rejections of my insistent attempts to get his attention, taught me early on that here was a man who had to be carefully watched. With him away, I could relax my vigilance. I do not remember feeling a sense of loss. My world was intact when my grandmother was there and I was safe in my haven on Miller Avenue.

There is nothing new about parent/child conflicts. Sharing yours with your grandchildren may help them not feel so alone when crossing similar bridges.

In relating stories of economic hardship or illness take care not to be too depressing.

Stories about how grandma "won first prize" and "felt good about what she had accomplished" make compelling tales.

On the social class scale, Miller Avenue was at least three notches above the Lower East Side, where almost all Jewish immigrants in New York began their rise to the affluent suburbs. It was a solid block of attached single-dwelling houses, each with a small front garden and a larger rear one, and each with its own old tree at the curb. The curbside trees turned Miller Avenue into a valley with an arching arbor canopy, and the street into a summer fairy garden. Until the city came to cut them all down because the roots were clogging the sewers. Goodbye horse chestnuts. Goodbye maple leaves whose stems we braided together into long leaf-trains, in which we costumed ourselves to play East of the Sun and West of the Moon. Our toys and our shade lost along with the dignity of Miller Avenue.

My father returned one day, in an ambulance, to spend a long convalescence in the upstairs front bedroom. I was not allowed in, but I could wave to him from the sidewalk. There were secret and hushed family gatherings around the large dining room table. As my family's small savings had eroded away and with no prospect of my father's working on the immediate horizon, plans were being made for our moving out. We could not afford to stay in the house. We were already in arrears on the rent, and also in debt to friends and relatives for—I don't know. It sounded like a lot, but then, every sum seemed like a fortune in 1933.

Alabama Avenue was only eight blocks away, but clearly we had moved to the other side of the tracks, into the rear flat of a four story tenement, which housed seven other families. From the kitchen window, across a small open air shaft, you could almost touch the sill of the window of the apartment in the next building. And if the neighbors were truly neighbors, this proximity promoted the most close and enduring friendships. All manner of troubles were shared across the air shaft, and the pain and misery that were constants in our lives during those Depression years filled those wells of sorrow many times over. (Do those shared miseries linger behind in those alleys to haunt new tenants, as we move on with our socially mobile climb?)

Our apartment was called a railroad flat—four boxes strung out in

Children are fascinated by stories of grandpa and grandma young and in love.

a line connected by open doorways. My room was the third in the line, between the living room and my parents' bedroom. In that way, I was sandwiched between the arguments about money, which ran a steady refrain under the harsh reality of our lives. My mother's tearful accusations about the state of my father's joblessness were a daily tyranny, and my father's deviousness and cunning grew with each new humiliation.

Alabama Avenue had some redeeming features. On the corner of Alabama and Blake, you stood right in the center of the teeming open push-cart market—a hothouse of activity that stretched for blocks in both directions on both sides of the street. A hodge-podge of peddler's carts, each merchant hawking an indescribable variety of wares—pickles and herrings in barrels, live chickens, fruits and vegetables, pots and pans, and clothing. Blake Avenue was an everyday circus, and it was business rain or shine, summer or winter, every day except Saturdays. At the end of each market day, the peddlers took down their makeshift awnings, lifted the handles of their wagons, and bearing their burdens, pushed off to—who knows what homes, leaving the detritus of their day's work to litter the redolent gutter. At dawn, they were back on the street.

On Blake Avenue, if I was lucky, an enormous lady named Sis, who was covered all the way around and down to her shoes with a white apron, gave me a slice of strictly kosher bologna, when my mother was shopping for meat for the Sabbath. Lung cost five cents a pound, and sometimes we had lung stew. But mostly we had freshly killed chicken, over which my mother haggled a penny or two off the price per pound each Thursday.

Without my grandmother's comforting presence I grew closer to my mother, and began to learn her foibles. She, having no other immediately available ally, drew me into her war against my father. I was glad to be my mother's comrade, but there were prices to pay. My father grew more and more resentful and distant. Even when he was able to get temporary work repairing fences as part of a W.P.A. project at Floyd Bennet Airfield, his sense of self and his connection to us

Write honestly. Phony sentiments diminish the power of your story.

were in serious jeopardy. It took many years of mending the tears in the fabric of our early relationship for me to learn to know my father. And even though he is long gone, I'm learning him still.

## My First Day of School

*(A grandfather writes for his grandsons, aged 8 and 10.)*
My father had a small factory where they made carpets. It was just across from the school. Since we lived in a very small village, the school and the factory were not very far from our house. I was five, and I was getting ready for my first day of school.

You know what it's like when it is the first day of school. You're all excited. You get dressed up in your best clothes. I was probably up all night long waiting for the big day! In the morning, my father said that he would walk along with me to school, and he would take me in. We left the house together. I was riding on my little new bike and he walked alongside with me. When we got to the factory, he told me to wait for him. He was going inside, and he would be right out. Then he would take me into the school. I waited on my bike, in the alley, across from the factory. It seemed to me that he was taking forever. I knew he had forgotten all about me and that I would be late on the first day of school. I sat there on my bike and cried. It wasn't a great way for me to begin my first day of school.

## New Year's Eve

*(A grandfather writes for his grandson, aged 14.)*
I was born in a very small fishing town, a very traditional place. Very Protestant. All my family lived there and even when we moved away, I kept going back often. All my friends were there, and all my social activities as well. One New Year's Eve, I, and some of my other friends, were baby sitting for some of the parents who had gone out. At midnight, we left the babies (some sitters!) and went out on the streets. There were only about five streets in the town and we must have

figured it was all right to do this. Well, everybody was walking arm in arm, and as I'm walking along with this girl, this great big guy tries to pull my girl away. I guess he thought I was a "foreigner" and didn't belong. We got into a terrible fight, and he was on the ground and I was on top of him, yelling, "Ik ben ook een gelle muneger geneduiden" in Dutch, which meant, "I'm coming from here too!" The next morning my mother told me, "Do you know what you did? You broke your nephew's glasses!" My nephew! I hadn't recognized him, nor he me. His mother didn't talk to my mother for six months.

## Skating on Ice

*(A grandfather writes for his granddaughter, aged 15.)*
In the wintertime in my village the townspeople would flood a great big pasture to make a skating rink. I was about fourteen or fifteen years old when this happened. When you went skating, if you could, you would try to get a girl. The way you did it was, you'd skate around and then you would select a girl to skate with you. Once she'd agreed, you knew that you were accepted! After skating, she'd walk back to town with you. For the first time in my life, I was walking with a girl! With very great nervousness, I put my arm around her waist. But she had put newspapers around her, underneath her skating sweater to keep her warm. And when my arm went around her, the newspapers began to crinkle. When I heard that sound I didn't know what to do. So I pulled my hand back and let it fall to my side and I escorted her in silent embarrassment back to her house.

## My Last Fire

*(A grandfather writes for his grandson, aged 6.)*
I know this was a terrible and even dangerous thing to do. We used to live in a very small town very near the railroad tracks and for mischief, especially in the summer when there was no school, and there was not much of anything to do, a group of us boys—we must have been

> Stories such as "My First Day of School" have strong universal appeal.

If your readers think "that reminds me of the time when…" you've hooked them.

twelve or thirteen—used to set fire to the grasses alongside the railroad track. You know what the summers were like in the prairies. Hot as anything and the grasses were completely dried out. So setting the fires was a cinch. The trick was, of course, not to get caught. We'd set the fire, and then when we saw the police coming, we'd get on our bikes and ride like hell out of there. Now that I think of it, I realize what a dumb thing it was to do; but we thought it was a great adventure at the time. One day, there we were, burning away. A freight train was coming and we watched it pass by, with the border of fire alongside the track. The engineer didn't seem to mind. We waved at him and he waved back. We were totally preoccupied with the train, and we were very pleased with ourselves.

When the last car passed, lo and behold, there was a policeman, on a bicycle, who had been riding behind the caboose. He had used the train to hide behind, so that he would be able to approach us without our seeing him. When we saw him there, we were all thunderstruck! He rounded us all up, and marched us off to jail.

It was a terrifying experience for me, to spend the afternoon in jail. I didn't know what my folks would say, or what hell I'd catch when they came to get me. Our parents did come later on that afternoon to get us out. It was the last fire we'd ever set. And being in jail was nothing compared to what I had to face when I got home. But I could never get over that guy on the bicycle, riding over three kilometers on those railroad ties behind the train, just to catch us. Now that's determination!

## Who Took the Strap?

*(A grandfather writes for his grandson, aged 8.)*
I went to a small country school and during those days, each teacher had a strap. It was issued by every school board, and in those days, this was the usual form of punishment for kids who did not behave. The teachers had to keep these straps in a certain drawer in their desks, and I guess that was a school board regulation too.

Every morning the kids arrived at school long before the teacher. And every morning before we got there, we'd do our mischief. The more mischief we'd do without getting caught, the more brazen we'd get! One day, we started opening the drawers of her desk. And every day after that, we got bolder and bolder.

There was a boy—we called him Pig Eye because he was so homely—he opened the teacher's drawer and found the strap. He gave it to me to hide. There was a hole in the classroom wall, and I poked the strap into the hole. Pig Eye said to me, "I dare you to drop it down there." I knew that if I did it would be the last we'd ever see of that strap. It would fall down between the wall boards of the schoolroom. Pig Eye kept egging me on. That was all I needed. Bye bye strap.

It took the teacher two days to discover the strap was gone. She looked everyone of us in the eye—the whole class. "Who took the strap?" Silence. "I'm going to find out, you know!" She began an in-quisition that lasted over two weeks. Nobody said a word. I was cool. After all, I didn't actually take it. It was Pig Eye that took it. The whole class had to stay in after school every day for two weeks, for two and a half hours each day. We even had our lunch hour taken away too. But still nobody said a word. They never found the strap, but that was not the end of strapping for bad behavior in that class. But to have done it and gotten away with it, ahhhh, that was sweet.

## I Wanted To Be the Hero

*(A grandfather writes for his grandson, aged 8.)*

I used to feel very insecure as a boy. Whatever I seemed to do, I gener-ally wound up behind the eight-ball. My brother, on the other hand, seemed to do everything right all the time. I kept messing up and he kept winning. And naturally, he seemed to get all the favors and all the attention. I remember that one day a team of horses came into our yard and I threw a root, so the horses acted up. My parents were furious with me. But my brother leaped out and brought those horses

While the emotions and sentiments are shared, it's the details that set one story apart from another.

The snake under the bed, the boogey-man in the closet, and the witch with the evil eye are common childhood fears.

under control. Once again, he was the hero and I was the villain. How could I get back in grace?

The next day, I was out in the yard with my brother, and we were talking to our parents. In the far pasture, this cow was yelling her mouth off! So I got an idea. Maybe, maybe if I could shut that cow's mouth, my parents would think better of me. But before I could do anything about it, my brother picked up this root and threw it—golly—it must have been 150 yards. I watched that darn root arc overhead and saw it come down and hit the cow right between the horns. The cow shut up right on the spot and my brother was the hero again!

## The Old Bubbe

*(A grandmother writes for her granddaughters, aged 8 and 11.)*
We lived in a house with two stories. Grandma and grandpa lived downstairs and they had the only kitchen. Upstairs, there was our living room, virtually unused, since we were always downstairs for meals and every other social occasion, my parents' bedroom, and my own bedroom, at the top of the stairs.

One day she was just there. I never knew where she had come from or how she had arrived. She was there, carpet slippers scuffling along the upstairs corridor, in her wrinkled eggplant face and brown wig. "She's your bubbe," my mother said. This was impossible, I knew, because my bubbe lived downstairs and there was no one in my world who was more familiar, more comfortable and who had a lap more warm and generous than my bubbe.

"She's your grandma's mother." A concept as alien as the woman herself. Impossible, I knew. My grandma didn't need a mother. She was mother to us all.

"Where did she come from?" I asked.

"From the old country."

They made it sound light years away. Far Rockaway was the most remote place I knew. It took over an hour to get there by car. But I couldn't imagine how the old bubbe could have come from Far Rockaway, a magic place of sand and waves and sun. This old bubbe did not have any of the Far Rockaway magic. She seemed more forbidding than inviting.

"Say good morning to the old bubbe," my mother legislated my social behavior.

"Good morning bubbe."

Her eggplant face cracked into a toothless smile and I saw a demon's face, in a tight brown wig of artificial hair. But her eyes were bright and spoke of her pleasure at my greeting. She answered in sounds which I could not fathom.

"Why doesn't she speak to me?" I asked my mother.

"She can't speak too well," my mother tried to explain.

"How old is she?" I asked.

"Maybe 90—we don't know for sure when she was born in the old country."

Impossible. She was surely old enough to talk. Even I, at four, could talk easily and even recognize the alphabet. And everybody knew when they were born!

Why were they making up these stories about this old lady? And who was she?

I caught her watching me and I told my mother. "The old bubbe keeps watching me."

My mother seemed alarmed. She told me, "Put your hand behind your back and cross your fingers like this." She showed me how to position my thumb between my first and second fingers. "Then say, 'Fig! Fig!' and spit three times." That would ward off evil spirits. She told my real bubbe that the old bubbe was trying to give me the evil eye and we had to be very careful about that.

The fear of the evil eye, the dark demeanor, the toothless, incomprehensible dialect prevented me from making any human contact with the old bubbe and I really don't know how long she stayed with us. But I do know with a child's sense of certainty that nobody really

The bitterness of sibling rivalry is felt in every generation. Knowing you've been there may make it easier for your grandchildren.

173

wanted her there. Not my mother, not my real bubbe, and certainly not me.

One day she was gone—as mysteriously as she had come.

"Where's the old bubbe?" I asked more out of a need to comprehend what was going on in my world than out of a sense of loss.

"She's gone," my mother said.

"Where to? Where has she gone?"

"I can't explain it. You're too little to understand."

The case was closed since I knew that to try to combat the "you're too little to understand" argument was useless. Years later it dawned on me that it was not my inadequacy to comprehend that was the problem, but rather her limited patience in attempting an explanation that would be understood by a child. Four years old always has a thousand questions, and the "But why?" of a child tends to provoke a confrontation with one's own values that many adults would rather avoid.

I don't know how many days, weeks or months passed since the old bubbe disappeared from her silent walks along the upstairs corridor. Fours live in a time warp that is unreliable, with weeks that seem like months, and months years. But on a warm summer Sunday afternoon, my real bubbe, my mother and I, and maybe my grandfather, too, got into my uncle's borrowed car, with my father at the wheel, to go to "New York." Even though we lived in a major borough of New York City, Brooklyn was Brooklyn and to make a trip into Manhattan was to "go to New York."

"Where are we going?" I asked, not really caring too much, because much of the pleasure was in the going, and especially in the going by car.

"You'll see when we get there," said my mother. "Get in."

I sat in the back, squished between the ample rumps of mama and bubbe. It was a long drive and I can't remember anything about it other than parking in front of a building with an awning that stretched to the curb in the lower east side section of Manhattan. The

If you can, in the telling, transport yourself back to the time and place of your story. You'll take your young readers with you.

family moved slowly into the building, and from the reception area we were all ushered by an attendant to a long room filled with rows of beds on both sides. There seemed to me to be a hundred beds in that room. As the double doors swung closed behind us the stench of incontinent old age, medications, and rotting food in bedside gift parcels, all heightened by the heat of that summer's day, made me gag. I felt immediately ill.

"Be quiet," said my mother. I choked down my nausea and my nose started to run.

"Say hello to your old bubbe," my mother's tone left no choice.

Her face with ten thousand wrinkles, and artificial hair, propped up by two less-than-white pillows, looked yellow, and the glittering demon eyes had turned flat. I approached the bed, my mother's prods in the small of my back urging me forward, and my foot kicked the pail underneath. The stench was overpowering and I thought I would die right there. I wanted to hold my nose, but even at four felt that such an indiscretion would be a social gaffe of momentous order.

"Hello, bubbe," I gagged out my words and took several steps back.

She didn't speak to me, but I saw the pain and fear in her eyes and I remember them still. Even though she wasn't my real bubbe.

("Bubbe" is Yiddish for grandmother.)

## The Nickel

*(By a grandmother, for grandchildren aged from 8 to 18.)*
In September, I entered first grade in the immense four story brick building on Williams Avenue, two and one-half blocks from my home. This distance I was permitted to walk by myself,  having been repeatedly warned, many times over, about talking to strangers. I made the trip easily each day with a growing sense of adventure that came from being finally allowed to cross the streets without supervision. I dearly loved the *idea* of school and its smells and its mysterious dark corridors and locked doors. But first grade I could take or leave

> Memories are often centered in powerful emotions and make strong stories.

Children are inundated with stories of virtue and obedience. A tale of some mischief you got away with gives you a fresh new persona.

alone. Under the iron fist of Miss Stellwagon, I learned many things that after all these years I am still trying to forget: that I was poor, fat, and lacking in "class." Miss Stellwagon kept most of us at arm's length, but I, because of my size and weight, was even further removed. A by-product of "size-place seating," my first grade destiny meant sitting permanently in the last row, last seat. And because I couldn't bear to endure the snail's place of oral reading, I never knew the place when it finally came round to my turn to read. This did not do much to endear me to my teacher, either.

In P.S. 174, each day during the mid-morning, a monitor came from an upper grade class to deliver the milk order—individual containers of milk which could be bought by those children whose parents could afford the penny-per-carton fee. When the milk was delivered to the class, the teacher produced, from a locked cupboard, a large box of cookies, sometimes chocolate marshmallows, sometimes cream filled chocolate and vanilla sandwiches, sometimes chocolate covered graham crackers. There might have been perhaps twelve dozen cookies in each box. These were sold to the children for one penny each, turning the mid-morning snack into a feast. When the supply of cookies in a box was consumed, a new carton magically appeared, and so we moved from biscuit box to biscuit box.

I remember the smell of chocolate and vanilla that greeted each box opening, and the direct connection between nose and saliva glands. I remember never having a penny for a cookie, or for milk. To my requests for precious household pennies, my mother would tell me that I was too fat anyway, and that I did not need a mid-morning snack. I remember feeling as if I were the only child in the whole world who was too poor to buy milk and cookies in school, and my poverty hung onto me inside of Irma Klebanoff's cast off clothes. Life would, I knew, have been vastly more endurable if I could only be on that cookie line.

That midmorning snack became for me the main event of the school day, to be lived through with the most intense and unfulfilled longing. No gourmet meal ever beckoned as tantalizingly as those double-strawed milk containers, and those boxed biscuits. I ached to be included in the feasting, as I ached for the end of my alienation, my acceptance into the group.

On one morning when my father and I left the house together—he heading for work and I for school—he said quite surprisingly that he'd walk along with me. It was out of his way and I, unaccustomed to being on good terms with him, went uneasily at his side. He kept his giant legs in stride with mine, and we walked the two and one-half blocks without speaking, but I could smell the putty on his overalls. When we got to the school, the man I thought I'd never love didn't hug me goodbye, but dug into his pocket to let a nickel slip from it into my hand. "Here," he said. "Buy yourself some candy." I'd never had a nickel of my own before. I felt all the hugs in the world embrace me as I ran off to my class!

When Miss Stellwagon opened the biscuit box that morning, I was in the line-up. "Four. I'll have four." Four chocolate covered graham crackers were counted into my hand, and I used the last penny to buy a container of milk. I ate my father's love right down to the very last crumb, and when it was finished, felt wonderfully full.

Being the "odd man out" should strike a chord of sympathy if not empathy with most youngsters.

# 12

# Grandma Gets "Wired"

HIGH-SPEED Internet connections. HTML, XML, URLs. E-Commerce. Websites. Hyperlinks. E-mails. Search engines. Dot-com companies. It sounds as if the aliens have landed and are talking in tongues! But in fact, these strange acronyms and buzzwords are part of techspeak—the language of the Internet, a virtual world in cyberspace that has given communication new meaning. If you are "connected" you are a cool grandma. But even if you are, your grandchildren are probably already outpacing you in their understanding of, and in their use of, the wide world of the Web.

## The Wide and Wonderful World of the Web

If computers have changed our lives radically in the past dozen years, the World Wide Web and its infinite hyperlinks have made it possible for us to communicate globally in a way that was undreamed of, even a few short years ago. Today, nearly everyone is "wired"—connected to each other by a complex, invisible network of linkages that allows us to chat across the miles, without the use of a telephone handset; to send photos of the new baby to grandma and grandpa on the other side of the world; to send information instantly, anywhere in the world; to purchase books, tools, works of art without stepping outside in the rain; to buy and sell stocks on our own trading accounts, from the privacy of our homes; to do personal banking without waiting on line at the teller's wicket; to search for addresses and telephone numbers of long lost friends; to look up information from the Encyclopedia Britannica, the U.S. Library of Congress, the National Archives.

Looking for the best recipe for chocolate brownies? Search the Internet for recipes and for critiques from people who have used them. You're traveling to Barcelona and don't know what clothes to pack? Check *www.weather.com* for a three-day forecast. Forgot to buy the newspaper? Several different sites give today's news and it's updated three to five times daily! Can't decide on a movie? Film archives provide reviews without charge. Want information about flights to Hong Kong? About cheap fares, budget hotels, film festivals, concerts? Want to find an apartment or a new house in your own town, or in a distant city? Looking for a vacation rental in Tuscany? Go online, and save yourself some shoe leather. How about taking a course without ever having to attend classes? More and more educational institutions provide courses online, with virtual access to your teacher and your classmates! The wonders of the World Wide Web are enough to knock your socks clear across the room.

Finding what you need on the Internet is as easy as pushing the right buttons. A mind-boggling array of resources all lie within your reach. But what about the problems involved in entering such a high-tech world? Is it possible for grandparents, born and raised when dinosaurs walked the earth, to learn their way around computers? Perhaps you are already thinking, "I'm too old for this new stuff!" thereby retreating gracefully behind the barrier of age. It is a comfortable place to hide; but those of us who wish to become involved with

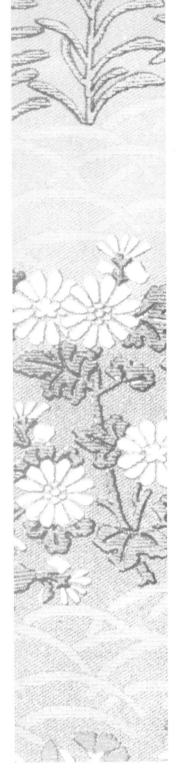

Grandchildren will be full of admiration for a grandma who surfs the Net with them.

this endlessly fascinating tool will, without doubt, become much more connected to our grandchildren and the world in which they now live.

With a computer, you have access to the Internet, a fantasyland that lies at your fingertips. And whether you are a grandparent with your own Palm Pilot, cell phone, fax machine, scanner, ADSL connection, and all the toys of the high-tech trade, already literate about the possibilities in cyberspace, or one who is just interested in learning a little bit more about what is possible, you will find that the Internet offers new and exciting opportunities for not only long distance connections, but for keeping in closer touch with what is happening in your grandchildren's lives.

## It Starts Here

The tool that allows you access to the wired world is the computer. One of the pivotal pieces of computer equipment needed for Internet access is a *modem*. A modem allows your computer to "dial up" the Internet, much the same way as you make a telephone call. It's not important that you understand how this works, just as you don't need to understand the workings of the internal combustion engine in order to drive a car. All you need to know is what this particular tool will allow you to do. If you are purchasing a new computer, whether a Mac or a PC, make sure to purchase a modem as well. If you are using an older computer and do not already have a modem, you can purchase one at any reliable computer store. It will come with instructions for installation; and an informed clerk at the store can be very helpful in advising which wires connect to which terminals. Of course, you have to be able to plug the modem into your telephone jack.

Having the hardware you need (a computer and a modem) is the first step in the process of becoming connected. Next, you need to obtain an account with an *Internet service provider*, or ISP, a company that will connect you to the Web, for a monthly fee. Your Internet service provider establishes the connections that allow you to be linked up with everyone in the world who is also "connected."

One way of finding a good Internet service provider is by asking friends and neighbors who are already connected which service provider they use. Some important questions to ask are: Are the lines often busy? Do the lines disconnect when a message is being sent? Is the provider helpful when calls are made for help and for information? What are the monthly charges? Are there any introductory offers? Any free time allowances? There are dozens and dozens of ISPs, and you should shop around for the best service, support and value that you can find.

It will not be surprising to learn that your city's *Yellow Pages* is a rich information source about the Internet. A quick search through my own *Yellow Page Directory* (for the Greater Vancouver area) reveals that there are 46 pages of listings under the Internet heading, beginning with this introduction:

> The Internet is the world's largest computer network, or more simply, many computers that are linked together. An easy way to understand the Internet, is to think of a telephone system. Phones are linked together through a network of telephone lines. A computer network is connected in the same way. When a large number of computers are connected together, they form the Internet. Unlike the telephone, the computer can utilize the network not only to transmit sound, but text, pictures and graphics as well.
>
> (Telus, *The Yellow Pages*, Vancouver, B.C., 2000, p. 1065)

Under the title *Internet Access Providers* (or IAP) you will find an exhaustive listing of options. But as with all lists, it is always a good idea to get feedback from an informed source as to their reliability and ability to deliver the service.

Perhaps the best source of help and information is your neighborhood "geek." If you haven't already heard this term, you should know

The Internet can be used as an accompaniment to regular mail. It is as fun to get messages from Grandma onscreen as it is to get your own letter from the mailbox.

that it is far from derogatory, and refers to those super-knowledgeable people who are at the cutting edge of the high-tech world. Very often, "geeks" are kids—and I must confess that it's a bit intimidating to see the expertise with which a teenager is able to navigate her way around a computer. If this isn't off-putting, and if their language is only barely comprehensible (they tend to talk fast, and in a language of their own), many "geeks" are eager to be of service and to help you become wired. It would not be surprising to discover that your own granddaughter or grandson is a "geek" and has far more sophisticated knowledge of the Internet and its capabilities than you ever imagined. Getting your grandkids to help you find your way online turns the tables nicely on intergenerational connections; our kids LOVE helping grandpa learn what they already consider to be first grade stuff!

## You've Got Mail!

Once you have signed up for Internet access with your ISP, you'll be given an e-mail address. At that point, you will be asked to choose a (secret) password that allows only you to access your mail. You can now send and receive written messages to and from anyone else who has an e-mail address. "Logging on" means keying in the protocols that signal your computer to dial up your ISP for you. (As this occurs, you will be able to hear the same kinds of sounds from your computer terminal that you hear when you are dialing long distance on your telephone.) When a successful connection has been made, you can now send a new message and/or check your mail to see if there are any messages waiting for you in your "mailbox."

If you wish to send a new message, you use the appropriate command to call up a message form on your computer screen that looks something like an old fashioned telegram blank. A line at the top of the form will ask for the e-mail address of the person to whom you are sending your message (i.e., "To") and another line asks what the mes-

Talking to your grand-child on the computer will require the same guidelines as communicating on the phone. It's a good idea to establish times with your son or daughter when it is convenient for you to chat with your grandchild.

sage is about (i.e., "Subject"). Very important is the accuracy of keying in the correct e-mail address of the recipient as the Internet is very unforgiving about inaccuracy. If you have even a single letter wrong, or missing, the message will be returned. If you have set things up correctly, your "Reply to" e-mail address is already in place on the message form. This is part of the protocol that you can arrange when you create your account with your service provider.

The bottom section of the form contains a large blank space for your message. In fact, the space is virtually infinite—you can write as much as you want, or just a few words. When you have completed your message, just click your mouse on the "Send" button, and your message will travel, immediately, over the Internet, to the virtual mailbox of your sendee. Of course, you pay your service provider for all the time you spend online; but you will find that the costs are very much cheaper than regular long-distance telephone charges.

Each time you log on, you will probably want to check your mail. This is done by opening your e-mail program, and clicking on the "Check Mail" or "Send and Receive" button. You'll first be asked to enter your (secret) password. A message will then appear, telling you whether or not you have new mail. If you have new mail, the headers of the new messages will appear, in a list, in your "Inbox." Double clicking on a message will open it up for you to read.

While it is true that there are many different e-mail programs, and not all of them look and work in exactly the same ways, these guidelines should be, nonetheless, sufficiently basic so that they can be "translated" to decipher the systems of most e-mail programs.

Both of my teenage grandsons are computer geeks. Each has his own e-mail address and both grandma and grandpa can send and receive messages from them more easily than we can reach them on the phone. When we call, they are usually "out"—doing what teenagers do—school, library, girlfriend's house, soccer, swimming, sleeping in. If it weren't for our e-mail connections, our contacts would be seri-

Kids are fascinated by computers and learn very readily. By joining your grandchild online you will be entering your grandchild's world.

Games on the computer are like games in person. Games teach about cooperative playing and keeping a sense of fun.

ously reduced. Because we are all now fully "wired" we can chat as easily as if they were sitting right across from me. We share the news; we raise questions about recent events and activities; we send messages of love. Being wired has made THE difference to maintaining our long distance connection in these wonderful teenage years.

Needless to say, e-mail is not for connecting only with grandkids who are teens. Think of the many ways in which written language skills are developed through the simple messages between younger grandchildren and grandparents. And the most wonderful part of

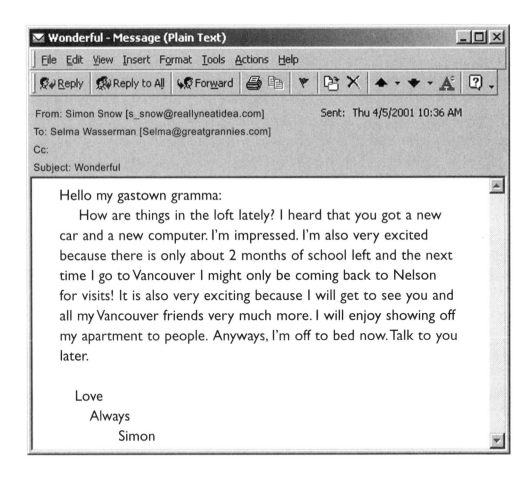

e-mail is that there are no worries about correct spelling, punctuation, grammar—no impediments to the free flow of messages of love. Being wired is a true bonus to long distance and even short distance relationships.

Even long e-mail messages take up very little room in cyberspace, making it possible for them to travel across the Internet very quickly. So if you are online, and your grandchild is also online, messages can be sent back and forth, allowing you to "chat" with each other in almost "real time." (More about this below.) Otherwise, you will need to wait to see if the message you sent to your grandchild at an earlier hour has resulted later in the day in that most welcome response, "You've got MAIL!"

## Connecting through Cyberspace

Clearly, the Internet is the stuff of high-tech legend, and whether you are a grandparent who is already an experienced "Netscape Navigator" or one who is just interested in exploring new options for keeping in touch with distant grandchildren, you will find the possibilities of connecting through cyberspace both exciting and "very cool." Some of those possibilities are described below; but it should be noted that in the cyberworld, what is new today, is history tomorrow. Even as this message is being word processed, geeks and techno-wizards are at work in their garages, brewing technological revolutions that defy even the most sophisticated imagination.

## Chatrooms

Another wonderful electronic means of communication via the Internet is the chatroom. There are thousands of chatrooms available, and they are usually free to use. Chatrooms allow you and your grandchildren to "talk" to each other in real time. Of course, you would have

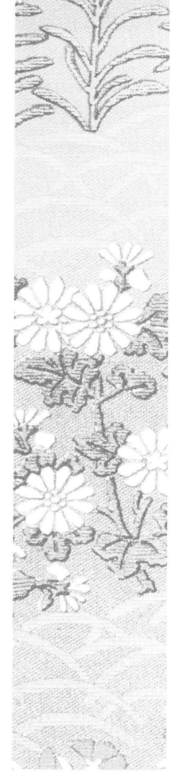

to arrange with your grandchild to be online at the same time as you; this is something like talking on the phone, but instead, you are "chatting" electronically, and in written form.

If you are a novice to computerland and the Internet, it may be a good idea to (once again) find your "geek" helpmate to see you through your first chat. Again, it would not be surprising if your grandchild is already quite knowledgeable about chatting—perhaps even chatting regularly with his or her own friends. The value of engaging your grandchildren in such a helping role cannot be overestimated. Think of how important it feels to be the one to whom grandma and grandpa turn for high level technical help! For ego boosting, seeking advice and help from grandchildren is a sure-fire winner.

## Beyond E-Mail (Far Beyond)

When Isaac William was born in San Francisco, his proud dad took some birth photos of the baby and sent them online to the new grandparents, who live several hundred miles away, in Northern California. Not only were the photos received instantly (is the post office worried?), but they could also be "downloaded" (printed) so they could be passed around to friends and neighbors. With a color printer, gramma and grandpa could even see the color of the baby's hair, his eyes, and the blush in his sweet cheeks.

Even if you are new to the world of the Internet and the marvels of the computer, you must already know that e-mail and chatrooms are just the tip of the iceberg of what is possible. And while I will describe other ways of connecting with long distance grandchildren here, it should be noted that the one constant that typifies this high-tech world is rapid change. That is why it is inevitable that what I write today is likely to be already out of date by the time this book winds up in your hands. Not only passé, but surpassed by other, more ingenious, more dazzling technological toys.

Today, the possibility of sending photos, maps, illustrations and other graphics via your Internet connection is taken for granted. With a scanner (another piece of equipment that can be purchased in your favorite computer shop), you can scan pictures and illustrations that are digitized into your computer. Once on the computer, these can be sent out over the "information highway" to whomever else is connected online. So, for example, if you have found some interesting information that is particularly relevant to your grandchildren, you can scan that into the computer, and send it as an "attachment" to an e-mail message. If you have found an illustration in the library that you'd like to scan and send, that too is an option. You can, of course, refer grandchildren to children's interactive programs that are available online. If you have found a website that you think may be particularly appealing to grandchildren, you might bring this to their attention by providing them with the URL to the website in your e-mail message. Young children and teens have their particular favorites, but in your surfing, you may come across something altogether different, whose recommendation may elevate your status to that of "way cool, grandma."

The installation of another computer tool—the webcam—allows you to make movies and take pictures that may be sent via the Internet. About as big as a tennis ball, this miniature camera has the potential of adding live video to your computer, so that you may communicate visually. It gives you the option of taking still pictures, or making movies. A built-in microphone lets you record voices. What this tool does is to allow long distance grandparents and their grandkids to turn their computers into video phones! The cost of these cameras should be weighed against the communicative possibilities they provide.

Because the amount of video and audio information being transmitted is enormous, video images will usually appear choppy, and the sound, if there is any, will break up at the receiving end. That is because the modem connected to your video camera just can't transmit

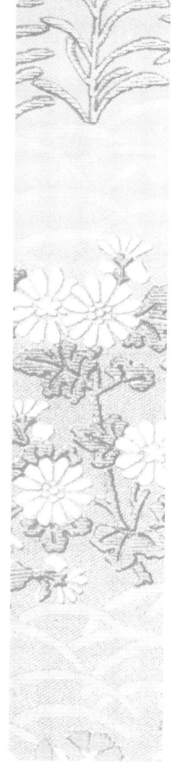

the information fast enough. In order to transmit or receive smooth full motion video, you will need a higher speed connection to the Internet than your modem can provide.

## High-Speed Internet Connections

There are currently two different high-speed technologies available for home use: ADSL and cable. Cable Internet access is provided by a cable TV company, while ADSL is provided by the phone company. In this high-speed, high-tech world, this may be the same company! While these technologies both offer high-speed connections, the ADSL is the much faster connection.

ADSL, the acronym for Asymmetric Digital Subscriber Line, refers to the high-speed connection made available through conventional phone lines, creating an alternative way to gain access to the Internet other than through a modem. The operational words for ADSL connections are *speed* and *ever-present access.* This means faster access to the Internet and to multimedia (e.g., video, music, games, entertainment, live events, etc.).

ADSL connections are available through most telephone companies, and they do not require the installation of expensive additional equipment. However, they do require a special high-speed connection (port). This is usually twice as costly, per month, as a regular (modem) connection. The critical difference with ADSL is the high speed in which connections are made. In fact, for only twice the price of a regular modem, the speed of your connection is increased by a hundred times. For those whose primary concern is speed between sender and receiver (everyone wants faster and cheaper connections!), and ever-present access, ADSL offers amazing speed at relatively low cost.

High-speed technologies, such as ADSL and cable, are being readied to bring entertainment and Internet content to your computer screen with the same quality and speed as your television. In the very near future, we will be seeing more sophisticated uses, like video conferencing, interactive television, and other far-reaching, high-tech applications made as easily as we now use e-mail.

# ICQ (I Seek You)

ICQ is an Internet tool that informs you of who's online at any time, and enables you to contact them at will. ICQ will alert you when your grandchild logs on to the Internet and allow the two of you to chat in real time. The need to conduct a direct search each time you want to communicate with him or her is eliminated. ICQ does the searching for you.

With ICQ, you can chat, send messages and files, play games, or just "hang out" with your grandchildren. The program runs in the background, taking up minimal memory and computer resources. If you are working on other applications at the same time (such as word processing), ICQ alerts you when your grandchildren log on. Among the functions available are chat, message, e-mail, URL and file transfer. All these functions are consolidated into one easy-to-use program.

Like many other applications available on the Web, ICQ is a free program. You need to visit *www.icq.com,* to find out how to download the program and get started. Once you've set up ICQ, you can compile a list of your grandchildren, friends, and associates and ICQ will use the list to find your friends for you. Meanwhile, ICQ "waits quietly in the background" without interrupting whatever else you may be doing on your computer. As soon as you log onto the Internet, ICQ will automatically detect the Internet connection, announcing your presence to the Internet community and alert you when your grandchild signs on or off.

Once you know who's on, all it takes is a click on an icon to begin a chat, send messages, or exchange files.

The ICQ site will provide all additional information you may need. This information is available, with a click of your mouse, in English,

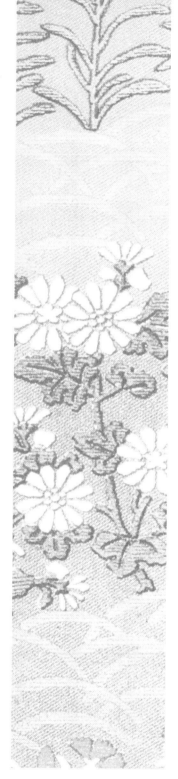

Chinese, Dutch, French, German, Italian, Japanese, Portuguese, Russian, Spanish, and Swedish. Welcome to the wonderful world of the Web!

## Long Distance Gaming

Since writing the chapter on the Internet for the third edition of this book (1996), in which I noted that it was possible to play long distance games with grandchildren on the Internet, what is now possible is far more extensive, more sophisticated, and much more fun. Games are available from the quite simple, for use with younger grandchildren, to the more complex. One of many available sites is Yahoo! Games. Check out *Yahoo.com* and enter into the world of cybergames. You may never want to leave. If you should happen, in the process, to get compulsively stuck on Klondike Solitaire, don't blame me.

When you find your way to the *Yahoo.com* site, you will notice that it is not devoted solely to games. Yahoo is a vast search engine that provides information about shopping, media, the stock market, television, and weather, in addition to games. At the *Yahoo.com* site, click on the Games icon, and you will be presented with a list of what is currently available. (Keep checking; new games are added all the time.)

On the Games page, the link *Yahooligans! Games* lists those that are particularly suited for use with younger children. These include Chess, Tic Tac Toe, Go Fish, Yahoo! Towers, Backgammon, Dominoes, Checkers, Word Search, Reversi, and Maze. The main game selection includes Board Games (Backgammon, Checkers, Chinese Checkers, Chess, Go, Reversi), Tile Games (Dominoes, MahJong), Card Games (Blackjack, Bridge, Canasta, Cribbage, Euchre, Gin, Go Fish, Hearts, Pinochle, Poker, Sheepshead, Spades) and "Other" Games (Bingo, Yahoo! Towers, Word Racer).

All games are free and require no extra plug-ins. The *Yahoo.com* games link provides information about software limitations, privacy policy, and software requirements.

## What Else is Out There?

I must confess that I am delighted to have achieved status as "a cool grandma" in my grandsons' eyes. This may have more to do with the "sporty" car I drive (and perhaps how I drive it) than it has with my computer skills! However, I do know that being connected to both boys on the Internet means that our long distance relationship has evolved in new and delightful ways. Not only do we e-mail regularly, but we also share the same language. I am more in tune with their world when Arlo explains to me how he has designed a computer game, and how it was conceptualized and executed. Even if I don't fully understand the lingo, I'm not totally out in the cold and can raise questions that suggest to him at least some understanding of the process. With Simon taking off for a two-year post-secondary program in Web design, I know that I can, at the very least, begin to appreciate the nature of what he is studying.

As the boys share with me their new experiences with computers, I too share with them some of what I find that is of interest on the Internet. For example, when I hear about a particular site that might contain information relevant to their research or studies, I forward that URL to them and suggest they check it out.

A few of the sites that have proved of interest to my grandchildren in the teen years include:

*Canada's Native Peoples*
http://www.collections.ic.gc.ca/heirloom_series/volume2/
   volume2.htm
This site offers a history of native groups within different regions of Canada.

*Canadian War Museum: Exhibitions*
civilization.ca/cwm/cwmeng/cwmexeng.html
Links to this museum's permanent and temporary exhibits.

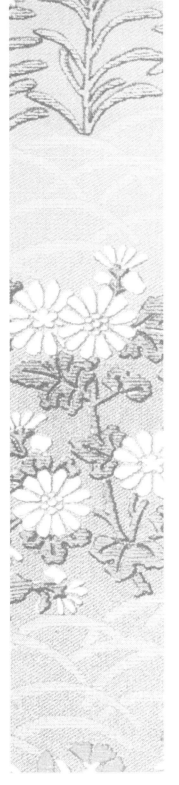

*The Cave of Lascaux*
http://www.culture.fr/culture/arcnat/lascaux/en/
This is a two-part site. Part I, "Discover," is a virtual tour through the Lascaux cave. Part II supplies the archaeological and artistic background.

*CMCC Virtual Museum Level 1: First Peoples Hall/Archeology Hall*
http://www.civilization.ca/members/level01.html
Over a dozen exhibits on the history and culture of First People in Canada including the Arctic.

*CMCC Virtual Museum Level 2: Folk Arts and Fine Crafts / Cultural Traditions / Treasures*
http://www.civilization.ca/membrs/level02.html
Features exhibits on Canadian crafts, artisans, and folk artists; a number of Canadian cultures; and selections from a collection of Canadian heritage treasures.

*CMCC Virtual Museum Level 3: Canadian History Hall*
http://www.civilization.ca/membrs/level03.html
Offers a variety of exhibits detailing various aspects of Canadian history. Early Canadian history can be explored in a virtual tour of Canada Hall; the history of hats, glassworks, pottery, the canoe and fancy dress balls are also exhibited. A history of Canadian Labour is exhibited in the Social Progress Gallery.

*Conversations With History [RealPlayer]*
http://www.globetrotter.berkeley.edu/conversations/
Created in 1982 by Harry Kreisler and produced by the Institute of International Studies at the University of California at Berkeley, Conversations With History features interviews with over 150 distinguished men and women from all over the world. Users can now read, and in many cases view, a large selection of these interviews online.

The interviews can be browsed by year, guest name, profession, or topic. In addition to RealPlayer video segments, many interview pages also include photos and relevant links. The guests and topics span the world and engage an excellent variety of pressing and important issues.

### Elizabethan Costuming Page
http://www.dnaco.net/~aleed/corsets/general.html

Intended for people who participate in reenactment activities, this site gives descriptions of the clothing worn during the Elizabethan period, in addition to the specific instructions on how to create the actual costume itself. Many of the links are to pages within this site but there are also plenty of links to outside resources.

### Endangered Animals of the World
http://www.geocities.com/rainforest/vines/1460/index.html

The Endangered Animals of the World site contains information about different species of endangered mammals, birds and fish. Although there are only a few pictures included the information is well written. The site also provides many links that can help in finding further information on endangered animals.

### Endangered Species Project
http://www.schoolworld.asn.au/species/reports.html

This site contains reports on endangered animals created by students from around the world. Sections include mammals, birds, fish, amphibians, insects, and reptiles. Each section is arranged to give information on the problems faced by each animal and what can be done to protect it. There are lots of bold and realistic pictures.

### Everything Shakespeare
http://www.field-of-themes.com/shakespeare/

This site contains, unbelievably, the complete Shakespearean works

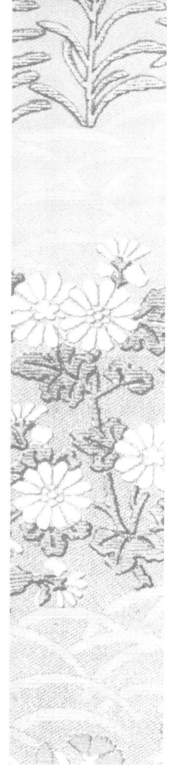

online. There are also summaries of the plays, a history of Shakespeare, a number of essays on various topics about his works, and links to other sites. For related resources, see the Shakespeare Theme Page at:

http://www.cln.org/themes/shakespeare.html

*HyperHistory*

http://www.hyperhistory.com/online_n2/History_n2/a.html

World history, going back 3000 years, with a combination of colorful graphics, lifelines, timelines and maps.

*The Physics Classroom: Einstein's Special Theory of Relativity*

http://www.glenbrook.k12.il.us/gbssci/phys/Class/relativity/
    reltoc.html

On this interactive site, children can explore time from a different angle.

*The State of the World's Children 2000—UNICEF* [.pdf, RealPlayer]

http://www.unicef.org/sowc00/

UNICEF State of the World's Children report for the year 2000 includes an appeal for a new international coalition on behalf of children. The report also summarizes progress made since the 1990 World Summit for Children and the challenges that remain. Included in the report are a number of photographs, maps, tables, and a glossary. A summary, features (a collection of children's own words on important issues), RealPlayer videos, and a .pdf version of the report are available from the main page.

*Virtual Labs and Simulations*

http://www.home.stlnet.com/~grichert/applets.html

A collection of links to sites on the Web that have computerized simulations of physics principles that allow students to see a visual demonstration of a scientific concept, often in animated form. In addition, the student may be given the opportunity to manipulate one or more variables underlying the concept and then witness the changes. There are close to 300 labs/simulations in senior high physics. Category headings include Mechanics, Momentum, Rotational Mechanics, Machines, Measurement Tools, Fluid Physics, Electricity, Thermodynamics, Simple Harmonic Motion, Wave Phenomena, Light, Color, Geometric Optics, Astrophysics, and Nuclear.

*Virtual Museum of New France*
http://www.vmnf.civilization.ca/somm-en.htm
In this site the period in Canadian history when the French explored North America and founded the colony of New France can be explored. Especially recommended are the Explorer and People sections.

*Web of Online Dictionaries*
http://www.facstaff.bucknell.edu/rbeard/diction.html
An extensive collection of specialized dictionaries from foreign language collections to dictionaries on many topics from advertising to travel (and everything in between).

**For children ages 4–12**

*The Endangered Animals of the World Project*
http://www.tenan.vuurwerk.nl/indexusa.htm
Fifty-two schools contributed to this site. It would be great for all students who are interested in animals. The Animals section lists threatened or endangered animals of the earth, grouped according to regions—where they live, what they eat and how we can help. The site is bright and interesting and invites further exploration by linking to other sites.

*EndangeredSpecie.com*
http://www.endangeredspecie.com
This site offers an interesting and fun way to learn all you need to know about endangered species. It not only contains useful information, but also supplies an exciting way to help endangered animals. Images at the site are realistic and informative. There are many sections to enjoy such as the teachers and kids sections and an entire book category as well as a search option. This site lists endangered species laws and suggests a number of ways to help endangered species.

*Grimm Brothers@nationalgeographic.com [RealPlayer]*
http://www.nationalgeographic.com/grimm/
National Geographic presents this site that will read you a bedtime story, from the unexpurgated Grimm Brothers' Fairy Tales from a 1914 translation. Cautionary note: These tales are not exactly your "soothing bedtime fare." The twelve tales here are full of wicked stepmothers, hungry wolves, bewitched wild beasts, and all manner of spells and curses. All of the stories include at least one illustration, and audio is provided for several. The site also includes biographical information on the Grimms, kids' activities, and links to other fairy tale resources on the Web.

*History of the Cherokee*
http://www.Pages.tca.net
This site is a tribute to the strength and determination of the Cherokee people to survive centuries of trials and oppression. The links include History of the Cherokee; Images and Maps, Genealogy; Books and Newspapers; and Related Links to other sources.

*National Oceanic and Atmospheric Administration*
http://www.websites.noaa.gov

This site is maintained by the U.S. office of the National Oceanic and Atmospheric Administration, and offers hundreds of links to topics for information about the weather, satellite imagery, space weather, and related topics. It is fascinating, fun, and very entertaining for those who are interested in weather phenomena.

*United States History*
http://www.usahistory.com
This extensive link to United States History offers a vast data source about Presidents, Trivia, Statistics, Wars, State Pages, and the Constitution. The information contained in this site is both relevant and trivial—a fun and helpful source of data.

*United States History*
http://www.ushistory.org/
This vast and extensive data source is referred to as the Congress of Websites. It was created and is maintained by the Independence Hall Association of Philadelphia. Its mission is to bring American History to life on the Internet. Included are such fascinating links as: Philadelphia Oddities; Carpenter's Hall; Declaration of Independence; Benjamin Franklin. The amount of material contained on this site is nothing short of staggering!

## I'm Too Old for This Stuff!

A dear friend recently lost her husband of fifty-five years. Devastated by his sudden death, she nonetheless allowed her grown children to introduce her to the world of computers, partly to divert her from dwelling on her deep loss, but also to help her connect with grandchildren who live on three different continents. When she wrote to me, she had a very dim view of her ability, at age seventy-seven, to look the computer in its one eye and tame it so she could use it to connect with her family. The computer was an entirely new world for her; she was intimidated by everything about it—everything was new and unfamiliar. Each time she pressed the "on" switch, she thought that she would do something terrible and profoundly wrong, causing the machine to self-destruct and perhaps a total blackout of the entire middle-Atlantic grid.

Her son, who lived close by, helped her through her first days of using the computer in his free time. In a few weeks, I was receiving e-mail messages from her. These were a little shaky at first, but after a few months she became more experienced and accomplished. She may never become a geek, but she is able to find her way around the Internet and communicate regularly with her many friends who live far from her, and of course, with her beloved grandchildren. These connections are especially vital for her now because, ironic as it seems, cyberspace allows her to feel closer to her distant family and less alone.

In an earlier chapter, I wrote about how difficult it was for some grandparents to take up pen or pencil, and write stories for their grandchildren. I have heard it from all corners of the globe: I can't write! Yet, with a little encouragement, grandparents have, more and more, begun to write personal stories for their grandchildren. And the more they write, the more they find that they enjoy the process. And the more their grandchildren find pleasure in their stories.

It is also likely to be difficult for grandparents who have never faced a computer screen to avail themselves of this tool to make a long distance connection with their grandchildren. The beginning stages of finding one's way into the world of the Web is not very different from finding one's way to writing stories. The first time is the hardest! The equipment seems foreign—like an enemy! The descriptive language is alien to the ear and tongue. Yet, with a few keyboard strokes, and a supportive, informed teacher, a beginning can be made. As with all other new tasks, experience is the best teacher.

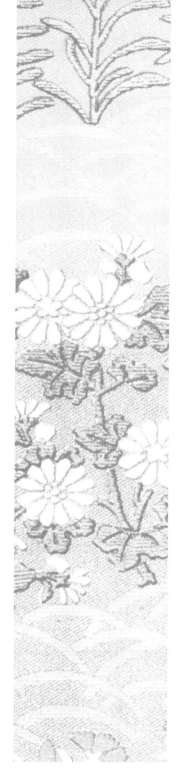

But perhaps you don't want to invest big bucks and buy a computer without testing out how it might work for you. Trial "lessons" can be had at Internet Cafes—coffee and Internet hang-outs, where, for approximately $2.50 an hour, you can approach the World Wide Web by just putting one toe in the water. Then, if you like what you find, you can take the giant step to the computer store. You may never become an addict, like so many of us chained to these machines, but you will discover a whole world of possible connections to your grandchildren.

## Conclusion

It is unlikely that grandparents who are coming to Internet use for the first time will want to jump right in and immediately pursue all of these ways of connecting. However, for those who are interested in what the options are, and who wish to pursue the variety of creative ways in which the Internet can strengthen long distance intergenerational connections, some basic reading in the field might be of value. While there are literally dozens of books that might be helpful, the ones I have listed below are particularly recommended:

John Levine, Carol Baroudi, and Margaret Levine Young. *Internet for Dummies.* Now in its seventh edition, this basic book is considered one of the best user's guides to the Internet now available. Not only does it contain clear advice, and information on every aspect of the Internet, it also includes a list of service providers throughout the United States and Canada.

Rick Bolton and Galen Grimes. *Ten Minute Guide to the Internet and the World Wide Web.* If you are in a hurry and need a quick tutorial, the Bolton and Grimes book may be for you. But given its lack of breadth and depth, it only scratches the surface of what the Levine, Baroudi, and Young book offers.

If you do decide to make an Internet connection with your grandchildren, be prepared to spend much more time with your computer! This is a unique way for you to enter into your grandchildren's world and become a part of what is happening in their lives. While first experiences with the technology may be daunting, once we have overcome initial resistance and our feelings of intimidation, we are likely to find that the potential of this tool to bring us closer together is greater than we could have dreamed.

# 13

# Grandparenting Children With Special Needs

*"I think a grandma should be nice and
strong and help me. She would love me."*

## Children With Disabilities

SHE SITS by the telephone, a cup of cold tea at the table beside her. She has been there for four hours, waiting for news about her third grandchild. She knots, unknots, and knots again the white handkerchief in her lap, giving her fingers something to do through the interminable waiting time.

When her son-in-law telephoned that morning to say they were unsure if her new grandson had Down's syndrome, and the doctor would be sending blood samples over to the lab to check this out, she felt a cold hand reach out into her chest and squeeze her heart. Here she was, two thousand miles away. What could she do? What could she do if she were right there?

She felt a thousand years old, powerless to cope at such a distance with this potential family crisis. What if the doctor's diagnosis was confirmed? What if this long-awaited and cherished baby had Down's syndrome? What would it mean for her daughter and son-in-law? What would it mean for her? What kinds of life expectations are there for Down's syndrome children? Would this child break everybody's heart? Should she make immediate plans to move there?

Nearly every mother who receives her baby in her arms for the first time asks, "Is my baby whole? Is my baby well?" When all the parts are there, and all appendages tallied up, she assures herself that this means the baby is a complete new being. And given the wonders of modern medicine, and our improved preventive health care during pregnancy, our prospects for "healthy and complete" babies increase all the time.

Yet, in spite of all this, there is still much we do not know and much we may not prevent. Children may be born with birth defects, like Turner's syndrome, hemophilia, or Down's, with learning disabilities, like dyslexia, or with a physical handicap. All of these conditions put a great deal of stress on the child-victims as well as on the entire family.

The best, most current books on how children develop tell us that between twenty and forty percent of children in North America under the age of eighteen suffer from one or another form of disability. Some of these are inherited, while others come from childhood diseases. Children may have speech problems, eating problems, like anorexia or bulimia, problems with bladder control, or with hyperactivity. When children with disabling chronic disorders come into our families, no matter what the cause and no matter what the specific condition, they require our special help, our special understanding, our special love. And while these children may tug at our hearts in sometimes heartbreaking ways, they also give us a very special kind of love in return.

The M.'s third child, Erin, was a Down's baby. The M.'s knew about Erin's condition during Holly's pregnancy and welcomed this baby into their lives. Now that she is two, Holly says, "She's brought more joy and more love into our lives than we ever dreamed possible. And we have all—especially the other children —come to a fuller understanding and appreciation of each other's individual differences and unique gifts. I think with Erin we have been especially blessed."

Children with disabilities present profound challenges to parents and grandparents.

# In the Eye of the Beholder

The child who is different must wrestle with his own demons. He may have physical differences that set him apart from his peers or his siblings. He may have handicaps that require special consideration and individual treatment. He may find difficulty dealing competently with the "simplest" tasks. How we accept our "special" grandchild, in our long distance (or close) personal relationships, may make his life happier, more fulfilled, and more productive. Or it may add to his growing sense of frustration and lack of self confidence. It is how the attitude that each of us holds about disabilities shows in our behavior that will make the difference between love and acceptance, and subtle, but still very clear, rejection.

Our attitudes are very much a part of who we are. As adults of the senior generation, we have been a long time in growing them. Many are already deeply entrenched, and they are not easily changed. But as adults who are in charge of their own lives, we do have the option of changing our attitudes, and of turning something that we do not like about ourselves into something that we *do* like. While this is difficult even for seniors to do, we at least have a greater potential for self awareness.

While, for example, Erin's parents were originally concerned about their ability to receive a Down's baby with love and affection, they were able to examine their attitudes, to understand their fears, work on them and deal openly with their concerns. In that way they were able to build their love, affection, trust, and acceptance. The more they were able to express these positive feelings, the more they were revealed to Erin. And as with all babies, the more love is received, the more is returned. Love is always a two-way road.

But suppose Holly was trundling Erin down the avenue to the supermarket, and suppose the group of women talking at the corner observed Erin's broad flat face, her oval, upward-slanted eyes with the epicanthic fold, her sparse, fine, straight hair, her stubby hands and

While we may pay lip service to the credo that "self-acceptance comes from within," many of us care what others think.

203

Don't berate yourself for not being able to do or say the perfect thing. It takes time to adjust and learn appropriate coping strategies.

feet. Would they think she was cute, as Holly does? Would they turn away? Would they feel pity? Would they whisper to each other that this child was a "Mongoloid"? Such attitudes would be very different from those of Holly and her family. Our attitudes about *all* children are rooted in "the eyes of the beholder." We see grace, beauty, generosity, capability, and other personal qualities from our own biases. Though we may see, for example, a perfectly homely little boy next door, his parents and grandparents think he is the next Paul Newman!

## Are Our Expectations Realistic?

Some of our special needs grandchildren may have difficulty in understanding what we say. They may take longer to learn to walk and talk than most other children. They may have trouble with certain (or all) subjects in school. They may be "clumsy." They may be more timid or more aggressive than we would have preferred. They may be unable to carry a tune, ride a bicycle, get A's on their report cards. Will they still be adorable to us? The answer is, only if we can, in our hearts, be genuinely loving and accepting, appreciating the special qualities they have, and refusing to measure them by more trivial, popularized standards. And only if we can appreciate that children's gifts come in many different shapes and forms, knowing that to measure all by a single standard is to condemn and reject all that "do not measure up." And only if we can open ourselves up to the love that our special needs children have to give us.

We are the mirrors in which our children and grandchildren see themselves and learn about who they are. If our attitudes mirror that we believe in them, and that they have the potential for growing and learning—wherever it may take them—that is what they will learn. They will be able to learn about their capabilities and their unique gifts. Their self confidence will grow, and so will their self respect.

Only a few short years ago, our attitudes toward handicapped children were grounded in false assumptions about their limited capacity. We believed that disabilities invariably meant drastically reduced lives and dim, bleak futures. Yet, when we opened our minds instead of sticking our heads in the sand, we learned that some people with even extreme physical handicaps could lead productive and satisfying adult lives, and that a physical disability need not interfere with intellectual functioning. Helen Keller's intelligence was not an anomaly, nor are the seriously physically handicapped adults who graduate from universities, drive cars, paint landscapes, join marathon races, marry and have happy families.

To be a person with special needs is to be different, not less. And that, perhaps, is the key to our understanding and acceptance of brain damaged grandchildren. They will have many real limitations to face and parents may feel taxed to the limits of their endurance in the day-to-day demands of raising these very special children. We grandparents, even at long distance, may be especially helpful to parents and to grandchildren in very important ways. We may provide understanding and emotional support on the telephone and in letters. We may help with the finances, if we are able, to provide quality day care and special schooling. We may offer to come and visit more frequently, insofar as we are able, to assume some of the care-giving, and allow parents a "breather" or a holiday away by themselves. At gift giving time, we may take special pains to find out what kinds of gifts would be most welcome, from "purchasing" extra baby-sitting services, to the toys and equipment that would bring pleasure to the child. Rather than guessing it is always best to ask.

Expectations for our "special" grandchildren must neither be too limited (and thus limiting), nor exaggerated, and the best way is to find out whatever we can about the child's special circumstances. The neighborhood librarian will be able to offer invaluable assistance. It is important to read *only* up-to-date information, keeping abreast of all the new knowledge. (Refer to the Resources section at the back of the

Children learn by example. If you respect and accept them they can accept and respect themselves.

Check with your son or daughter before purchasing gifts for special needs grandchildren.

book for where to find out more.) The better we are informed the more helpful we are likely to be.

As we pay particular attention to our "special" grandchildren, we must not forget about their brothers and sisters, who may feel overlooked. It is all too easy to be caught up in one child's special demands, ignoring the children with more "ordinary" needs. To give of ourselves equally, ensuring that none feels neglected, is a real challenge that will take our most serious efforts.

## Some Long Distance "Do's and Don'ts"

Connecting with special grandchildren at long distance does not require any additional talents. But you will want to keep in mind some of the following guidelines. And at the very top of the list is your acceptance of the specialness of your grandchildren—their unique limitations and gifts.

- Be sensitive to their special needs in your letters, your stories, your gifts.
- Do not patronize them.
- Do not put them into positions where they will feel frustrated and inadequate. If, for example, your grandchild is dyslexic, sending sophisticated books and stories is not a very good idea. If your grandchild has difficulties with coordination, do not send gifts or toys that require dexterity.
- If stress is adding to your grandchild's difficulties don't contribute to it still further by emphasizing his difficulty and urging him to "get over it."
- If your grandchild is visually handicapped, make special books with large print, and write your letters with large handwriting.
- Tread the midpath between condescension and expectations that are too high.
- If you know your grandchild very well, you will know more about how his needs may be met. Find out, in whatever ways you can,

Get informed. You may have precious time at your disposal that your children don't. Use it to learn all you can to help them and your grandchild.

what he feels, and how your responses to him may strengthen him as a person.
- Add to your own background of information about his disability. In gathering your information, be sure to go to authoritative and current resources.

## The Special Problems of Talented Grandchildren

There are, of course, children with special gifts and talents. Some may show intellectual gifts at a very early age, while in others, special talents appear only later in life. For example, Einstein learned to speak late. Even at the age of nine, he did not speak fluently, and it was feared that he might be "slow." There are also many gifted and talented adults who emerged from a childhood with extreme physical handicaps, like Helen Keller, Toulouse Lautrec, Henry James, and William O. Douglas.

We have learned that if a talent appears early, it is good to provide the conditions that will allow it to flourish. We know, too, that gifts appear in many different forms, and that to be especially gifted in music, for example, does not mean we are also equally gifted in other areas. We also know that very bright and precocious children may, as adults, show no remarkable accomplishments. Overzealous parents and grandparents can, with their untempered enthusiasms, create a talented neurotic adult who may be brilliant in his special field, but who is unable to live a happy or satisfied life.

If your grandchild is outstanding in a particular skill, you can help to nurture her talent with your attention. For example, in your long distance connections, you are likely to want to write and talk about her special interests. When gift giving time comes around, you can find out how you may contribute in some special way to her talent. You can give her opportunities to talk and write about what she is doing and how she feels about it all. You will want to encourage, to respect.

A special needs grandchild may require special attention or consideration, but take care not to treat your grandchild as though he or she is helpless.

Gifted grandchildren's personal rights and needs must be protected from those who would manipulate them to their own advantage.

All children, no matter what their gifts, flourish best in supportive environments.

Children's gifts may be destroyed if their growth is forced. Pushing too hard, unrealistic expectations, and the crushing conditions created by "that's not quite good enough" will kill any budding talent. To love and cherish a child primarily for what she can *do,* instead of for who she is, may warp even the strongest youngster. And if, because of a child's precocity, we encourage him to grow up too fast, we will have robbed him of the most precious gift of all—his childhood, never to be replaced throughout his entire life.

## Our Expectations for Talented Children

We all have secret and not-so-secret expectations for our talented children and grandchildren. But we must take care that we do not communicate expectations that destroy, rather than appreciate their talents. It doesn't matter if our unrealistic expectation is stated outright or whether it leaks out in tone of voice or facial expression. The child can "read" it and knows it's there. He will grow up with the idea that what he does is never "quite good enough"—a terrible and defeating mind-set.

We may expect our grandchildren to be academic giants, twenty-first century Mozarts, or the sports heroes that we had always wanted to be ourselves. We may expect them to take over the family business when we retire, or to be doctors or lawyers. Though it's all right to dream, it may spell a future full of disaster if we impose our own expectations onto our grandchildren. Learning what our own expectations *are,* and sifting out those which are encouraging and those which are defeating, may help us keep them under control.

But are all expectations wrong? Should we never communicate expectations to grandchildren? On the contrary. We may certainly expect that they do their best in school, but there is a difference between "the best that she can do," and insisting that she always do better. And understanding this difference may be the key. This is often a problem for grandparents of gifted and talented grandchildren. We want to be supportive and appreciative of a talented child's amazing abilities, but we must tread carefully lest we create a talented neurotic.

## Who, Me?

"She's not talking about me, surely," says Grandma Nettie, flipping over these pages and into the more lightweight stuff. "I don't have expectations that are hurtful! This part does not mean ME!"

It's not easy to look at our expectations for our grandchildren, and own up to the fact that some of them may be more hurtful than helpful. It is hard to see ourselves as we really are, rather than as we hope we are, and to allow ourselves to become aware of behavior that is less than wonderful. Becoming aware can mean a rude awakening, but if you are "up for trying" to examine your expectations realistically, the payoffs can be great, for both yourself and your grandchildren.

## Listen to Your Heart

There are no easy paths on this road, and no magic, quick-fix solutions for getting there. If you choose this path, you will need to "listen to your heart" to hear what it is telling you about your expectations. No, don't shut out the messages you don't like hearing. Listen to them all and learn about the ones that reveal hidden expectations that might be hurtful for your grandchild.

Pretend you are sitting in front of a mirror in which you can watch yourself when you write or talk to your grandchild. What are you writing or saying? Think about it and the expectations being communicated. In writing, this is easier to do because we can write, reflect, and change what we've said that we don't like. On the telephone or in person, the words may fall off our lips before we even realize what has been uttered. But we can *listen* to what we have said. We can say, "Whoops, I'm sorry. I didn't mean that." We can profit from the experience and use the wisdom to help us the next time.

Discipline and hard work make fine taskmasters, but drive anyone too hard and they can break, or else rebel.

Owning your own feelings can be a painful process. It's hard to look at yourself without the rose-colored glasses.

Learning to monitor and to take charge of our expectations for our grandchildren may not be as easy as learning to play lawn bowling, but the results will doubtlessly lead to improved relationships between the generations.

## When Families Change

Family breakdowns create other special circumstances for children. They must deal with all sorts of upheavals in the lives of all the family members—and especially in their own. The accompanying uprooting naturally causes deep emotional stress, as it does for all the adults involved. But children are less equipped to handle it. They require our most sensitive understanding to help them deal with their profound sense of loss, and to sort through the turmoil and make sense out of their new lives. For grandchildren who are going through the experiences of family breakdowns, grandparents, even at long distance, may be the single stable relationship they feel they can count on and trust.

There may now be two distinct and separate residences with "my own bed" in each. There may be new mates for one or both of the parents, or new siblings and even new grandparents! A parent may move to another city, and even out of the child's life altogether.

At the very least, no matter how sensitively the parents are tuned to the child's needs, and however hard they try to be considerate of them, the child will at first feel insecure. While an agreed upon separation may, in the long run, be the best course for everyone who must live day after day in an unhappy household, the wrenching apart of the fabric of the family will take time to mend.

Of course, where grandchildren are suffering the loss of a parent through death, the situation will be greatly magnified. And because the parents are so caught up, themselves, in the thick of the turmoil or in their own grieving, the grandparents may become key players in bringing the child safely through.

Children often blame themselves for family break-ups.

It is at these times of crisis that long distance relationships seem more frustrating than ever. These are times when families need to be

210

together, to find support and sustenance in their reaching out and touching. When we are ill or unhappy or our life is in shreds, we will want our family close by, in intimate contact. You and your daughter or son will decide together what is the best plan. Should you go? Should you stay? For how long? Should you wait it out at home? Should your grandchild come to stay with you? Decisions such as these should not be precipitous. You are not the avenging angel nor are you the Mary Poppins fix-it lady. You must talk with your daughter or son and decide together about what to do, for that is the respectful way.

There may be reasons that make it impossible for you to go. You may have to "be there" at long distance, making more telephone calls and sending more letters. This may not seem adequate, but do not underestimate the value of the telephone and postal connections. They are a potential source of comfort for your grandchild as well.

In either long distance or close connections with grandchildren experiencing traumatic loss, what we say and how we say it is important in helping them through the crisis. And this communication may be in person, on the telephone, in the mail, or all of them. Be in touch as frequently as is feasible for you. At long distance, once a month will not do in times of crisis. You may have to telephone more frequently. You will want to write several times a week. You may want to "talk" to your grandchild on a cassette tape, reassuring him and telling of your love. You might choose stories to read that tell about other children in similar situations. Keeping the connection and "being there" will probably require a special effort on your part, at least during the more critical period, and until your grandchildren have come to terms with the loss.

## Helping Grandchildren Through Troubled Times

Once again, the way we offer help may be for better or for worse. Good intentions here will not count for much. It's what we actually *deliver*—what we say and how we say it—that counts. For grandparents who want to take on a key role in effectively helping grand-

> Learning not to judge or take sides in the event of a divorce or separation is vital to preserving the integrity of the grandchild-grandparent relationship.

Make an extra effort to "be there" for your grandchildren in times of loss.

children with traumatic loss, here are some guidelines. They apply equally well to telephone, postal, taped, or close personal connections.

- Encourage your grandchild to speak his heart out about the loss.

A child, even as young as age four, can be encouraged to talk about some of the events in his life that are causing problems for him. It makes it okay for him to have his feelings. And it also tells him that you have understood how he feels. Communicating that understanding to your grandchild is one of the most powerful gifts you can give towards helping him to feel more secure. And it is done in caring and non-critical ways.

With the death of a parent, we must not shirk from our responsibility to allow the child to express his feelings. Death is an issue we'd rather avoid. If we had our "druthers" we'd avoid it altogether! (If we don't talk about it openly, perhaps we can pretend it never happened, or it's not going to happen to us.) Such avoidance would be both confusing and disastrous for the child. He might have no other outlet for his feelings, no avenue to help him to examine, explore, and come to terms with his loss. In the event of such a loss, grandparents must take the intrepid route, allowing and even encouraging children to unburden themselves of deeply held feelings.

- Don't diminish his feelings, or tell him that he "shouldn't feel that way."

It's hard to explain why so many of us take off in the other direction in the face of expressions of powerful feelings. Open expressions of love often make us feel uneasy. When we see anger expressed, we shrink from it. With children, we are apt to tell them, "Don't feel bad." Not only is it useless to tell this to a child who *does* feel bad, and has every reason for feeling this way, it also subtly tells him that his feelings are unacceptable.

Children need an outlet for the feelings if they are going to heal.

Children who have experienced traumatic loss *will* be upset, and are likely to be upset more easily over small things. They may cry more, for "no apparent reason." They may show anger at the slightest provocation. They may seem more moody and prefer to be left alone. Or their general behavior might take a turn for the worse, and grandparents may be astonished to see them behave in more infantile or aggressive ways. And the children may be feeling an overwhelming sense of despair, a powerlessness to deal with the events in their lives. Schoolwork may suffer, and teachers may write notes home like "Jane's getting into fights with the other children."

Without going into a psychological explanation, suffice it to say that there are good reasons for these things. We may not like the behavior, but it is the child's way of expressing hurt, pain, anger, and confusion. And naturally, they will express these feelings to the adults who matter to them most. Hard as they are for us to bear, we know that the expression of feelings is healthier than bottling them up.

Children who show their pain and anger in response to traumatic loss need from us the very best that we are able to give. We must leave behind the temptation to advise, direct, or be critical. We must not try to talk the child out of his feelings, or suggest he is bad for having those feelings, no matter how difficult it may be.

Do say:

"You're having a hard time of it today."

"You're really missing your dad."

"You're so unhappy."

"You're so angry. You'd like to break things!"

Don't say:

"Don't be so angry."

"Try to control yourself."

"Good boys/girls don't do that."

"I can't love a boy/girl who does that."

- In a separation, don't add to the war between the mates by taking an active, belligerent role. Don't encourage your grandchild to take sides and align himself with one or the other parent.

Acknowledge and deal with your own feelings concerning the break-up or loss. It will help you understand your grandchildren's "acting out."

Above all else—
be a good listener.

In some marital break-ups, the conflict between the mates may be intense. In others, there may be a polite agreement to separate. In the former, surely the partners do not need another belligerent to increase hostilities. And if the agreement to separate is amicable, surely the partners do not need an agitator to lead them to war. Neither conciliator, mediator, belligerent, nor adviser are good roles for a grandparent. They are best left to others. But grandparents can be enormously helpful by being supportive, respectful, loving, and non-critical.

•   Be supportive in helping your grandchildren cope with new mates.
    Much confusion occurs with the addition of a new mate. The child will have divided loyalties. Should she like/hate the man who is now the adult male in the household? What if he is kind and loving to her? If she likes him, will that mean a betrayal of her own dad? Should she be angry with her mother for replacing her dad with another partner? When there is a new baby, where will she fit in her mother's affections?
    If there is a marriage with children from a former marriage, there will be instant new brothers and sisters. There may be another set of grandparents, new aunts and uncles. Today it is not uncommon for a child to have two sets of mothers and fathers, a group of half sisters and brothers, and four sets of grandparents. Having to negotiate between all of these family branches can be very confusing to any child, and learning to do it well may call for her growing up before her time.
    The best plan for grandparents of children facing new family situations is to become very sensitive to what may be the child's confusion. Once again, allowing the child's feelings to be expressed and being a good listener are all-important. Encourage your grandchild to talk or write about her feelings and give her the chance of ultimately making sense out of the confusion. And not requiring that she grow up too fast to meet the new challenges will add immeasurably to seeing her through.
    Grandparents of children in special circumstances will feel more

Jumping in to "fix"
other people's
problems invariably
backfires on the "fixer."

acutely the need for close physical contact and will mourn their inability to be nearby. It would be nice if we could be together, if we had unlimited spending money to fly back and forth as often as we wished, and if we could re-establish our lives around the needs of the grandchildren. But most of us cannot do this. Our long distance connection may not be perfect, there will be missed opportunities, and times we would have preferred the loving touch.

But if nurturing at distance is second best, it need not be second rate. We can reach out through the various connections written about in this book, touching deeply, affectionately, and respectfully those we love. We can give them the best of us, letting them know that we *know,* that we care, and that we understand. And in that way we can fulfill our traditional roles as grandparents.

# 14

# The Long Distance Grandmother Comes to Visit

## A Personal Experience

I AM AN authoritative person. I have no difficulty taking charge—in fact, I prefer doing so. I like organizing events and delegating authority. Orchestrating a learning experience for sixty-five adults is a challenge I readily undertake. And I enjoy the task! Many years ago, and long before grandchildren were on the horizon, when I made my first visit to my daughter's own home, I had no sooner put my suitcase down than I began to organize lunch. Without a thought for her feelings, I took charge in my daughter's kitchen and gave everyone a job, efficiently dispatching and delegating. I cringe when I think of it. It hadn't taken me but a few moments to usurp my daughter's role as mistress of her own home. After all, I was the mother. She was my child. Isn't this what mothers should do?

In the face of this assault on her dignity, she had great sensitivity. She did not confront me with charges about my colossal nerve. She allowed me to play out my managerial role at lunch, but talked with her father later on about her feelings. He, in his most caring and thoughtful way, brought me up short that evening when we were alone. When I heard what he had to say, I immediately rose to my own defense. My intention was to be *helpful!* I didn't want to burden my daughter with

If we are able to behave respectfully to others we will feel no need to control them.

the additional work of guests for lunch! I wanted to relieve her of the chores! I had all the best arguments. I felt misunderstood and wrongfully accused. I did not want to look at my bossy behavior from my daughter's point of view. I wanted to hold onto the view that what I did was noble and good—because that was what I had intended.

I was hurt and angry, and it took until the next day for me to see things from my daughter's perspective. How would I have felt if someone (my mother) had taken charge in *my* kitchen, bossing me around? I would have hated it, and resented the person who had done that to me. Then I remembered with discomfort how I felt when my own mother came to my home on her weekly Saturday visits. No sooner had she hung up her coat, than she waded into the housecleaning with the vigor of a woman obsessed. While it was true that as a working mother I devoted less time to the household chores than she thought acceptable, and while it was also true that her intentions were to "give me the gift of her help," it was a gift that pierced my heart like an accusation.

My daughter's strategy of talking first with my husband was a good one. In that way, it was he who took the brunt of my defensive and angry response. Since he was a neutral party, he could listen more charitably. Also, it allowed me to vent my feelings, and gave me time to reconsider the situation. By the next day, I could be more objective and understood how my daughter felt. When I spoke with her that morning after breakfast, it was adult-to-adult. I apologized for my indiscretions, and hoped she would understand that my intentions were honorable. She, in turn, told me how she felt. At the end of our talk, we were friends again, and I vowed to myself that I would exercise constant vigilance when visiting my daughter, to make sure I would not exceed my place as guest in her home. This is never easy. Having learned to be a "driver" it is difficult to play the role of "passenger." One must be constantly alert for the "director" that emerges, without invitation, to take over the show.

You will be comforted to know that I do not show these managerial

Your son or daughter's housekeeping and child-rearing practices may be quite different from yours.

Receiving that long-awaited hug is worth all the jet-lag or travel discomfort it took to get there.

excesses when I visit the homes of friends. You will not see me jumping up and taking over in their kitchens. Even when a friend asks me for help or advice, I do not tell them what I think they *should* do. To me, helping friends means helping them to figure out for themselves what they want to do. How is it possible that I can be so different with friends? Why is it that I do not have to prevent myself from taking over and managing their lives?

Each of us is, of course, a complex product of all of our life experiences. We have learned parenting from many cumulative experiences, programming ourselves to take charge in caring for our children. By the time they are grown, our habits are deeply entrenched, and not easily given up. It takes conscious effort to behave differently, even though we know our children are now adults. In fact, we must consciously "re-program" ourselves to behave otherwise.

With friends it is different. There is no early history of having to "take charge" of them, and of being responsible for their health and safety. When we go to their homes, we go as guests, not as parents. As guests, we behave respectfully to them, and with the greatest consideration. And this happens naturally, without conscious effort. With our children the umbilical connection still lives! And so with them we must try to behave as we would with our friends—as respectful guests in their home. This is not easy for most of us. It may require some long-term practice, and even, perhaps, a sense of humor when confronted with a slippage into our old roles. For me, this respect is the bottom-line principle of visiting, and everything else in this chapter is built upon this foundation.

## Long Distances Lead to Long Visits

When my parents made their regular weekly visits to our home, the visit always ended after dinner. It was a long drive back to the city. My father was tired, and he liked sleeping in his own bed. Happy to see

218

them come, we were not unhappy to see them go. We could look forward to a quiet evening together, sitting in our pajamas with our feet up, talking only to each other. All during the day, our attention had been given over to them, and we had little time to ourselves. It was not hard to put our own activities on the shelf until then, and it didn't matter a lot, because the following day, we could return to our normal schedules.

Visits by long distance grandparents are more complicated, first, because they are a rarer event in the family's lives, and second, because the visits are longer. If you are going to be traveling 3,000 miles to see your grandchildren, you are likely to want to stay a while. Some grandparents may stay for two weeks, others for two months. Finally, long distance grandparents who come for extended visits are more than likely to be staying in the children's homes. All of these will have a substantial effect on the relationships in the home. And they might easily put stresses and strains on the visit for everyone. To know what these stresses might be, and to know how tensions arise, can be an important step towards making our visits pleasurable.

In the pages that follow, I will try to identify some potentially stressful areas around long-term visits, with respect to how they build. I will also describe some things that may create tensions, and some ways to reduce them. As in earlier chapters, take them only as suggestions that *may* be helpful. Read, consider, and choose for yourself those that seem, to your way of thinking, the wisest paths to follow.

## What Role Do You Wish to Play?

"Here's grandma," shout Billy Jean and Timmy, whisking her out of the airport and into the waiting car. In thirty minutes they are at the house, and grandma is billeted in Billy Jean's room, for the duration of her visit, while Billy Jean doubles up with Timmy. It's only for two weeks and this arrangement seems like it's going to work.

Extended visits call for special reserves of tact and diplomacy.

Before you leave on your visit, be clear about your own need for physical space and comfort.

"How about a cup of tea, mother?" asks daughter. The two sit at the kitchen table savouring the pleasure of this long awaited moment, while granddaughter and grandson snuggle close. There's a lot of news to catch up on, and grandma is enjoying just sitting down after the exhausting plane trip and the days of preparation that preceded it. Before long, however, daughter has given grandma a list of "things to do."

"Mom, I've been waiting for you to come! I have so much mending that needs to be done."

"I know you won't mind hemming those skirts. I just don't have the time to do it myself."

"I was hoping you'd help me make a new dress for the Christmas party."

"Arthur and I have a dance on Friday. Would you mind babysitting the kids?"

"You know how much Arthur loves your biscuits! Will you make some for supper?"

"I'm going to leave the breakfast dishes in the sink. You don't have to do them if you're too tired. I'll do them when I get home."

"I'm just going to run out to the market. I won't be gone long. The kids won't be any trouble."

"How about bathing the kids? Would you mind?"

"Gee, the ironing has piled up. Do you think you can give me a hand?"

"Dad, this closet just doesn't close right. Do you think you can get the doors to hang straight?"

"Dad, would you drive Timmy to school tomorrow morning? I've got some important chores to run."

"Dad, do you feel like doing some work in the garden?"

"Dad, could you look at my car? I think the clutch might be going, and it costs a fortune to fix at the service station."

"Dad, could you let me have $50? Don't tell Arthur."

"Dad, could you give the kids breakfast tomorrow morning? I sure would like to sleep late just once!"

Between all the requests for your help and your desire to be helpful, you will have to make some important decisions about the role you want to play as a visiting, live-in grandparent.

Do you want to be the maid? The babysitter? The gourmet chef? The chauffeur? The handyman? The gardener? The banker?

Most grandparents will want, to some extent, to play several of these roles. We *want* to help, and we very much enjoy the feeling of being needed and helping out. Yet, there are points beyond which we need not be prepared to go, and these will be strictly individual for each of us. It may be fine to make apple pie and biscuits, but not to land up with meal preparations every evening. It may be all right to help with the ironing, but not all right to end up scrubbing floors and windows. Babysitting once or twice may be all right, but not winding up with it as a permanent job.

In the extended visit you may often be consulting your feelings to decide between chores you take on willingly and those that are somehow being imposed on you. If you find yourself doing more than you want to do, giving more of your energies than you can comfortably part with, a critical point has been passed, and you will feel "put upon." When that happens, tension in the house will increase, and life together will cease being "happily ever after."

## Preventing Tensions

Preventing tensions like these may take some assertion on your part. Know what you are comfortable doing. Know what you feel all right about giving. And know where and when to draw the line. You can take the initiative about this before you get too angry and resentful. You need not be critical or hurtful. It's just a matter of stating your preferences:

When you are able to make your needs clear, all the family will be appreciative.

Some people find it difficult to state their needs and preferences. A humorous multiple-choice questionnaire may help break down the barriers.

*Daughter:* I have so much mending that needs to be done.

*Mother:* Golly, you know, I've lost my taste for sewing. I'd like to help you out, but unless it's a real emergency, I'd prefer not to.

*Daughter:* Dad, you feel like doing some work in the garden?

*Father:* You know, I used to love to do that. But it's getting so hard on my back these days. I could probably trim those hedges, but I don't think I'm up to doing the weeding.

*Daughter:* Would you mind babysitting on Friday?

*Mother:* I worry about not hearing the baby if I fall asleep. I'd much prefer it if you got your regular sitter. I could help her out, but then I wouldn't have to worry about going to bed early.

Give what you *want to* and *can* give. Your visit will benefit greatly from being clear about the roles you want to play, and the extent to which you want to assume responsibilities.

## Making Your Important Needs Known

LIST FOR GRANDMA
TO DO

DO LAUNDRY
VACUUM
DO DISHES
SHOP FOR DINNER
FEED KIDS
PUT KIDS TO BED

Children and grandchildren will push at your boundaries. Know ahead of time how you will respond.

Several years ago, we had a house guest for a week whose membership in the grandfather club was of long standing. What distinguished his visit from those of most other come-to-stay friends and relatives was that he was able to make his needs known simply and directly. Not only was this unique, but it also reassured us to know that we did not have to guess what had to be done to make his visit comfortable, or worry that we might not have done the right thing! We could count on the fact that he would tell us. It was refreshing! For example, he liked a certain type of high fibre cereal for breakfast. He liked to read in bed and required a reading light. He did not care for shellfish. His requests were never excessive, nor demanding. And he made his wishes known in the most polite and gracious way.

I thought of other live-in guests and could not help making comparisons. There were those who would "suffer in silence" before making what might be an inconvenient request. They are so determined not to inconvenience that they will *never* tell you what their preferences are. Instead of liberating us from worry this has the opposite effect: we worry constantly and their feigned selflessness drives us crazy! Then there are those who let you know what they need only indirectly. ("Aren't you cold?" is likely to mean, "It's freezing in here and why don't you turn up the heat?") With such guests, hosts must somehow know, without being told directly, what they really need. Perhaps that is why some live-in guests can be burdensome. With grandparents as live-in guests, there is the added possibility of our adult children feeling guilty because they haven't looked after our needs properly.

## Grandparents' Special Needs

As we achieve seniority, we are likely to have different physical needs than when we were younger, more flexible, and with vastly more energy. We may absolutely need a comfortable bed. We may need a night light to see our way down unfamiliar hallways to the bathroom. We may need prunes or bran for breakfast. We may need the house kept a little warmer than our offspring do, because our joints are a little stiff.

We may have other needs, such as time away from the hubbub of the house, away even from the beloved grandchildren. While grandchildren are wonderful in every way, their ceaseless energy and demands may easily exhaust us. The noise they make as part of their routine activities may wear us out. We may need to get away for a daily rest period. We may also need some personal space—a room with a door to close so we may be in private for a while. We may need free

Family members cannot read your mind. We should not expect them to.

223

Your opinions on housekeeping and child-rearing practices are exactly that: opinions, and not universal truths. Try to accept that your grown children need to do things their way.

time on our own in town, or to visit friends. We may just want to wander the streets by ourselves. Being clear about our own needs, and seeing that they are accommodated where possible, is the key to a happy live-in visit. And to get our needs met we must allow them to be known.

It is not wrong to have such needs, nor to let the children and grandchildren in on them. If we make them known, in direct and gracious ways, our hosts are more than likely to feel relief at knowing what will make us comfortable and relaxed. If we try to hide them, we are likely to feel stressed, thereby contributing to the discomfort and anxiety of those we love.

At the very opposite end of grandparents who "endure in silence" are some with excessive expectations. Their insistent demands to be looked after, to have things their own way, to be entertained, to turn everything around to their own satisfaction, will throw the entire household into an uproar. Instead of welcoming them, children and grandchildren will long for their departure, so that life can return to normal.

So with respect to personal needs, it is helpful to use the guidelines you yourself follow when visiting friends, treading the middle ground of making your important needs known, while at the same time being polite and gracious in respecting others' personal needs.

## Children's and Grandchildren's Needs

Good house guests can sense their hosts' needs, whether they come for dinner, for a weekend, or for a longer visit. We can see from the way our hosts run their homes what they are likely to enjoy or object to. Some hosts love it when you help with the dishes, some hate it. Good house guests respect their hosts' privacy if they retreat behind closed doors. Being good guests in homes of our children calls for similar discernment. And I'm not just speaking of helping in the kitchen, but rather all those things that are the cornerstones of good relationships.

## Making the Visit a Happy One

- Respect the family's rights to make their own choices. (Minding our own business!)

As live-in guests in our offspring's home we will be privy to virtually everything that is going on in their lives. Unless the family lives in a mansion we are likely to be sharing some close quarters. Living space just comfortable for the immediate family now has to accommodate one or two more bodies. We may be living in each other's pockets! So it is inevitable that we will be hearing and seeing everything—every family secret may be exposed to our eyes and ears.

Your daughter and her husband may argue, and you may have some strong opinions about who is "right"! We may object to the house-keeping standards. We may not like the furniture, the drapes, the room arrangements. We may disapprove of the number of times they go out for dinner. We may not like their friends, or that they enjoy sleeping late on Sunday mornings. We may have quite strong opinions about the way they are raising the children. There may be a very great temptation to criticize their "bad" habits and put them on the "right road" to a perfect life. But we mustn't do it!

Grandparents who butt in will not be appreciated. They will be seen as intrusive, as "not minding their own business." Visits, rather than being welcomed in future, will be anticipated as stressful for all concerned, and may be resisted, if not rejected. We may be older, but older does not necessarily mean wiser. And wiser, for ourselves, does not always mean knowing better what is wise for our children. If we love them, truly love them, we must allow them to make choices for themselves.

We may be called upon to give advice. Should we give it? It depends!

*Grandparents who interfere will not be appreciated. Try to remember that you are a guest in their home.*

225

Child-rearing habits are often rooted in necessity. But times have changed; perhaps the old ways are not so imperative today.

Can we *really* know what is best for someone else? We can always say, "In my opinion, this is how I see it." But to take charge of the decisions in another adult's life puts us in the position of being responsible for that adult—an awesome responsibility. Our adult children need to run their own lives and make their own decisions.

- Our way may not, in fact, be better.

We have had many years of practice doing what we do and we have learned to do many things well. After all, we raised our children successfully, made a living, and developed some competence in our work. By now, what we do and how we do it is a matter of habit, like growing a toenail. We are accustomed to those ways and they work for us.

In my case, my daughter's ways are different from mine, and she was far more relaxed about the children's "cleanliness habits." She did not shudder and quake when Arlo picked up a piece of his bread and jelly from the floor, and popped it into his mouth. (When she was small, had she done that, I'd have hit the roof!) I cannot see that her more flexible ways have wreaked havoc with the boys' overall physical health, either, and they are both (knock wood) healthy and strong. My daughter was also more relaxed about the boys' finishing their food. If one of them rejected his lunch or supper, that was not cause for hysteria, and no fuss was made. (Years ago, this would have caused me great consternation, and fears that the child would starve!) The boys did not starve and their bones are strong. My daughter was more easy-going about many other things in her child-raising, and my ways were very different from hers.

It would have been quite easy for me to tell her that her ways were wrong.

"How could you let him eat that from the floor!"

"How could you let him leave the table without any supper!"

How could you, etc., etc., etc.!

When we have become accustomed to "our ways" we assume that they are the "right ways." It takes a little bit of flexibility to remember that "our ways" are just different ways, and that others may be quite as appropriate and acceptable. And if "our ways" of child raising were so wonderful, we would certainly have the kinds of children who, as adults, would know the "right ways" for themselves.

- We must be sensitive to our son's or daughter's wishes for privacy.

He or she may need time alone, even if our visit is a brief one. Especially if our children are introverted types, time alone is important, restorative time, and does not mean that they do not enjoy or want our company. Avoid being intrusive if they want time alone. What we have to say can easily wait until later. If our daughter and her husband want time together, just the two of them, it is especially important that we avoid being intrusive. And if they don't ask for it, we can offer it. They will appreciate us all the more, and applaud and cherish our sensitivity.

- When speaking to our grandchildren we can tell them how we feel, rather than criticizing them. ("Grandma, get off my case!")

As live-in grandparents we will see our grandchildren doing things that we may not like, and that we take exception to. We will be sorely tempted to *tell* them how much we disapprove of their actions. Yet, if we choose to be a "critic," out to correct what we feel to be wrong, our grandchildren will feel constantly tested and evaluated. They may feel that they have fallen short of our standards, and that we do not even like them. And of course, nothing could be further from the truth. When we criticize, we do so with the best of intentions. But certain criticisms expressed in certain ways can make grandchildren uncomfortable and insecure, and may upset them terribly:

"What kind of hairstyle is that for a beautiful girl like you?"

"Are you sure you spent enough time on your homework?"

"Your teachers let you wear shorts to school?"

"You only got a B+ in science? I thought that was your favorite subject!"

Alone time is a precious commodity for today's working parents.

Today's children are raised to believe that respect is earned—not a right decreed by age.

"That's what you call cleaning up your room?"

"Isn't your skirt too short?"

"I think you are wearing too much makeup. It makes you look cheap."

"You spent all the money already?"

"The toy is broken already? You only played with it for five minutes."

"You're not wearing the sweater I made for you? How come?"

Though we may mean well in our criticisms, they are the shortest route to alienating us from our grandchildren. This is not to say that we should always agree with everything our children and grandchildren do, or that we should ignore all our own feelings. But there are important differences between expressing our feelings and being openly critical. To want to share our feelings is human and we can do so with respect.

## Expressing Feelings Versus Criticism

I really worry that Franklin didn't have enough to eat this evening. (Feelings.)

How could you let him leave the table without any dinner! (Criticism.)

I worry that he isn't going to get enough sleep. Will he be okay tomorrow and not too tired? (Feelings.)

He should go to bed now. (Criticism.)

Ugh! When he eats that from the floor, I feel repelled. (Feelings.)

Don't let him pick that up and eat it from the floor! (Criticism.)

And grandchildren:

I worry about your going outside in that cold weather with just a light sweater. (Feelings.)

Put on your warm coat when you go. (Criticism.)

I was so thrilled to see your report card. I can see how hard you have been working. (Feelings.)

I was sad to see your failing grade in math. You must have been very upset when you saw it too. (Feelings.)

How could you fail math! Didn't you study? A smart boy like you! (Criticism.)

I worry about your running off to school without a chance for breakfast. Will you be hungry? (Feelings.)

You call that breakfast? Sit down and put something hot in your stomach before you go to school! (Criticism.)

## Wanting to Be With the Grandchildren

By the time you have made up your mind to visit your grandchildren, you will begin to experience that craving for being together that you have barely been able to suppress since you saw them last. Now that the visit is imminent, you may allow yourself to feel that hunger which will only be sated by the real life touch of your grandchildren. As the time of the visit grows nearer, you cannot wait! All you can think about is being together and nothing else in the world seems to be as important.

When our own feelings are so overpowering and we have waited such a long time, it is harder to be sensitive to others. Our own wishes to be with the children seem *paramount!* Yet, grandchildren have their own activities, some of which cannot be pushed aside without contributing to household stress. Our adult children may have important rules about their children's routines that may not be broken without causing friction.

Because we are the guests, it falls to us to make the concessions. This, I believe, is the respectful way. Some visiting grandparents may feel otherwise—that as visitors, all rights and privileges are due *them.*

Grandchildren have lives too. Try to understand that they can't spend every waking minute with you.

229

Consistency in child-rearing helps children feel secure. Mixed messages and conflicting information will only confuse little ones and make them feel insecure.

My belief is that if we are a guest in someone else's home, whether that someone is daughter, son, aunt, mother, or best friend, the rules of respect still apply. I believe that when such respectful courtesies are observed, the visit will be positive, and the relationships of all those involved improve. This, of course, puts the greater burden on the visiting grandparent—a burden that might be difficult to carry.

## Learning the Family's Rules

It will be helpful, first of all, to learn the parents' rules, especially concerning younger grandchildren's activities. If you know what they are, you will be less likely to sin against them. You may also be able to ask whether or not negotiation is possible. For example, is naptime a must? Does a nap mean the difference between a cranky child and a pleasant afternoon? Is the child's bedtime set at a fixed hour? May there be active "fun and games" before bedtime, or would this prevent settling down to sleep?

If the child cries when put to bed, what are the rules about going in to comfort him? When he wakes up in the morning, what are the rules about his getting out of bed? Coming down to the kitchen? What may he have for breakfast? Lunch?

During visits to the shopping mall, what are the parents' rules about your buying gifts and trinkets for the children? What are the rules about buying candy and cookies for them, before, during, and after lunch? What are the rules about "horsie" rides? About video games in the arcade?

During play times at home, what are the rules about what might be played and where? Are there rules for paints and fingerpaints? Clay? Musical activities? Are there rules about more active games? About watching TV with respect to time, and the type of programs allowed? Are there rules about noise? About how the furniture is to be treated?

Are there rules about playing outside? About what outdoor clothing to wear? About any activities that need close supervision? About which friends may come to play? Which toys may be taken outside? How long the child may play outdoors?

Are there rules about mealtime manners?

When the child misbehaves, what are the rules about how he or she is disciplined? Will it break your heart to see him sent, in tears, from the table, because he has committed an atrocious social gaffe? Will you be able to keep your criticisms to yourself despite your own more "soft hearted" bias, or will you become the child's advocate against his parents' actions?

These are tricky situations, and a grandparent's heart may get in the way of exercising good judgment. So it is best to know the rules of the household, and to abide by them. If your grandparenting feelings are very strong, it is far better to try to negotiate with the parents about the rules, than to defy them. And it is also best to accept the parents' behavioral standards without assuming the role of ally to a grandchild.

There will, of course, be other circumstances as well. For example, older grandchildren will very likely want to "leave you behind" as they go off to play with their friends. Here you have flown three thousand miles, and are hardly unpacked, when he says, "Gram, I'm going out to play. I'll see you later." Heartbreak! Here the visiting grandparent skates on thin ice. Invoking guilt may keep him at your side ("You're leaving already? But I only just got here, and I wanted to be with you!"), but there will be a price to pay for it in his later resentment. If he goes, it does not mean that he does not love you. If we can allow our grandchildren the freedom to go as they choose, our loving relationship will be much enhanced.

There will be times during our visit when we may choose to go off by ourselves. "But gramma, how come you are going? Why do you *have* to go! Can't you take me, too?" Sometimes, we can't. Sometimes, we don't want to. Respect works in both directions, and grandparents have the right to have time away from the children, if they need it. If the child is hurt and angry, he will surely get over it. And from the ex-

At times you'll need the fortitude and resistance of a block of granite.

perience, he will learn that we too have rights and needs which are to be protected. If we give up our rights for our own space and our own time at a grandchild's insistence, we are not doing him or ourselves any favors. Over the long run, he will learn that he can manipulate us to his advantage, and that is hardly an appreciable accomplishment.

## Who Plays the "Heavy"?

I must confess that when I saw my grandson sent to his room amid a torrent of tears, it broke my heart. He had been perfectly odious to his younger brother, and after having been told several times to stop punching and shoving, his last offense demanded a harsher response. His mother took him to his room, where he wailed for what seemed to me to be an eternity. I sat there and cried, too! All my grandparental instincts were to rush to his side, comfort him, and strike out at all that had caused him pain. But I knew that my head must rule my heart, that in fact, parents must play out such scenes according to their own best and wisest judgments about child rearing. They, after all, know their children better than anyone, even than a grandparent! And what I have learned, through reading, teaching, and hard life experience, is that there *are* no perfect ways.

There is no question that limits must be set for children. Beyond these the child may not go, or he is in for "big trouble." Such limits are very important for both the child's physical and emotional security. Even though he may push hard against these limits, he learns that he is safe, protected, and cared about. Important as this part of child rearing is, it is a job that is, at best, difficult. At times, it may be hair-raising, and it is certainly exhausting.

Visiting grandparents should be exempt from "playing the heavy" in dealing with a child's transgressions. We have already done our work in this area and are now excused. In any case, this role belongs to parents, and must not be usurped, even by loving grandparents. I believe, too, that we must not intervene, no matter what feelings we must

You don't have to slink out the back door if your grandchild is being called onto the carpet, but a tactful exit at certain times may alleviate added tension and unease.

wrestle with, when parents are dealing with the child's behavior. If we have an opinion, we may offer it in private, afterwards, and not during a highly charged disciplinary scene.

Who plays the heavy? The parents do. Non-intervention on our part is the key to good family relations across all three generations.

## What Can I Do to Help?

She lives in a city on the West Coast with her husband and two children. Her mother lives in Florida. Each summer, her mother comes for a six-week visit and has been doing this for at least twelve years. And each summer, the entire family looks forward to her coming with great enthusiasm and delight. There is never a trace of resentment over her long stay, nor any feelings of being intruded upon. What makes this grandmother's visit such a special time for her, and for her daughter, son-in-law, and grandchildren?

She is, first of all, very sensitive to the family's needs for privacy. She is open and direct about her own needs, and makes her requests in a gracious and courteous way. She does not intervene in family matters, respecting the adults to handle them in their own ways. She observes the simple courtesies of being a guest in someone's home, and offers much love, affection, and warmth to the grandchildren and to her children.

She is a woman whose life was defined by mothering, and she has reconciled herself to the fact that this role is now behind her. It was a sad loss, and one that meant giving up some expectations. It is easy to deceive ourselves into thinking we may recapture the mothering role by insinuating ourselves into our daughter's place. It is tough to fade to the "back of the picture." We can try to fight against it—but we will always lose. Instead, we can accept our losses gracefully and with compassion for ourselves. These facts of life that accompany our aging we learn, not easily, with grandparenting.

With the loss of the mothering role, is there nothing of value for us

Relationships are not static. They are constantly evolving and changing.

Now you can be a friend to your grown son or daughter rather than a parent.

to do? Besides babysitting, baking buttermilk biscuits, helping with the mending, and loving our grandchildren to distraction, is there no primary role for us? Do we have to be content with being a second-class family member? What, exactly, does Mrs. S. do on her six-week visit that makes her stay such a happy one?

Mrs. S.'s daughter has said, "She's my friend. That's why I so look forward to her coming. She is more to me than mother now. I'm a big girl. I don't need a mother. But I need a friend, and this she is to me."

Mrs. S. is a "listening ear." She is warm, supportive, and caring. She is this with her daughter, her son-in-law, and with her teenage granddaughter, and pre-teen grandson. Anyone in the family may approach her comfortably, knowing that she will listen to what they have to say, and that she will care. She is rarely critical, and seldom offers advice. When she disagrees with something that is being done she will agree to disagree, and there is mutual respect for all points of view. On principle and without exception Mrs. S. does not criticize her son-in-law to her daughter, or vice versa, nor either to the children.

When she listens to what each has to say, she is warm and loving, and as her daughter says, "She is always there for me."

# 15

# On the Road with Grandchildren

THE FIRST TIME I took my grandsons on a major journey away from home was when the boys were five and seven. We were invited to a family occasion down in Orange County, California and it seemed like an opportune time to arrange a side trip to Disneyland—the stuff of kids' dreams. When I suggested this to my daughter, she was delighted that I wanted to undertake such an ambitious trip, albeit somewhat anxious about how grandpa and grandma would handle both boys, on their own, so far from home.

Our grandsons, who live in a small town in the eastern part of British Columbia, Canada, had never been out of the country, and barely remembered the long air trip they made when they were much younger to visit their paternal grandmother, in Toronto. This was going to be, from several perspectives, a major journey for all of us.

From all of the challenges of that trip, and all of the obstacles we surmounted, I learned much about traveling with grandkids, which I was able to use to advantage in subsequent journeys. Even if long distance grandparents yearn to have the uninterrupted, one-on-one time with grandchildren that an extended trip offers, advance knowledge and preparation can make the journey safer, more satisfying and more comfortable for all the travelers.

## Are You Ready for This?

Before even thinking about taking grandchildren on an extended journey, a critical question is whether they are ready for such a trip. It's impossible to specify an appropriate age, since children differ in levels of maturity and in their readiness to be away from their parents. Even loving grandparents may not be enough to comfort a child who wakes up in the middle of the night, crying for "mommy." Your grandchildren's readiness for an extended trip away from home should be discussed at length with their parents; and as in all matters of judgment relating to them, the parents should be the primary decision makers. It is they, after all, who know best how ready the children are to be away. I would not cheerfully undertake to invite children younger than five on an extended trip with me, since I consider five to be the dawning of the age of reason. At the age of five, most children are able to be reasoned with and can reason back; suggestions and requests can be negotiated with logic, and they are less likely to lose steam and get cranky en route. Of course, this guideline, like most others, is negotiable. Some children may not be ready at five; others may be ready to go the long distance at a younger age.

Consider, too, your own readiness for such an undertaking. Unless your grandchildren are of an age where they can function independently from adults, looking after them, full time, every waking minute, is a big job! If your energy levels are low, if your health is not up to par, or if you, for whatever reason, are having second thoughts about your stamina to travel with grandchildren to far-off lands, listen to your inner voices telling you to postpone, until you FEEL ready! You don't want to end up in a distant city or country secretly wishing you were home in bed, while your grandchildren press you to head off on the next adventure!

## Coming Attractions

One of the most delightful aspects of traveling is our anticipation of the journey. We make plans, look at travel brochures, consider different hotel accommodations, check out important sightseeing possibilities. All of this builds our anticipation for the journey, and whets our appetite for what is to come.

Children are not frequently invited into the discussions when travel arrangements are made, but I think this is a serious omission. Anticipation, whetting the appetite for the coming attractions, is, I believe, a significant pleasure. Talking to children about what travel arrangements have been made, and what the nature of the travel experience will be, adds to their understanding and prepares them for their new experiences. This is especially true for younger children. Pictures of and information about the places you will be visiting, as well as major sightseeing attractions, will all contribute to their anticipation and pleasure. What is the hotel like? What are its special features? What provisions will be made for the children? What arrangements will be made for meals? What schedules will guide our visits? What is unique about the flora and fauna of the area? It is also more than likely that your grandchildren will have agendas of their own, and insofar as possible, accommodations for visiting their special places should be built into the trip. In fact, older grandchildren might be encouraged to do a bit of research in the library or on the Internet to find out about the city or place of destination and its special attractions, and to make some decisions about what *they'd* like to do.

The importance of preparing children for the travel experience is not to be underestimated. They should know that planes may be delayed and they may have to wait at the airport. They should know how many hours the journey will take, and young children should have a measuring stick that gives them an idea about how long that period of time is (i.e., five hours = as long as a whole school day). They should know that the weather in the city of destination will be warmer (or colder, or the same) than it is in the one they are leaving from and that this may mean some climactic accommodation. They should know that the city of destination is considerably larger (smaller, the same size) than the one in which they live. They should know that the language in the city of destination is different (or the same) and if different, that may create difficulty in talking to people they meet. They should know about the hotel accommodations, the standards of behavior you expect when they are traveling, and the importance of staying close, so no one gets lost. They should know what the protocols are in the event that a grandchild does (God forbid!) get lost en route. When children know, in advance, they not only can anticipate more pleasurably, but they also increase their understanding and feelings of security about the journey to come.

## Preparing

The first time I took my grandchildren across the border from Canada to the United States, I went without a single thought about child abduction, missing children, or proof of identity. I had my passport but the children, ages five and seven, had no proof of who they were, or of any parental consent to travel with me. For all the immigration people knew, I could have been the Boston Strangler.

Oddly enough, we had no difficulty at Vancouver International Airport, from where we departed. The U.S. immigration officer looked at my passport, and at the three tickets, acknowledged that we were going to Los Angeles, and then to Disneyland, and saw, as well, our return tickets to Vancouver. He teased the boys about how lucky they were to go on this trip, and with a wave of his hand, smiled and wished us a good journey. We were off!

It wasn't until we reached Los Angeles International Airport, ready for the journey home, that we encountered difficulty. Where were the children's passports? We had none. Where was their identification? We had none. Where were letters of permission to travel from their parents? We had none. Airline agents were unprepared to allow this "strange" woman to travel to a foreign country with two young, un-documented children. After considerable begging, urging, and nearly weeping, we were finally allowed to board the plane.

That was not the end of the troubles. On the Vancouver side, we were met with the same concerns. Here, the children were taken from me and questioned individually. Who was I? How did they know that? Where did they live? Where did they go to school? Where were their parents? The children were untroubled by all the fuss—but I vowed never to go again without the appropriate documentation, in spite of the fact that I had been told by U.S. Immigration officials, whom I telephoned before leaving, that no documentation would be required. It could have been worse; and we were finally allowed to enter Canada and come home.

After my *a priori* reassurances from Immigration, it had not occurred to me that traveling without appropriate documents would cause such a furor. I didn't think about how many children are ab-ducted and go missing from their families. I just assumed that no one would question such an obviously harmless senior citizen; that my gray hair would automatically open all doors.

After that first unhappy experience, whenever our trips involved crossing an international border, the children carried "letters of docu-mentation" that were notarized, and signed by their mother. Later still, they carried their own passports. In preparing to go with grand-children, especially if you are going to another country, it's better to be safely documented.

Other preparations may also be worth considering. For example, in choosing accommodations, you may be very grateful if the place has special features for kids—such as a swimming pool, hot tub, exercise room, or other recreational facilities. After a hard day's trek, it is a wonderful respite for kids and grandparents to "take a break" at the poolside, where grands can sit and watch (whew!) while kids jump and splash and expend pent-up energies.

It may also be helpful, if tickets are needed, to order these in advance. This avoids waiting in lines (very boring for kids) and using up valuable sightseeing time. It is probably also helpful to know in advance what the opening and closing times of the featured attractions are; and if there are any days on which the place to be visited is closed. There's nothing worse than trekking to a museum that everyone is geared up to see, and finding it "Closed on Wednesdays."

It's important to determine if your grandchild is ready for such a trip.

Some grandparents will prefer to schedule each day's activities very closely—leaving little to chance. Other grandparents prefer a more open schedule. Whichever your preference, give some thought to how advance preparations can prevent on-the-scene disappointments, and make the whole trip easier, more comfortable, and more satisfying.

While it's not pleasant to contemplate losing a grandchild in the crowds of a distant city, it is better to prepare for such an eventuality in advance, just in case! Then, having prepared, make sure the grandkids know the first rule of travel: "Stick to me like glue!" The first line of defense if you look around and don't see your grandchild, is to arrange a signal between you. The child may just not be in your sight line; so before you run for the police or security guards, a whistle of particular tune may serve as a homing device. Whistles, which are piercing, carry farther than shouts; and the sound can be followed to its origin. Children should carry identification with them at all times; the name and telephone number of the hotel at which you are staying; your name; the name of your daughter and son, and their home telephone number—just in case. Children should also know whom to approach if they are lost, and what the strategies are for being found again. A few strategies in the pocket may avoid big problems; it is easy to get lost in a strange place, but knowing what to do is one giant step toward being found.

One final note about preparing concerns a grandchild's special needs. If your grandchild requires special medication, you will want to insure that not only do these come along and in carry-on luggage, but that you have a prescription, in case the supply is lost. You will want to insure that allergy medications, if required, are close at hand; and that the environments you frequent will not exacerbate an allergic reaction. If your grandchild requires a special diet, you will want to make requests to airlines well in advance of your trip. Making preparations in advance for children with special needs can be critical to a safe, happy and healthful trip.

## En Route

Whether you are traveling by car, bus, train or plane, it is a very good idea to have some "en route" activities for grandchildren to do while on the journey. Especially if you are traveling with younger children, for whom looking out the window quickly loses its appeal, play activities that engage them and help them to pass the time are heartily recommended.

These activities don't have to break your travel budget. A blank drawing pad and some felt-tipped pens provide a variety of possibilities, from drawing, to writing, to playing games. A deck of cards is easy to pack, and offers several options. Grandchildren may be reminded to carry their CD players and earphones or pocket computer games. They may have other toys or games that would be suitable and they should be encouraged to take what they have that will keep them busy during long hours of confinement in a tiny space. There are several reference books that offer suggestions for how to occupy kids during extended journeys. One of these is *Kids Travel: A Backseat Survival Kit,* published by Klutz Press. It provides suggestions for entertaining the "backseat gang" for miles! Puzzles, songs, stories, quizzes and projects help keep children from getting too restless, and are likely to reduce the numbers of times you get asked, "Grandma, are we there yet?" Grandchildren should be encouraged to plan what they want to take on the trip, and these things should be added to their

backpacks, which can then be carried along and easily accessed. Older grandchildren pose few problems; they know what they want to take that will occupy them, and may spend all their traveling time with noses pressed into a computer magazine, or staring out the window, listening quietly to the latest CD.

If the journey is to be long (several hours) and constraining, it is probably a very good idea to have some snack food on hand. Fruit juices and other healthful snacks may fill the bill, as well as the stomach. As you prepare for the journey, you will no doubt ask yourself what your grandchild's particular needs are, what are the essentials, and how they might easily be filled, en route.

While I am a firm believer in making a trip with grandchildren as fun filled and pleasurable as possible, this in no way precludes setting behavioral expectations for travel. While I love my grandchildren with all my heart, this does not prevent me from stating, quite explicitly, what behavioral standards are acceptable on a journey. Not only are there other passengers to consider, but also the teaching and learning of social awareness and social responsibility does not end when the journey begins.

Even young children need to know that running up and down the aisles of airplanes is not appropriate, because it is simply not safe; that putting one's feet on the back of the seat of the person in front of you is annoying; that yelling, fighting, pushing and hyperactive behavior is unappreciated. Not only are these behaviors annoying to other passengers; they may create conditions that are hazardous for the children and for others around them. If you are traveling by car, for long distances, it is easy to stop every two hours for a long running, jumping, and yelling break! If you are traveling by bus, train or plane, a walk up the aisle every hour takes the edge off sitting, and gives the muscles a chance to stretch. If you are not traveling from Hong Kong to New York, an endless and exhausting trek, your journey will eventually result in the final A-ha! We're here!

## Grandpa, I've Gotta Have It!

Loving grandparents will find it hard to resist giving in to all requests from their grandchildren for every souvenir, every t-shirt, every model of the Empire State Building, every stuffed animal, every memento of the trip. If you do give in, and if you are not in the higher income brackets like Connie's "Grandmoney," you are likely to deplete your travel budget pretty quickly and have to hitchhike home.

To avert constant demands and the need to make on-the-spot "yes" or "no" decisions each time a request is made, some grandparents provide their traveling companion grandchildren an allowance for each day's expenditures. This is probably a better option than a fixed allowance for the whole trip, which could be depleted with a single purchase on the first day. (There's a lesson there, but you may not want to face the consequences of subsequent days' denials.) Your allowance should be realistic, in terms of the currency and local prices; but it should also be within what your budget will allow comfortably. Providing an allowance has other attractive features. Not only does it get you off the hook with respect to every request for funding; it also teaches lessons to your grandchildren of budgeting, economy, and of making choices about what's important.

If a daily allowance is given, grandchildren should have a safe place for keeping their money—and cautions should be given about how to keep money safe. These simple rules of the high finance of travel are learned best en route, and they are then learned for all time.

## E.T. Phone Home

There's nothing quite as exciting as calling home when grandkids are away on a big journey without their parents. There are stories to be told, each day's adventures to be narrated—all the fun experiences and the travails of the journey are grist for the conversation. But more

important, what a delicious treat to hear mommy's and daddy's voices and to give them a share of the experience. No matter what the age of the grandchildren, it's a good idea to take special care to make sure that phone calls to mom and dad are frequent and regular during your trip. All will be enriched by this small gesture.

## Eating Out: Beyond Peanut Butter and Jelly

Unless you are going camping with your grandchildren, where most of the meals are cooked at the campsite or in the trailer, the experience of eating out in restaurants is likely to present some interesting challenges—especially if the grandchildren are younger, and most especially, if any of them has any food idiosyncrasies. Choosing a restaurant, and finding one with a suitable menu, may take a few creative maneuvers—but the problems of feeding grandchildren on the road are far from insurmountable.

One of the first orders of business is to be aware, with real clarity, of the type of food that your grandchildren prefer. Among the younger set, there are generally a few "acceptables" in limited repertoires: spaghetti, hamburgers, hot dogs, sliced meat sandwiches, pizza, turkey, roast, fried, or barbecued chicken, and spare ribs. If you know your grandchildren's "faves," calling around to restaurants to find out what their menus offer will help you make good choices. Inquiring about possibilities from the hotel concierge or motel manager will usually net some good advice. Often, hotels and motels come equipped with sample menus from local restaurants, left on the bureau as advertising flyers. Once you have found a place that fills the bill, repeat visits are more than acceptable.

When traveling with my grandsons when they were younger and their food preferences bordered on the bizarre, I gave up early on trying to find restaurants that would accommodate my more sophisticated tastes with their more plebian ones, and just opted for places that would please them. I could always find something on the menu for myself—even though it was a far cry from haute cuisine.

If you are traveling to a larger city, there is likely to be a food guide available that will give you information about restaurants, and the type of food being served. The *Zagat* guides for large cities in the United States and Canada are unfailingly helpful. For travels in the Pacific Northwest, *Best Places* is one of the most comprehensive surveys around, containing not only listings for restaurants, but including references to special attractions for children. Many states, cites and countries have their own guides. A visit to the Travel section of your local bookstore will point you in the right direction. If you are going abroad, you may already have your own list of places to eat; if not, travel guides abound. Access to the *www.Amazon.com* website will give you lots of information about travel books for the destination you are planning, along with reader reviews of the helpfulness of each of the books you are considering. Most helpful, I find, are recommendations from friends who have already been there, and gone the route.

While you will find that restaurant options are plentiful, I always think it is a good idea to bring the grandchildren into the loop when making a decision about a place to eat. This has many important advantages. Children are made to feel an important part of the process and they learn that their opinions and feelings are respected. They can contribute to making an informed decision, based on the data being considered. Being part of the process is enormously empowering. Of course, it must be a group decision—with all voters negotiating to yes. Even when children have the vote, they should in no way be permitted to overrule the strong preferences of their grandparents, who, after all, are wiser, more knowledgeable, and still paying the bills.

When all else fails, there is always the possibility of having pizza delivered to the room—maybe not exactly what you had in mind for yourself, but generally an acceptable standby for younger grandchil-

dren. With grown grandchildren whose food tastes have evolved with age, they are likely to be telling you where *they'd* like to go and what *they'd* prefer to eat! You need only to insure that the prices are within what your travel budget allows.

Even if you are not on a camping trip, where a mid-day snack is always accessible, you will want to make sure that when traveling with younger grandchildren you have some food on hand in your room. Something that doesn't necessarily require refrigeration—like a jar of peanut butter, crackers, fruit juices, fruit, and other snacks. Some children like to eat often—perhaps it's because they are growing so fast—and having something on hand can avert crisis when shops are closed or inaccessible. Better to be prepared!

## Trips Galore

One of the reasons for taking trips with grandchildren is to invite them to share in experiences we have had and loved, or experience together for the first time. We want to introduce them into our worlds—what's fun; what's beautiful; what's historic; what's important; what's just plain wonderful. When I traveled to San Francisco, arguably one of the most beautiful cities in North America, I used to send my (then) young grandchildren postcards with pictures of the cable cars, and the message: "One day, I want to bring you here and we'll all go for a ride on the cable car." It was my dream to bring my grandchildren into my experiences, to expand their horizons, to share with them what I enjoyed. In these ways, I built up their expectations for travel, and their anticipation of what good things were yet to come.

We've logged a few trips together over the years—Disneyland, the San Diego Zoo, New York City and its many attractions, Disneyworld, San Francisco. There are many places to go and many ways to get there. What follows in this section are some suggestions for where and how—from my own imagination and stories from other traveling grandparents. When you add your own dreams for sharing personal experiences with your grandkids, your list will grow immeasurably.

## Camping

One of the dreams that Grandpa Ruby had was to own an RV and spend months camping, during his retirement. When his grand-daughter Melissa came of an age to spend an extended holiday with her grandparents, a two-week camping trip was planned. The trip would center around visits to four different hot spring sites. Melissa was brought into the planning early on; maps were used to show the parts of the journey, and reservations made early for securing camp-sites en route. Melissa brought some of her favorite toys, books and games, so she would not be bored during the days on the road. Grandpa planned the trip so that the traveling days ended early—and no one felt totally exhausted from an overlong drive. Each afternoon, Melissa's help was enlisted in setting up the campsite, getting dinner ready and cleaning up. Melissa learned to fish and caught her first trout, which was cleaned and eaten that evening for dinner. Best of all, four hot spring sites, the culmination of four small journeys, gave respite to weary travelers and a focus to the journey.

Traveling by RV or camper is one of the pleasures of many grand-parents, and bringing grandchildren along is an obvious way to share experiences. Camping holds many opportunities for grandkids—and there is much to be learned, as well as enjoyed, on a camping trip. The United States and Canada are rich in natural parks, campgrounds and campsites in some of the most spectacularly beautiful geographical areas. Wildlife abounds, and the scenery can be breathtaking. If you are a camper and enjoy the recreational activities of the out-of-doors, camping is a "natural" way of sharing a holiday with grandchildren.

## Other Out-of-Doors Possibilities

There are lots of out-of-doors possibilities for holidays with grand-children. While a major expenditure, skiing, for those who love the rush of downhill, is exciting and challenging. Resorts and inns offer cross country skiing as well, which gives a chance to see more of the

outdoors during the winter months. Hiking, for the more rugged, provides opportunities to get closer to the land, see the flora and fauna, and engage in some serious exercise. Whale watching, for those of us who live near the coasts, is a chance to see these wondrous mammals in their natural habitats.

Grandparents who are boaters and sailors might consider first short, and then longer, holidays aboard with their grandchildren. Like camping, boating offers opportunity for children to "learn the ropes" about boats, become more experienced sailors and learn a healthy respect for the sea.

Grandpa Bill has been taking his two grandsons to the beach at St. Augustine every summer since they were very young. There, the children have learned not only how to swim and build sand castles, but also have become voracious readers since many of their days at the beach are pleasurably spent reading fiction. Now, when they go to St. Augustine, the first item on their list is the library books that will accompany them!

Grandparents Loretta and Marv made a historic bicycle trip across Canada, from coast to coast! While their grandchild was too young to make such a journey, it is not impossible to consider an extended bicycle trip with older grandchildren, if two-wheel transportation is "your thing" and you are up to the rigors of marathon bicycling.

When traveling with grandkids, remember to "take a break" yourself.

## Historic Sites

Historic sites are plentiful in North America and one can make a career of attempting to visit them all! If it is your plan to visit historic sites with your grandchildren, my advice is to select carefully, to bring the grandchildren into the planning stage, and to make sure that what you are planning falls within the interests and the experience of the young travelers. Visits to historic sites are a wonderful way of learning about a country's history—and should be taken when the children are old enough to understand both the significance of history, and the relationship of what you are seeing to the historic event. Some advance planning, prior to the trip, is seriously recommended.

## Amusement Parks, Theme Parks, Amusement-Shopping Malls, and other Entertainment Centers

Is there a child in North America who hasn't dreamed of going to Disneyland or Disneyworld? Or to West Edmonton Mall? Or to. . . ? (You fill in the blank!) If this is your grandchild's biggest wish, and if it is within your means, such a holiday can make for a dream come true. But if you do not live geographically close to the site, such a trip will involve considerable expense, time, and energy. Amusement centers can fill the children's day entirely; and you should plan to spend several days at the sites, as there is much to see and do. The caveat is: Bring a lot of money.

## Major Cities

Of the many cities that one can take children to, there are several that stand out as exceptional and worth considering as a holiday destination. New York is a once-in-a-lifetime experience for children. It is, arguably, the city that everyone should see at least once. Two weeks is barely enough to scratch the surface of what is available—museums, historic societies, art, theater, shops. Just walking the streets is fun and exciting. San Francisco offers much, but on a smaller scale; and the views are unsurpassed! Los Angeles and San Diego both have many wonderful attractions for children. The variety of historic sites and museums in Washington, D.C. is exceptional; the Smithsonian itself is worth the trip! Vancouver, B.C. is a holiday paradise during the summer months. You will, doubtless, have your own special cities, with special attractions that are worth sharing with grandchildren. And of course, there's always Paris!

## Cruises

From the windows of my home, I see the cruise ships in port each summer, beginning in May and extending through the end of September. These are the Alaska cruise lines only and there are forty-eight ships that make this trip each week! Given that each of them carries more than a thousand passengers, that's a lot of cruising!

Many ships offer special deals for grandparents traveling with grandchildren, and if this is what you are looking for, you should check out the options. One of the advantages of cruising is that all the recreational facilities are self-contained. Everything is at your fingertips, and you will have no worries about finding a restaurant, transportation, or of selecting a destination for the day. All has already been organized for you. If you are looking for an "easy" way of traveling with grandchildren to scenery that is quite literally awe-inspiring, and you like the feeling of being totally pampered en route, you might do worse than considering cruising.

## Take a Break, Mona

Before embarking on our first holiday together accompanied by our grandchildren, my daughter warned me in advance. "They will make you tired. They will run you ragged! Don't forget to schedule some rest and relaxation for yourself—otherwise, you will be exhausted!" Her words of advice were worth heeding. Even though I have a great deal of stamina, I nevertheless found that I needed some quiet time each day—free from the constant exercising of due caution when we were "on the march." Like many other grandparents, I renew my energy supply from rest and quiet. Making sure that I got some every day was critical for my mental and physical health on the trip. As much as we love them, having to pay constant attention to our grandchildren can be exhausting; and grandparents are entitled to replenish their resources, and make some time for themselves.

The logistics of arranging this are not difficult. I find that the best approach is the direct one: "Grandma needs to have an hour of quiet time now, you guys—so you have some choices of what to do during this time. When I've rested, we'll go on to [whatever activity is scheduled next]." My grandsons never objected to this; in fact, they honored my request and found things to do which interested them. My hunch is that they, too, appreciated a little "down time" and were grateful that this was included in the schedule.

Now that our boys are at the age where they can go off on their own, I find that giving them this freedom not only is good for them, but also allows me to take a needed break. When they do take off, however, I give them my cell phone, for my own peace of mind, since wherever they decide to wander, I can still maintain that slender thread of connection. It just makes me feel better to know that they are safe.

## Off to the Wilds!

A dear friend, and grandfather of two, is planning to take his grandchildren, ages six and nine, to the Galapagos next spring. This is serious traveling, but he is preparing well and carefully, and the children have been learning about the unique and extraordinary animals they will find there. It may be the trip of a lifetime—but knowing Grandpa Buddy it's hard to know what he has up his sleeve for next year!

You don't have to take your grandchildren to the ends of the earth to include them in your holiday experiences. Less extravagant travel plans, where they are invited to share with you some of the things YOU enjoy, and some of the attractions you'd like to see, work equally well. When long distance grandparents invite grandchildren to share in and enjoy the trips that they enjoy, these journeys can serve as one more means of bridging the distances between you.

# 16

# Grandparent to Grandparent

A WAVE OF responses from grandparents who have read the earlier editions of this book makes it clear that the subject of long distance grandparenting, from the perspective of grandparents, their children, and their grandchildren, touches an important chord in families who live apart, and that relationships at distance are never free from the pain of longing to be close. While some grandparents generously shared ingenious ideas they had invented to bridge the distance between them and their loved ones, others raised heartaching questions about seemingly insurmountable problems.

This chapter includes some of these messages—the different ways of reaching out, problems in relationships near and far, and the ways we have each learned to cope with our longing.

## Marketplace of Ideas

A letter from a grandmother who lives in Phoenix included some new ideas for using tapes:

I don't have much of a voice, and I don't even play the piano very well, but it didn't matter. When my grandson and granddaughter, aged four and six, were here, their grandad and I took them to see Snow White and the Seven Dwarfs. We enjoyed trying to sing the songs together at home. When the children left, I wanted them to remember their visit, and I thought it would be fun to make a tape for them with the songs. I played, sang, and taped our favorite songs from Snow White, and sent it to the kids. And even though it was strictly amateur, they loved them!

A grandmother from Dallas wrote to tell about how she follows up the children's visits with letters and notes that recall special highlights of their time together. She gives an example:

When the boys were here last, one of them had fun reading me a poem about "The froggies jumping on the bed." And his brother fell in love with the expression, "And that's the truth, Ruth." So I cut out two long strips of paper, and on one, I wrote, "No more froggies jumping on the bed." And on the other, "And that's the truth, Ruth." I put these into envelopes and sent them to the grandchildren. When I do that, it helps me to remember our happy times, and I think it does the same for them.

A student at university wrote to suggest that the ideas in *The Long Distance Grandmother* be extended to include other long distance relations—for example, aunts, uncles, stepsisters and stepbrothers. Her letter said, "Your ideas should not be limited to long distance grandparents only! My young stepbrothers live far from me and I have been trying to think of ways, besides letters, to keep in touch with them between my twice-a-year visits to their home. I've started to write short stories for them, and I illustrate them, even though my drawings are so gross! But I love doing that, and I get such a sense of satisfaction from it. And they love to get my stories."

One grandmother who lives in Toronto sent several letters describ-

*Your creative endeavors will earn you more than rich and satisfying relationships with your grandchildren.*

*Send your version of popular show-time songs.*

How do you send hugs and kisses through the mail? Mould lips out of plasticine; stuff arms with soft scraps.

ing the many ways she has of reaching out to her two beloved granddaughters who live in the Yukon. That is a dickens of a commute. When she became a grandmother, she received from a friend a framed poster with this message:

*You don't have to live close to be close!*
*Loving, thoughtful, imaginative grandparents*
*Really live in the hearts of their grandchildren.*

It became a way of life to find ways of being close to her grandgirls, in spite of the four thousand miles that separated them. "And so began my saga of keeping in touch with my family," she says. "In the last six years, I have become a collector of beautiful garbage—such wonderful things to make for little kiddies. With my scissors and paste pot and magazines, I'm off and running. My husband says it is more therapy for me than laughs for the grandchildren. Such masterpieces would made Grandma Moses sit up and notice!"

These grandparents are only able to see their granddaughters about every ten months, but when they visit them, "the kiddies stay with us in a motel, and we have ice cream *before* they go off to school in the morning, and we *tell* the mommy and daddy all about it. Who gets ice cream *before* school if you see your grandparents regularly?"

Some suggestions for using "beautiful garbage" to keep in touch:

• I make little scrapbooks. Each page has a picture, cut out of a magazine, that I think has some special appeal for my girls. Sometimes I stick a piece of gum, or another sweet treat, right on the page.

• From newspapers (grocery ads are great for this) I cut out the number of the child's birthday (for example, I cut out all the different sevens), and make a birthday card, with the numbers pasted all over it.

• We have a game called "Finger Time." You just can't help wanting to hug and kiss the children all the time, so we play "Finger Time." If we're visiting, when Grandma, or Grandpa, or one of the children calls "Finger Time," we all hug and kiss and touch fingers, and then go back to whatever it is we are doing. And I collect pictures of fingers, and every piece of mail I send includes fingers. There are so many pictures around of hands! I even found a hand stamp! We took pictures of touching fingers, and put these up on the refrigerator. When we're talking to each other on the telephone, we're supposed to go to the fridge and touch the picture whenever one of us says "Finger Time." (All these finger pictures are pasted on recycled envelopes and cards.)

• I had read a real cute suggestion about having kids lie on the floor, and have someone trace their arms on a newspaper to send "hugs" to grandparents. So when we were visiting the grandchildren, I traced their arms myself, and took the tracings home with me. Then, I told them I'd send them my arms just as soon as I returned home. I made a long hot-dog-like pair of arms, out of corduroy, stuffed them with tissue paper and plastic bags, and then decorated them with junk from the sewing box. I even found a little frame to sew on with my picture in it.

These are only some of the vast numbers of creative, ingenious ideas that flow from the fertile minds of grandparents. Here are some others:

A grandfather from New York, himself a professional musician, made an entire series of tapes with music that he felt appropriate to his grandson's different stages of growth. For example, when the grandchild was only a few months old, grandad made tapes of lullabies and other gentle-sounding, sleep inducing tunes. During toddler years, tapes were made of music with strong, rhythmic beats, so that grandson could clap or march or dance along with the music.

How much sweeter is that card, that letter, that gesture of affection, when it arrives unasked for.

Now that the boy is past six, grandpa is building up the musical repertoire with melodies from Mozart, Bach, Beethoven. Developing a love of music across the miles? Why not?!

"It works both ways, you know," a teenage grandson from Los Angeles told me. "My grandparents have been very important in my life. They were always there for me when I needed them. When everything in my own life was breaking apart, when my parents were getting a divorce, it was my grandparents who represented stability and support. Now that I'm older, and they are older too, I have a chance to do something for them in return. They live in a retirement village, too far for me to visit very often, but I make sure I reach out to them often, so that they know that I love them and am thinking of them. It's easy to remember to send a picture postcard at least once a week. We've got this shop in town that sells these hilarious cards—they're not gross or anything like that, but really whimsical. And I always write just a few "dumb" words, just to add to the humor. I know they get a kick out of the cards and I know they feel good to know I'm thinking about them."

"The most important thing I can do now that I'm grown and my grandad is in his eighties, is to get his 'stories,'" wrote an adult grandson from Pittsburgh. "Every time I go to visit, which is not often because of the travel involved, I bring my tape recorder and ask grandad to tell about his life as a kid, when he was growing up, when he married grandma—all that stuff. I know he's not going to be around for very much longer, but I'll always have his stories and the sound of his voice. It adds to our family history, like photos in an album."

A good way to overcome a fear of technology is to turn the "on" switch.

"My granddaughter, who is eight, is very interested in science and math," tells a grandfather from Vancouver, "so when I write to her, I like to send ideas for math and science projects for her to think about and to do. My own background in these fields is quite limited, but I can get good ideas from books I find in the library. In each letter, I include a suggestion like some of these:

• Try to figure out a good way to measure your hand. Try to figure out a good way to measure your head. Try to figure out a good way to measure your feet. Write and tell me how you did it.

• Try to figure out how fast a bird flies. Write to me and tell me how you did it.

• Go into the garden and see how many different kinds of insects you can observe. Make a drawing of an insect and send it to me.

• How may different birds can you spot in one day? Make a list of your birds and send it to me. Maybe you can make a drawing of your favorite bird.

"You have to be an extrovert to do this," wrote one grandmother from Miami, Florida, "but it works for us. We have a Camcorder and we gave another for my son for his birthday. Now, we are able to make and send videotapes to each other. At first, we weren't very creative about what we recorded and sent. But now we're getting more inventive and having even more fun. If we are doing something special in our community, we videotape that to send to the kids. For example, if we dress up in costumes for the community Halloween party, we film that and do some clowning, too. We'll film grandpa in the pool, doing his laps, or grandma doing a lip-synch with a Madonna record. In return, we get videos of our grandchildren at birthday parties, learning to ski, riding their bikes. When we get lonely for the sight of their adorable faces, grandad and I sit down and watch one of their tapes. Then we have a good cry and we feel better."

It's clear that there are many, many ways in which grandparents reach out to their grandchildren, and it's not so important what form the ideas take, or how elegantly or amateurishly they are executed.

Out of sight, out of mind. Perhaps not for you, but in the constantly shifting and changing world of children there is much that competes for their attention. Stay in touch.

When the message is "I love you, I am thinking of you, you may be miles away, but you are in my heart," whatever you send will do the job of keeping you close.

## Reaping What We Sow

The burden of developing and maintaining the long-distance relationship with younger grandchildren falls, of course, upon the grandparents. If we wish to take these steps, we can build warm and loving relationships with our grandchildren, even at distance. If we do not take the steps, grandchildren will have no chance of knowing us at all, as this mother's story shows:

My husband's father lives in California. He's been to our home several times, and we've visited him there, too, but beyond that he's never taken any pains to build a warm and personal connection with the children. It's too bad, too, because he is their only grandparent. When we learned that he had had a heart attack and was not expected to live, we told the children about his illness, but we weren't prepared for their response. They didn't seem to care! They shrugged the news off as if we were talking about some person they'd never heard of. I was stunned. When I gathered myself together and asked them why, my son, who is eleven years old, answered, "I don't even know him." My daughter, aged fourteen, agreed. "I'm sad that he's ill and I'm sorry for you and dad. But really, mom, he's a stranger to me." Through my anger and sadness I pondered this. Grandad had been to visit us a few times. We had been there a few times, to keep the connection alive. Yet these visits were not enough. I think it's because that's all there was—an occasional visit, and a card at Christmas and at birthdays. He *was* a stranger to them.

Another grandmother writes, "Last month, when we visited the kids, now four-and-a-half and seven-and-a-half, I felt certain that

258

they felt a closeness to us that wouldn't be there after a year away, if we hadn't been sending all those priceless parcels. I really feel that there should be special 'granny postage' rates!"

What grandparents actually send to bridge the gap of distance, whether it be letters, tapes, games, or stories, or even "beautiful junk," is not so important as the act of sending itself, and the frequency of keeping in touch. When we can send these messages of love, and do this regularly, we *are* able to create those close personal bonds that would more easily occur if we lived nearby. When we fail to reach out, we stand to lose that precious relationship, and we are the poorer for it.

## Problems in Long Distance Relationships

There are as many interpersonal problems in human relationships as there are waves in the ocean. When two people form a bond, be they husband and wife, friend and friend, grandparent and grandchild—there will be tensions, conflicts, and problems that run the gamut from, "She always leaves her stockings dripping from the shower," to "My grandmother is losing her eyesight and I feel so bad about it. I don't know what to say to her when she calls and tells me that she cannot see to read or knit any more." Sometimes these interpersonal tensions are lumped together as "problems in communication." Perhaps that is because dealing with them effectively requires good communication skills. However, putting a label on what is wrong does little to help resolve the problem. Such conflicts can also result when people are unable to "see the problem from the other person's point of view."

Grandparents, their grown children, and their grandchildren will inevitably (even in the very best of relationships) come up against problems that strain the relationship. But when the lines of communication are open, when problems can be dealt with in loving, and non-defensive ways, when all parties can appreciate how it feels to be in the other person's shoes, we have a much better chance of a happy

If you can say how you feel you are half-way to solving the problem.

resolution. When the interpersonal crisis is muddied with angry accusations, rigid expectations, defensiveness, and an inability to be sensitively aware of the other person's feelings, the likelihood is that everyone in the situation will lose. That is, the "sparring" players will retreat to neutral corners, but each will feel a victim—misunderstood, hurt, resentful.

Both in the letters I receive and during talks to grandparent groups, I have encountered many painful questions—and for all, there are no simple answers. Yet, following the guidelines of openness, non-defensiveness, and a willingness to experience the situation from the other's point of view will help a good deal towards understanding how to deal with the conflicts.

Though you may have questions about your own relationships that are not included here, I hope that the dialogues that follow may help you develop your own resolutions.

## When Grandparents Come to Visit

*Question:* My daughter-in-law just gave birth to her second child. Naturally, I wanted to be there. So did her mother. With two sets of grandparents, both coming from distant cities, I was worried that this would be too much for her, what with the new baby and a four year-old to look after. So I told her that Dad and I would make arrangements to stay at a nearby motel during our visit. She said that she wanted us to stay with them, and she would find a way to put us up, and make us comfortable. I thought of how I would feel in her place, and decided it was really best that we stay at the motel. Do you think we were slighting her by refusing her offer?

*Response:* Your decision was thoughtful and considerate of your daughter-in-law and son. Very few households can stand the stresses created by adding two more adults for a long-term stay, let alone four. Add to this the stresses of a new baby, and the likelihood that your

Visiting grandparents can be an added burden to households turned upside down by the arrival of a second or third child. Alternative accommodation may be wise.

daughter-in-law is not yet herself physically, and it's clear her invitation may have been more generous than wise.

If by now she is still feeling somewhat miffed because you refused her offer, it's a good idea to write to her, or to talk to her on the telephone to explain to her why you chose to stay at the motel, rather than in her home. Once she understands that you did this out of consideration for her and for the rest of the family, and if you do this in a way that is responsive to her feelings ("I know you really would have liked us to stay with you, and under normal circumstances, we would have loved to.") I'm sure she will appreciate your thoughtful gesture.

## Grandparents and Treats

*Question:* When I go to visit my grandchildren, which is not too often, I love to take them out and give them special treats, like cookies, ice cream, and candy. The children love these sweets. Their mother (my daughter-in-law) has told me that I should not buy them sweets any more. She says they are bad for their teeth and she doesn't want them to get a "sweet tooth." Since I only come to visit them about every six months, I don't see how it's possible for them to get bad teeth from such rare occasions for treats. Do you think my daughter-in-law is being unreasonable? Shouldn't a grandmother be allowed to give grandchildren special treats on their infrequent visits?

*Response:* It's natural for grandparents to want to indulge their grandchildren with candies and other treats, especially when they only see them every six months! On the other hand, it's natural for parents to be concerned about their children's dental health and well being. So you've got a dilemma. The fact that your sweet treats come only occasionally apparently doesn't satisfy your daughter-in-law, who feels that even occasional sweets can be harmful to children's teeth, or perhaps make it hard for the children to return to the family

Mom and Dad's child-rearing practices and house-rules may seem strange or unreasonable to you.

Don't be afraid to set rules in your own home.

In order for grand-
children to be able to
process their feelings,
it is important that you
be open and honest
about death, debilata-
tive illnesses and
senility.

rules after your visit. Unfortunately for you, in the case of raising children, and especially in the case of children's health and well being, it's
Mom and Dad who make the rules. Whether you love it or not,
grandparents have to play by these rules. Can you find other treats for
the children that will satisfy both your need to treat them, and the
parent' rules about sweets? How about other kinds of treats like going
to the zoo, or the water park, or the aquarium? How about the
movies, story time at the library, a ride on the trolley, or the rapid
transit? Talk to your daughter-in-law, too, and see if you can come to
some kind of compromise on what non-sweet treat-foods would be
allowable. Perhaps pop corn? Hot dogs? Pretzels? Nuts? Children do
love to munch on something, and perhaps if the two of you can talk
together, you might come up with some goodies that will satisfy the
children, and your need to treat them, and meet the parents' rules.

## Coping with Visiting Grandchildren

*Question:* When the grandchildren come to visit us, it doesn't take two
minutes before the house is in a mess! Toys everywhere! Clothes lying
about in the living room. Shouts and screams and fights! I feel as if I
have been invaded, and the aliens have landed and occupied my territory. There's nowhere to retreat. I want the children to come. I want
them to love coming to our house. But after two days, I'm a nervous
wreck. Is there a middle ground between no visits and total chaos?

*Response:* It's clear that your grandchildren's visits are becoming
more and more of a burden. And you are becoming more resentful of
the way their toys are scattered everywhere, of their habits of leaving
their clothes around, and of the noise they make. Between their behavior and their complete takeover of your home, you feel driven right up
the wall. In your heart of hearts, you may be wondering if they should-
n't have been brought up to have better manners!

It won't help much to point out that such troublesome behaviors do diminish as children get older. Your problem is now: how to cope and make the visits less stressful for you.

It does not harm your grandchildren to tell them that there are some rules that are followed in your home. First, toys are put away when the playtime is over. Explain to them that this is important, because it is not only dangerous to leave them about (someone may trip and fall), but because you like a tidy house! It's all right for you to like a tidy house, and it is perfectly within your rights to make these rules! You also might expect clothes to be folded and put away. Noise is to be held at decibel levels that do not shatter your ears.

Even young children are amenable to such rules; children are not hurt nor are their rights trampled on when they are asked to follow reasonable and legitimate requests. Loving one's grandchildren does not have to include letting them have free and uncontrolled reign in one's home.

These are not, of course, the only rules that might be appropriate. Other households, with different points of view, might establish different rules. What is important, however, is how you communicate these messages to them. When you can tell them what the rules are and give your reasons for asking them, and when you can do so without heavy-handed tones of martyrdom or built-up anger, then children are not likely to suffer a bit in having to live by them. By all means, tell your spirited grandchildren that you have these needs when they visit, and tell them directly, honestly, and without reproach. They may surprise you by living up to your highest expectations.

## When a Grandparent Dies

*Question:* My husband has cancer and is not expected to live very much longer. While we live fifteen hundred miles from our grandchildren, ages six and nine, we have had a close and loving relationship with them. I need some advice on how to break the hard news to them.

Many people are unaware of how hurtful their words and actions are. Gently letting them know can clear the path to a more enjoyable relationship.

*Response:* There is, unhappily no good way to break sad news. Your grandchildren will feel the pain of this loss. It is reasonable that you want to spare them that pain, but when you love, there is always pain when the love is lost. The alternative is not to love, and that is a very poor option.

In breaking the news about Grandfather's death, I believe it is very important to be honest and direct, while at the same time being supportive and loving. The children will likely have questions that they want answers to, and truths, although difficult to bear, are a better policy than fictions. In all of this, I think it is essential that children be allowed to express their feelings, to cry if they need to, and to mourn their loss naturally. To tell them "not to feel bad," or "not to cry," is to deny what children feel, and such an approach is likely to lead to deeper and more prolonged hurt.

Time and distance will make the loss more endurable, and it will be very therapeutic if children, parents, and grandmother can remember together the happy times they all had with Grandfather, to cherish his memory in their hearts.

You yourself may wish to consider an emotional support group to help with the difficult time of your own bereavement. Perhaps with that help, you may be even better able to help your grandchildren. While talking out one's feelings seems hardly enough to ease the pain, it is the healthiest way known to cope with the tragedy of the death of a loved one.

## Coping with a Grandfather's Criticism

*Question:* When I hear that my grandfather is coming to visit from Florida, I already start to worry. I know he is going to start asking me what my marks are in school, and why I don't clean up my room, and how come I'm not helping my mother with the dishes. He's on my case all the time, and I feel that he's watching me, just waiting for me to mess up, so he can say, "Gotcha!" Why does my grandfather have to be

Don't forget that your special needs grandchild has able brothers and sisters who need to feel special too.

so critical of me? He always seems to be ready to point out all my faults, which I admit are many, but he never remembers to appreciate the good things I do. I'm not such a bad kid, even though I'm only twelve years old. What can I say to him that will get him off my case?

*Response:* It's getting harder and harder for you to anticipate your grandfather's visit with any pleasure. You are full of worry about how he is going to find fault with you this time! He seems to want to pounce on your every move, criticizing you for not doing a good job and making you feel small, stupid and inadequate. It sounds as if you are becoming more and more resentful of the way he treats you. He's your grandfather, after all. He *should* know that there are wonderful things about you and he *should* remember to appreciate them.

It's disappointing to you, and you wish that he would behave differently. It's probably hard for you to tell him how you feel, but if you could, that might help a lot. Hearing it directly from you, for example, "Oh, Grandad, it makes me feel terrible when you pick on me like that," might help him to see your situation more clearly. If you can't bring yourself to tell him (and it *is* a hard thing to do), you might talk to your parents about it. Perhaps they are the ones who will be able to tell your grandfather to lighten up, to tune down his excessive criticisms, to remember to appreciate you more. Maybe he just needs to be told how much you resent his behavior and that you are beginning to resent him, too. Maybe he needs to hear that directly, if he is to change his ways.

## Dealing with Favoritism

*Question:* My grandmother has always been partial to my brother. She says it's because he has "special needs" and he needs more attention than I do. I know he is special because he is disabled. I wish my grandmother would know that I'd like her to think I'm special, too. Is there a way I can get her to know how I feel?

*Response:* It's hard for you to find yourself as "second best" when it

Child abuse is every-
one's business. If you
have suspicions, act
on them.

comes to how your grandmother treats you and your brother. She has singled him out for special treatment because of his disability and you are not getting the special attention that you'd like, too, from her. You may have even begun to believe that your grandmother loves your brother more than she loves you.

There is a very good chance that your grandmother does not know that you feel neglected by her, and would like more of her time and attention. While telling her your feelings is hard to do (you'd probably like it better if she knew this without your having to tell her so), you may want to find a way to let her know. She may be very glad that you did, since it's unlikely that she wants to hurt you by her behavior. She may not realize how unequally she has been giving her time and love. You could help her by telling her that you love her, and that you, too, would like more of her special attention.

## Differences in Lifestyle that Cause Problems

*Question:* My beautiful granddaughter has turned into a teenager! Her hair looks like it is made of steel wires, and she has shaved off parts of her hair over her ears! She wears three earrings in each ear! Her clothes look like she has bought them at an outer space rummage sale! She talks a language I can barely understand! I keep telling her that she is hiding her beautiful self under this bizarre costume, but she always tells me, "Oh, Gram, you don't understand anything!" Am I crazy, or is she?

*Response:* When you see your very attractive granddaughter wearing clothes and hairstyle that, according to your standards, take away from her natural beauty, you wonder about her reasons for this kind of costuming. It seems incredible to you that teenagers might choose to look "weird" when they could look beautiful. Seeing your granddaughter this way is very distressing for you.

It's hard for grandparents and even parents to understand a

teenager's need for a separate identity. This is a time when many teens seem to reject altogether the values of their parents and become members of "weird-looking" peer groups. Most teens go through a time of rebellion in appearance, in speech, in their decisions—all of which causes great consternation among the adults.

You may remember when you were a teen. Maybe you didn't spike your hair, but I'll bet something you did gave your parents problems! What about your son (daughter) when they were teens? How did they show you their need for independence? Your granddaughter also, through her "weird" choice of hair and clothes style, is trying to show her independence. When such choices are not dangerous to the child herself or to others, we don't have to love the choices, but we may find it healthier all around to voice our protests with grace and a sense of humor. If you are harshly critical, especially if you see her on infrequent visits, you may alienate her, cause deep resentment, and even worse, drive her into more rebellious actions. The good news is that in a few years, your granddaughter will grow out of her rebellious teens. Fortunately for us adults, the teenage years do not last forever!

## Long Distance Grandparents and Child Abuse

Among the many letters I received was one that asked for help with the tragic problem of child abuse. It seems only yesterday that child abuse was considered rare—a remote occurrence in some distant community. Yet, today, we know of abused children in frighteningly large numbers.

What should grandparents do if they suspect grandchildren are being abused? What role should a grandparent play in determining if a child is a victim? What should be done if suspicions prove accurate?

A long distance grandparent may not need radar to detect if grandchildren are at risk. Even infrequent visits can yield information. If you are picking up danger signals and are worried, but not sure, a visit to confirm is necessary. It's better to find out right away, than to have regrets later.

Any sign of hard to explain bodily injury is a cause for alarm. Multiple bruises are a three-alarm signal. Unusual cuts, bruises, and burns, or clear physical neglect, such as unattended medical needs, should be investigated. If you have suspicions, report them. Every city and town in the United States and Canada has access to a hot line for such reports. (See page 000 in the Resources section.) If the services you contact recognize any signs of abuse, they will consult with supervisors who will arrange that the child's situation be assessed within 24–48 hours of the report.

For children in such danger, grandparents may be their only reliable haven, and their responsibility to the child is clear. Report your concerns to a professional trained for the job of identifying child abuse, and let them evaluate what action should be taken. In taking such decisive action, you will face the dilemma of divided loyalties. You may worry that you will be cut off from both the family and the child. But failing to report will risk the health and well being of your grandchild. The professionals in this line of work are all agreed: You must report your suspicions.

You will have some very tough decisions to make if you are certain that a father or stepfather is being abusive, and that the mother, as sometimes happens, has ignored the evidence, keeping up a pretense that "nothing is wrong." You must decide if it's a better plan to try to open the mother's eyes to reality, or by-pass her altogether. There are no rules to follow, other than the cardinal rule about protecting the life and health of the child. If the mother knows, but is terrified of disclosing the situation to the authorities, you can be her ally and partner in determining the most appropriate course of action. If the situation is reversed, and the mother is abusive, the same suggestions are offered. Try to find out if the father will become your ally in protecting the child, and in seeking professional help for the mother. Determine if you have to by-pass the father in order to bring the situation to the attention of the authorities. You will agonize about what you must do, and you will worry about what this is going to mean to your ongoing relationship with the child. Yet, you cannot choose *not* to act when the life and health of your grandchild is at risk.

There may be a thin line dividing the actions of an "interfering" grandparent and a grandparent's legitimate concern about welfare and safety. Before making a report ask yourself these serious questions: Is what I see a difference in child-raising values between my grown children and me? Or is this a sign that my grandchild is being neglected in fundamental ways?

There may be psychological rather than physical difficulties for the child. The child may be frightened, anxious, highly subdued, or extremely withdrawn. If the child does not appear to be in immediate danger, family counseling can help. If you, yourself, are in doubt, there are professionals who can advise you. That's what the hotline numbers are for. (See page 269 in the Resources section.)

What do grandparents do who live with such tragedy? In some extreme instances, they may be called upon to act as parent surrogates, and to provide shelter for the grandchildren. When the children continue to live with their parents, grandparents can nevertheless play a key supportive role. Finally, grandparents may seek out support groups of other grandparents with similar problems. (Such groups do exist across the United States and Canada. Check with your local Seniors' center or community center.) It can help a great deal to learn that you are not alone, to share some of your grief and anguish with people who care.

Some grandparents are role models for their grandchildren, who then carry parts of their grandparents within their beings all of their lives. But in some extreme situations, grandparents can make the difference between life and death for their grandchildren.

Children grow up all too quickly, but they needn't grow apart from you. All it takes is a little effort and a little creativity to forge fast and lasting bonds with your long distance grandchildren.

269

## Postscript

Over the years it has taken to produce four editions of this book my grandchildren have grown from toddlers to young adults. Simon, having graduated from Grade 12 in June, is going to be living on his own (arrrrggggghhhh!) and studying new media computer design in a post-secondary school in Vancouver. Arlo, now in Grade 12, is already writing applications for university. I have missed being a constant presence in their growing-up years, and there was so much more I wanted to share with them, but the bonds we have forged in our long distance relationship are solid. This much I know to be true: we are good friends and good companions and we take great pleasure from being together. Their feelings for me could not be stronger if I had, in fact, lived down the block.

Long distance grandparenting means a lot of lost opportunities to be there to watch and feel joy in each special new day, each new growth stage, each new accomplishment. These are only some of the prices we pay for the hard and sometimes unendurable fact of the miles that distance us.

But as I have learned from my own experience, distance in miles does not have to mean distance in our feelings for each other. There are ways to build closer relationships that do not depend on close physical proximity. We may not have it all, but what we can have, through these relatively simple, but active involvements, will, nonetheless, bring our grandchildren closer to us, in spirit and in the heart—where it really counts.

"Grandma," Arlo says, hugging me close before he boards the plane that will take him back home from his three-day visit to see us, "you make your grandchildren very happy."

"Dearest," I tell him, trying not to weep, "it's my job."

# Resources

## Easy lettering

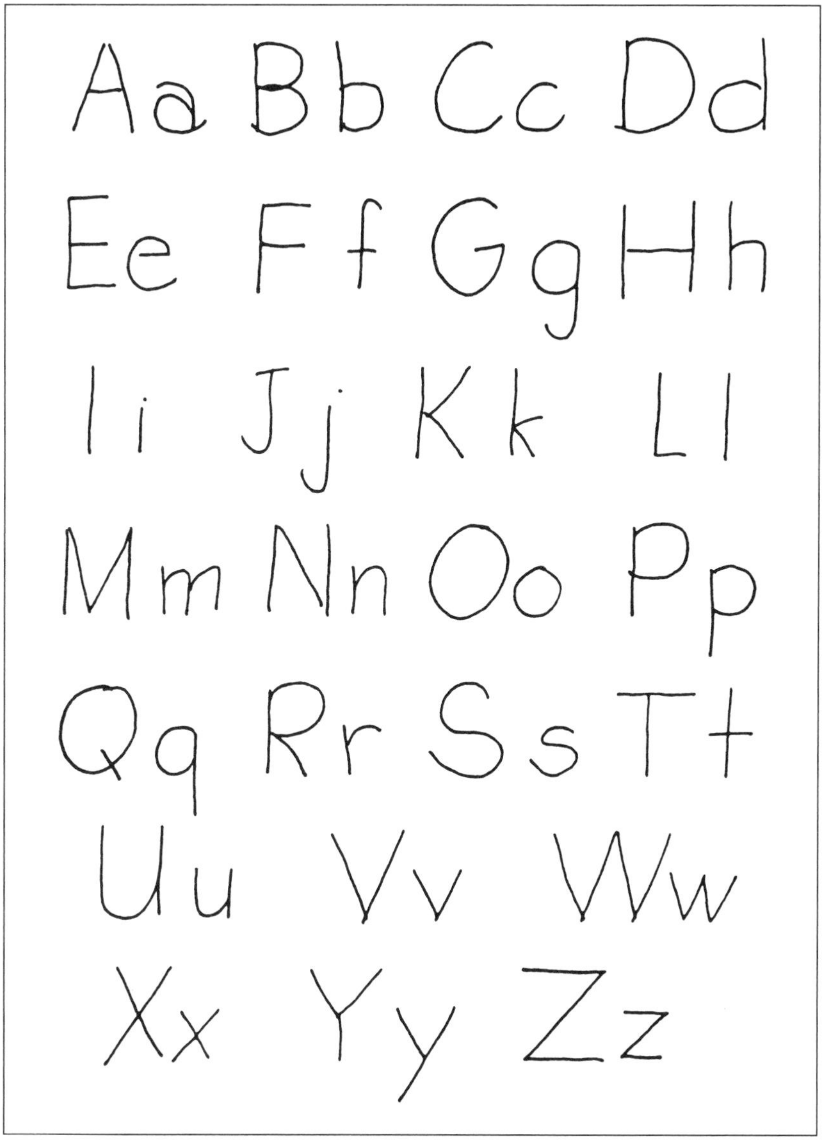

Aa Bb Cc Dd
Ee Ff Gg Hh
Ii Jj Kk Ll
Mm Nn Oo Pp
Qq Rr Ss Tt
Uu Vv Ww
Xx Yy Zz

# Sources of Information and Help

In the United States:
The National Information Center for Handicapped Children and Youth with Disabilities
P.O. Box 1492
Washington, D.C. 20012-0285
Telephone: 1-800-695-0285
Or, (202) 884-8200
E-mail: nichcy@aeo.org

Hotline number for help where child abuse is suspected:
1-800-4-A CHILD
This number is operative 24 hours a day, and may be called from telephones in the United states, Canada, Guam, Puerto Rico, and the U.S. Virgin Islands.

In Canada:
Disabled Peoples' International
#101-7 Evergreen
Winnipeg, MB    R3C 0B9
Tel.: 204-287-8010

Where child abuse is suspected:
The 1-800-4 A CHILD number works for Canadian residents. As well, many provinces list an emergency number at the front of the telephone directory. Children may call the **Kids Help Phone** which is accessible throughout Canada: 1-800-668-6868.

# Index